NEVER PUT ALL YOUR EGGS IN ONE BASTARD

ALSO BY PETA MATHIAS

Fête Accomplie (1995)
Don't Get Saucy With Me, Béarnaise (1996)
Salut! (1998)
Burnt Barley (2000)
Insatiable (2000)
Sirocco (2002)
Noodle Pillows (2003)
A Cook's Tour of New Zealand (2005)
French Toast (2006; updated 2010; first published in 1998 as *Salut!*)
Can We Help It If We're Fabulous? (2008)
A Matter of Taste (with Fulvio Bonavia, 2008)
Just In Time To Be Too Late (2009)
Culinary Adventures in Marrakech (2010)
Beat Till Stiff (2011)
Hot Pink Spice Saga (with Julie Le Clerc, 2014)

NEVER PUT ALL YOUR EGGS IN ONE BASTARD

PETA MATHIAS

RANDOM HOUSE
NEW ZEALAND

RANDOM HOUSE

UK | USA | Canada | Ireland | Australia
India | New Zealand | South Africa | China

Random House is an imprint of the Penguin Random House
group of companies, whose addresses can be found at
global.penguinrandomhouse.com.

Penguin
Random House
New Zealand

First published by Penguin Random House New Zealand, 2016

10 9 8 7 6 5 4 3 2 1

Text © Peta Mathias, 2016

The moral right of the author has been asserted.

All rights reserved. Without limiting the rights under copyright reserved above, no part of this publication may be reproduced, stored in or introduced into a retrieval system, or transmitted, in any form or by any means (electronic, mechanical, photocopying, recording or otherwise), without the prior written permission of both the copyright owner and the above publisher of this book.

Cover design by Carla Sy and Anna Egan-Reid © Penguin Random House New Zealand
Internal design by Sam Bunny © Penguin Random House New Zealand
Cover photograph by Sally Tagg

Printed and bound in Australia by Griffin Press, an Accredited
ISO AS/NZS 14001 Environmental Management Systems Printer

A catalogue record for this book is available from the National Library of New Zealand.

ISBN 978-1-77553-387-0
eISBN 978-1-77553-388-7

penguin.co.nz

THIS IS NOT THE LIFE I PLANNED

Dedicated to my adorable father
Harvey Mathias
who died as I was finishing this book.
He has gone to that big whisky distillery in the sky.

CONTENTS

PROLOGUE 13

CHAPTER 1   In which I decide to sell a house in Grey Lynn to buy a house in Uzès 17

CHAPTER 2   In which my fantasies are interrupted by new babies, primary school and the murder house 39

CHAPTER 3   In which I discover Uzès, *brocantes* and food markets 59

CHAPTER 4   In which television arrives, I go to secondary school and then become Joan Baez 79

CHAPTER 5   In which I buy the house in Uzès, and discover truffles 91

CHAPTER 6   In which I go nursing, lose God, find the pill, turn to revolt and fall in love 107

CHAPTER 7   In which the Uzès house saga continues 125

CHAPTER 8   In which I embrace the social revolution, endure the first sexual attack and dump nursing 133

CHAPTER 9   In which I emigrate to Canada, move to London, then on to Paris 151

CHAPTER 10   In which I live in Paris, get married, get real and open my first restaurant 167

CHAPTER 11 In which my Parisian life continues, my mother visits and I endure more sexual assaults 177

CHAPTER 12 In which I return to New Zealand to become a writer but only because I insisted 187

CHAPTER 13 In which the property situation in Uzès proceeds apace 209

CHAPTER 14 In which I fall into television 211

CHAPTER 15 In which I indulge my inner gastronomad and get paid for it 229

CHAPTER 16 Uzès and La Maison de la Diligence 241

POSTSCRIPT 257

LIST OF ILLUSTRATIONS 263

INDEX OF RECIPES 271

'We must be willing to get rid of the life we've planned, so as to have the life that is waiting for us.'
— *Joseph Campbell,* The Hero's Journey

PROLOGUE

This book is a memoir of sorts, viewed in the context of a (potentially insane) determination to buy a house in Uzès in the south of France. Looking back, it seems bizarre that this bid for domesticity ever became such a focus, because I am a nomad at heart. I've escaped more houses than I've said Hail Marys. As you will see, I grew up with experiences of the quarter-acre dream. I tried to be the conventional daughter my parents hoped for, safely cloistered within the nursing profession — answering the missionary complex instilled in me from birth — and accepted that I was being prepped to become perfect wife material. That was the plan. But how conventional can you be with a name like mine? Normality was doomed from baptism.

So, I have to ask: was my wanderlust an attempt to flee those expectations? Certainly my travels have often been triggered by men — running away from them as much as to them. But perhaps my love of travel is purely that — or rather a quest for the next gastronomic experience in the next exotic setting. If so, why does it look like I am trying to settle down in Uzès? Well, I'm not really trying to settle down, it's just that I'm easily bored and like change — everything was becoming a bit predictable so I needed a jolt. This seems to be part of the next phase of my life to add to all the other phases.

This book is my attempt to explore these interwoven elements that, like a refrain in a song, have recurred through my life: food, travel and love. It's not an *Eat Pray Love* thing — it's more a pay-the-rent thing and have-adventures-while-doing-it thing. Writing this book enables me to look back over my past as I battle glacial bureaucracy, mercurial sellers and the ravages of time on an ancient building, all in the hope of creating a new project, and a new cooking school, in a place that has been my other home since 2005: Uzès.

When Dorothy Parker realised she was pregnant, she said, 'serves me right for putting all my eggs in one bastard'. I have stretched this to encompass the idea of diversification: I like to have my fingers in many pies so in the case of famine I am not left with only one pie to eat. Of course there is always the risk of ending up with no pies at all, but I am prepared to take that gamble.

CHAPTER 1

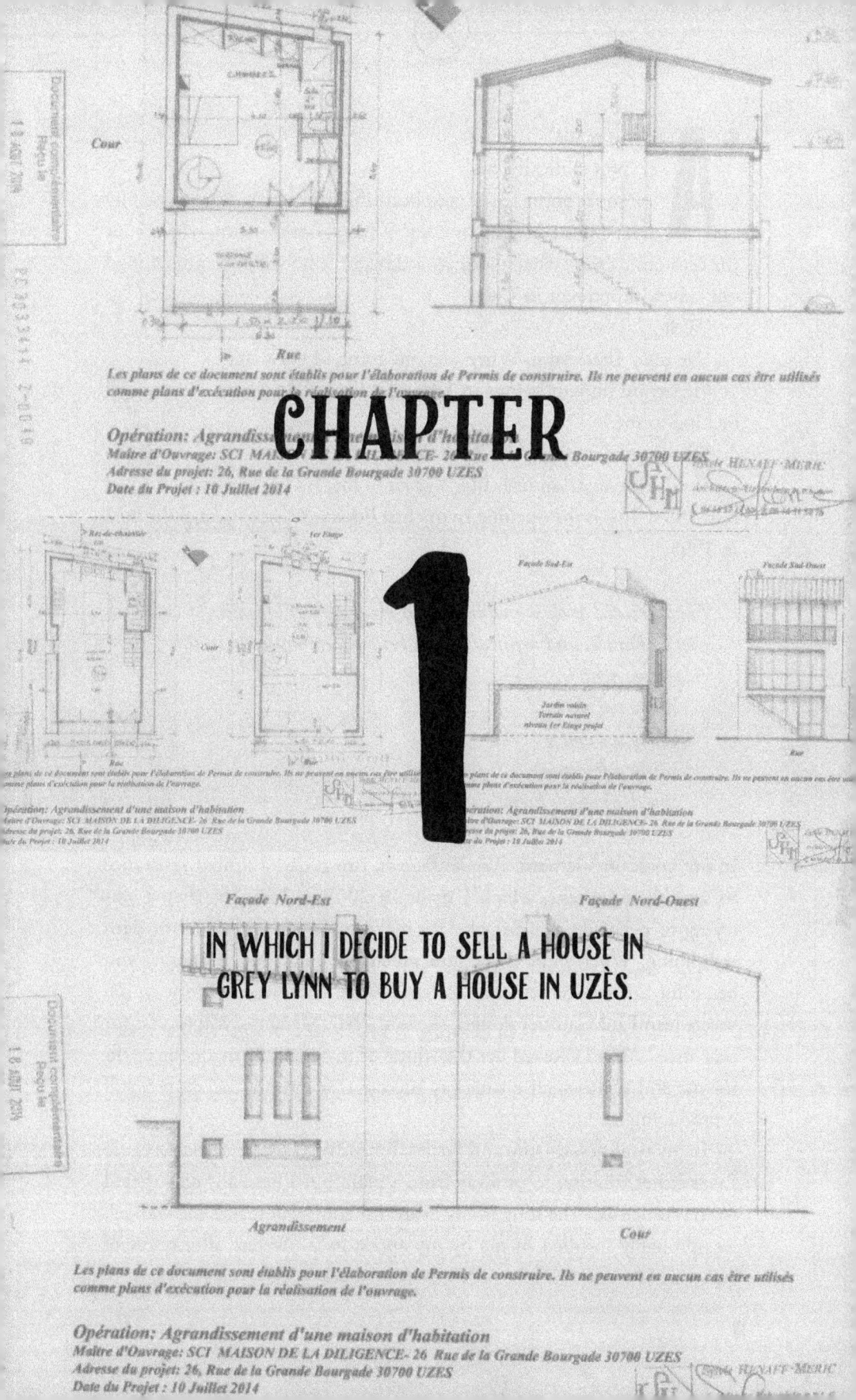

IN WHICH I DECIDE TO SELL A HOUSE IN GREY LYNN TO BUY A HOUSE IN UZÈS.

'Are you mad?'

'Not clinically, no.'

'You're going to sell your beautiful house in Auckland and buy a rat-infested dump in Uzès? What about the euro, what about the economic crisis, what about your dotage? Who will look after a mad old lady with red hair in Uzès?'

'Well . . .'

'No one. That's who. When are you going to grow up?'

'There are human beings in Uzès just like in Auckland. People will be kind to me.'

'They're not family, Peta. They don't count.'

If this conversation feels like *déjà vu* to me, it's because it is — I had it in 1985. This is the opening to my first book *Fête Accomplie*, published in 1995:

> *I had decided to do something about my dream of becoming a chef in France, and my friends and betters were touching in their encouragement:*
>
> *'You're too old . . .'*
> *'You're a woman . . .'*
> *'You're a foreigner . . .'*
> *'You don't speak French . . .'*

In my book on Vietnam, *Noodle Pillows*, I recorded a similar resistance to sensible argument, which I made in 2003 in Hoi An when I was trying to persuade a dressmaker to make me a lime-green outfit with red piping. When I chose the lime green, she said, 'No, Madame, you beautiful but too ol' for that colour.' When I showed her my *áo dài* meets Jean Paul Gaultier design, she said, 'No, Madame, you too fat for that style.' After I showed her the whites of my eyes, she made the outfit for me and it was such a runaway success that I think the shop is still reproducing it.

In my twenties, thirties and forties, I mostly moved countries because I was either running to or away from a man, but I have always suffered from wanderlust. The song in my heart, the song that makes me wander, was probably instilled in me by my ancestors — we are all a result of our history melding together from the past. Eventually I became so used to this part of me that I created a job where I was obliged to indulge the inner nomad. Since 2004 I have spent half my year in New Zealand and half travelling around the world with my gastronomic tours and living in Uzès. I have two separate lives, separate friends, different jobs, separate lodgings and speak different languages. I even speak French and English in different voices — the French voice is higher.

Every year, when I spend four months in Uzès teaching cooking, writing, and lying about teaching and writing when I am actually sitting around drinking Pastis, I rent a different apartment. This system has resulted in a terrifying variety of living arrangements — a tree is possibly the only place I have not lived in Uzès. The first year I struck gold when I was introduced to Gina, a Swiss woman living in one of the most famous grand old mansions in Uzès: the 'Albiousse' on Rue du Dr Blanchard in the best part of town. Gina and her then husband, Michael, had sold the *château* St-Victor-des-Oules outside Uzès and bought Albiousse. They took me on as their boarder for the summer — it was there I tested all my traditional southern French recipes for the cooking school I set up the following year. Overleaf is one of them.

Sometimes people offered me dumps to live in, like the year an acquaintance who has a house outside Uzès kindly expected me to live in a place that was still filthy from the last occupants, had stinking rubbish outside the door and no privacy whatsoever. I arrived at night and actually had to put clean sheets on the bed before I could sleep in it. This generosity forced me to find something more suitable, and I ended up in a very nice place in the back streets of Uzès on Impasse de la Trompe ('trompe' is defined by the *Collins English Dictionary* as 'an apparatus for supplying the blast of air in a forge, consisting of a thin column down which water falls, drawing in air through side openings'). It was beautifully decorated in the typical Uzès colours of biscuit, dove and clotted cream, but was closed-in and depressing. As I'm a light addict, it was a desperate situation for me: I had to drink my morning cup of tea outside on the street so I could see a tree and another human being and not burst into tears. This was also the year I felt the full force of a campaign of social exclusion, for the first time since my childhood, from the 'friend' outside Uzès, so it could have been that that made me cry into my tea. It was also the year

GINGER MADELEINES

Makes 45

185g butter
2 tablespoons grated fresh ginger
230g flour
1 teaspoon baking powder
¼ teaspoon salt
2 tablespoons diced crystallised ginger
4 large eggs
200g vanilla sugar

This recipe requires madeleine pans, which are readily available from most kitchen shops. They are like muffin trays but with fluted moulds to produce madeleines that look like scallop shells.

1. Melt the butter with the fresh ginger over a low heat, then set aside to cool to room temperature.

2. In a bowl, sift together the flour, baking powder and salt.

3. Add the crystallised ginger to the bowl and gently rub it into the flour mixture so that each piece of ginger is coated with flour to keep it separate.

4. Beat the eggs and sugar together until thick and pale. Fold in the flour mixture, then the cooled butter mixture.

5. Grease 2 madeleine pans and spoon a generous tablespoon of batter into each mould so that it is about three-quarters full. Refrigerate the filled madeleine pans and the remaining batter for half an hour.

6. Heat the oven to 220°C and bake the madeleines until they are golden and puffed — 8 to 10 minutes.

7. Turn the madeleines out of the moulds, and wipe out the moulds. Let the moulds cool, then grease and fill them with the remaining cold batter.

8. Eat immediately while still warm.

my principal employer, Television New Zealand, tried to pull the plug on my long-running television series *Taste New Zealand*.

Another year Gina came to the rescue again. By then she and Michael had sold Albiousse for a stately *maison de maître* in the countryside outside Saint-Quentin-la-Poterie. This huge four-storey mansion had other buildings on the property that Gina converted into luxury rental apartments with her sensual, theatrical taste. She had bought the property because she needed room for her horses. That summer I rented an upstairs apartment *chez elle* with gold curtains and black-and-white tiled floors. To access the wifi I had to sit in the courtyard outside the kitchen with her dogs.

In 2010, I sent out the tom-tom call to New Zealand friends Paul and Charmaine in Uzès to find me accommodation — something suitable to my status, please. Soon after Paul called me in Auckland and said, 'You are not going to believe what I have arranged for you — can you play the piano?' When I arrived in Uzès I moved into a converted luxury loft in the centre of town, part of an old church complete with three bedrooms, three bathrooms, two kitchens, a grand piano and a rooftop terrace. 'You owe me,' said Paul. This place was so big that it took me half a day to travel from the bedroom to the kitchen, and all the walking left me exhausted. I was very popular, needless to say — dinner parties, cooking lessons, concerts, parties, lovers and wall-to-wall housekeeping. At the end of the summer it was sold, so I was not able to rent it again. Opposite is one of the dishes I cooked there.

The following year, Gina came to the rescue again, and put me in contact with her friend Erick who had a large apartment right on the Boulevard Gambetta in the middle of town, on the corner of Avenue Jean-Jaurès. This first-floor apartment was in bad shape, roughly furnished and eccentric to say the least, but the location was sensational. People loaned me things, and eventually the place looked quite good, because all you really need is a kitchen and a laptop, right? Whenever there was a parade, a festival or a fight on the boulevard below, I had ringside seats. I could watch people doing drug deals on shady corners or having domestics in the apartments across the road, café owners cleaning up at the end of the night, and well-heeled visitors strolling home from classical music concerts. I was very popular in this location, too, because

FENNEL AND PASTIS SOUP WITH QUENELLES

Makes 10 small bowls

FOR THE SOUP

- 3 large fennel bulbs with fronds
- 1 medium onion
- 2 cloves garlic
- ½ preserved lemon plus 2 tablespoons of the juice
- 2 tablespoons olive oil
- 1½ litres vegetable stock
- sea salt and freshly ground white pepper
- 3 tablespoons Pastis or other aniseed liqueur like Ricard or Pernod

1. Trim the fennel of any brown bits, cut in half, remove the woody heart and discard it. Save the tips of the fronds for the garnish. Wash and chop the fennel into pieces.

2. Peel and chop the onion and garlic. Remove and discard the flesh from the lemon and slice the skin finely.

3. Heat the oil in a pot and quickly brown the vegetables and lemon.

4. Add the stock and preserved lemon juice and simmer, covered, for 15 minutes. Add salt and pepper to taste.

5. Add the Pastis or other aniseed liqueur, blend to a smooth soup in a food processor, then pass through a sieve.

PTO

TO SERVE

Serve chilled with the following quenelles on top, and drizzle with a little extra virgin olive oil. Sprinkle with chopped fennel fronds or tarragon.

FOR THE QUENELLES (MAKES 30)

2 slices of white bread, crusts cut off
50ml milk
250g white fish
150ml cream
1 heaped tablespoon fresh tarragon
½ teaspoon sea salt
freshly ground white pepper
¼ teaspoon freshly ground nutmeg

1. Soak the bread in the milk.

2. Cut the fish up and place in a food processor with all of the other ingredients. Blend until very smooth.

3. Using 2 teaspoons, shape the fish mousse into quenelles or little footballs, and lay in a steamer lined with baking paper.

4. Steam for 10 minutes. They can be plopped into the soup at room temperature.

of the ringside seats to *abrivados* (bull running), street parties and dubious fashion statements. The downside was the noise: it was like living in a tent on the boulevard. When the cleaning and garbage trucks arrived at five in the morning it was Armageddon — the apartment actually shook.

In 2012, I was unable to rent Erick's apartment again, as his next tenant, whom I unfortunately had recommended to him, refused to pay the rent and also refused to leave. In France it is extremely hard to evict a squatter from your property: you have to go to court, and if the squatter has mental health problems, which this woman did, you can't evict; if they have children, same thing; and you can't throw someone out in winter. In New Zealand if a bad tenant won't leave, you go to court quickly and they have to leave quickly. This woman, in spite of (or perhaps because of) her mental problems, moved from squatting to fraud to theft quite quickly. If you mention her name in Uzès to this day, fire issues from people's noses.

Fortunately, my friend Amy, the American organic winemaker whom I had interviewed in the television series I made on Uzès in 2010, emailed me to say that I could rent the flat attached to her house in Saint-Quentin-la-Poterie if I hadn't found anywhere else. I hadn't, would have preferred to live in Uzès, but wasn't going to look a gift horse in the mouth, so gratefully accepted the offer. The flat was rustic and pretty primitive, but very cheap and it was fun getting to know Amy better, along with her lovely husband, Matt. By the end of the summer, I was even on speaking terms with their pesky dogs. They — Amy and Matt, that is, not the dogs — make their own organic pasta, *focaccia* and fruit pies, and have a little wine truck they drive to markets to share their organic wine and food with the good people of the Uzège (the area around Uzès).

I stayed in Amy's flat with the broken shutters, and cleverly figured out how to access the BBC news online so I could watch the Olympics in London. Okay, so cancelling third-world debt is probably more important, but the isolation of the flat and the fact that the kitchen was so small that I couldn't entertain, little by little forced me into a catharsis. In this flat I was not popular — no parties, no dinners, no visitors.

'I can't understand why you don't buy a place here. We can't keep going through the anxiety and stress of finding you somewhere to live every year and then worrying where you might end up,' said my friend Pat as we slithered *rosé* and marinated sardines down our throats, sitting under the parasols outside the gorgeous and fashionable Les Terroirs café in the Place aux Herbes. Pat is a very chic, attractive older American lady who lives in a dramatic, artistic apartment with her handsome husband, Bob. They look like movie stars, and their best friends are Pam and Dan, so we talk of them as one person Pat&Bob&Pam&Dan. New Zealand friends who have visited me in Uzès often ask after Pat&Bob&Pam&Dan.

'Strangely enough, I've never seriously thought about it. As I'm a borderline commitment-phobe, I'm still trying Uzès out — mustn't rush and all that stuff.'

I started considering how helpful it might be to have a consistent kitchen in which to teach students how to rip out the entrails of a rabbit.

'How many years have you been coming here every summer? Nine? I know of a place on Boulevard Gambetta for sale, and if you don't like it we'll find another one.'

And that's all it took — one conversation over lunch. Two weeks after the conversation, I was due to leave Uzès to host my culinary trips in India. Having spent the entire summer in the area, I now had two weeks to find a place to buy, an agent, a French bank account, a notary and money. Easy, *n'est-ce pas*?

Amy told me about our friend Lucy's apartment for sale on Place d'Austerlitz in Uzès, I looked at it, fell in love with it and wanted it immediately. It was on two floors, had huge French windows opening out onto the pretty square, and a medieval turret at the top. Lucy said sure, let's start negotiating. My real-estate friend Pierre took on the job of agent and, to be sure Lucy's apartment was right for me, he looked at various other places in Uzès. One of them was an ordinary little two-storeyed stone house in the very same impasse where I had stood outside drinking my tea. It was empty but not for sale. In the interim Gina had separated from Michael and had sold the mansion in the country. She had bought the place I had hated living in on Impasse de la Trompe, mainly for its huge garage, which she had transformed into a sensuous Baroque split-level loft. I didn't even bother finding out who the owner of the little stone house was, so I didn't look inside — I mean how interesting could four rooms and a dunny be? Not a patch on Lucy's place, I was sure. The only things I could see that it had going for it were that it was on a quiet street away from the busy centre of Uzès . . . and now it was next-door to Gina.

There were other pressures to act quickly: in a summer 2012 article on real estate in *Le Républicain*, the local newspaper, it said prospective buyers shouldn't worry: unlike elsewhere in France, prices in Uzège aren't falling, and investing in real estate in Uzès and Uzège is still a good idea. In fact, it is becoming a buyer's market and most buyers hail from outside the area — Paris, Lyon and Europe, with the Swiss and Belgians leading the pack and Australians and New Zealanders taking up a distant rear. Most buyers are paying cash, it said. I later found out that the article was written by Pierre. A New Zealand friend, Guy, sent me a piece which appeared in the *New Zealand Herald* soon after called 'Chateau in France or House in Grey Lynn', regarding a do-up villa in Grey Lynn (similar to mine, also in Grey Lynn) which had sold for $1.006 million. Because the New Zealand dollar was more than holding its own against the euro and the American dollar, it seemed it would be churlish not to immediately sell in Auckland and buy a much better property for your money in the south of France.

But in September I had to fly to India for my gastronomic tours, so from the jungles of Goa, the mountains of Darjeeling, the traffic jams of Kolkata and the wifi-challenged hotels of Jaipur, I found an agent in Auckland and set in motion the sale of my beautiful, much-loved home in Grey Lynn. Every half-hour, I changed my mind — should I do it, shouldn't I do it? I imagined myself losing all my money in the move and living out my dotage in a mud hut in Rajasthan where they put elaborate silver shackles on women's ankles so they can't run away. I could become the Mother Teresa of disenfranchised widows, as I was about to become one myself. Organising this sale and all the legal papers that had to be signed from the middle of nowhere while simultaneously hosting two over-full gastronomic tours drove me absolutely bonkers. This is an email I sent to the friends looking after my Auckland house:

Dear Tanah and Sarah-Jane,

Yesterday in Pushkar there was no internet AT ALL in the hotel. Not only that (I almost fainted at reception), but Pushkar is an alcohol-free town (almost fainted again when I heard that). I said I seriously hoped they had some bhang (hash) lassis, at which they all smiled shyly. Pushkar is also a vegetarian town, including no fish, so you get paneer, paneer and paneer and some sloppy masala vegies. And heroin if you move in the right circles.

I marched out into the town with my laptop to find a fax or a scanner for the fucking contract — may as well have walked into the sacred lake and shouted loud, hoping the agent would hear me. First stop was a filthy second-hand bookshop where the owner was so morbid-looking I almost cried myself. He DUSTED OFF his fax machine (that's how often he used it) and tried to send a fax (with use of instruction manual). I sat there sandwiched between The Secrets of Kundalini, *Rudyard Kipling's* Kim *and* Zen and the Art of Motorcycle Maintenance *— talk about revisiting my youth!!!!!!!!!!*

Half an hour later the electricity failed, so I gave up with Mr Morbid and struggled off to an internet shop. Here I met the man of my life who is now my new best friend on Facebook. It took him half an hour to scan the papers, but at least it worked. I had a great time with him sipping masala chai, learning about his life and listening to his favourite hits from old Indian movies. Pushkar is famous for its fabulous camel fair, but frankly it's a dump — full of hippies, special twelve-hour alcohol licences and fake fakirs.

Mr Pushkar Facebooked me for a year until he finally fell in love with someone else.

My house in Auckland was on the front page of the *Herald Homes*, dozens and dozens of people viewed it, dozens more drove slowly by (Tanah was very amused and said you would think Madonna lived there), then it was passed in at auction, proof that my buyers and I lived in two different worlds. I wasn't too worried as I don't set much store by auctions, but agents seem to love them.

Soon after the auction, a woman viewed the house at the open home and fell for it like a ton of bricks — like I had six years previously. When I saw this heritage cottage on its heritage street — ridiculously pretty, beautifully restored with high ceilings, polished floors and French doors, and flooded with sunlight, I had to have it. I wasn't even looking for a house, couldn't really afford it, and bought it anyway. My friend Gail said, 'Buy it and figure out how to pay for it later — it will make you happy and you'll manage.' Very good advice as it turned out, because the universe does abhor a vacuum and we spend our lives being terrified of risk . . . Well, not me personally, but the great unwashed.

My prospective Auckland buyer and I then began our courtship dance wherein we spent a whole unbelievable month-and-a-half counter-signing conditional offers. I counter-signed all over India, in airports, up mountains, and continued practising my signature when I returned home to Auckland. I knew she was my buyer right from the beginning, but she certainly led me a merry dance. In the meantime, this had all taken so long that Lucy's apartment, the very reason I had sold my lovely house, had been sold to someone else — an American couple. Lucy gave me the option of putting in a counter-offer, but at that point I didn't yet have the money, so regretfully I told her to go ahead and give it to the other buyers. I subsequently met this couple and they are adorable.

I asked Pierre and Gina to look more closely at the stone house on the Impasse de la Trompe. Gina had been through it previously as she had considered buying it before she bought the one next door. She had drawn up a plan for the renovation, which included constructing what they call a *tropézienne* in the south of France, a small rooftop terrace, capturing every drop of sun and searing heat the region can provide. The house was inexpensive, and she guessed she could transform it for around €80,000. This would mean I could buy it with cash, do it up with cash, and not scramble around for a loan. It would mean freedom from mortgages and debt. Freedom, freedom, freedom. Pierre then went in, took photographs and measurements, and costed out a plan of his own design for the renovation. Inside the plain stone house, which was a two-up two-down box with a sordid little courtyard, were a living room and kitchen downstairs and two bedrooms and a bathroom upstairs.

Gail's advice was different when it came to selling my house in Auckland. She warned that if I changed my mind and decided to sell the Uzès house and return to Auckland, I would never be able to afford to buy back into my heritage area ever again. No bank would give me a mortgage either (not true as it turns out). So there I was, selling a gorgeous house in a high market to buy an ugly house in a low market, hoping like hell the whole deal wasn't going to ruin me, and that my plan to make the Uzès house work for me and pay for itself would materialise. The master plan was to rent it to holiday-makers when I wasn't there (which should be hugely profitable in sought-after Uzès) and teach cooking classes when I was there. The whole deal would leave me mortgage-free with no debt and a house that was producing income for me. This was ignoring the possibility that having debt and a mortgage is not necessarily a bad thing if house values are going up. But I'm old-fashioned and have a quaint idea that there is something honourable about being debt-free — I have always felt a noose looks better on a bull. Living a life of quiet desperation is not my thing. I don't want to go to the grave with the song still in my heart.

The second I had sold the Auckland house, I jumped on the blower to Pierre and asked him to meet up with the owner of the Uzès house. This is Pierre's report of that meeting:

27/11/2012, at 11:19 AM

Hi there,
 End of a very long day.
 I drove to where the house owner, a Berber from Morocco, manages a 15th c. castle with 400 acres of land around it. I got lost in the mountains, after I picked the wrong entrance to said estate. Then I visited the castle — a rare sighting I have to say. A private property not opened to the public — AT ALL. The castle owner hired Mr Morocco (19 at the time) in 1981 to do some building/renovation work. The Moroccan hasn't left and is very proud of the work he has done in there. Rightfully so, as I have never seen such a (private) castle in such a good state. The owner spends around 15,000€ a month on the estate (upkeep, staff, renovations, gardens, etc).
 While listening to Mr Morocco, I learned more about his personality. Our little negotiation took place over only 20 minutes at the end of the 3-hour session. For some (unclear) reason he has decided he won't sell under 115,000€ so it was kind of clever of me to start the bidding at that level — I wasn't sure but guessed right. The guy isn't loaded, but doesn't need money really. He is more than

capable of renovating the house in Uzès to a high standard, but has reached the conclusion that he simply can't invest the time. He now has two large properties on his boss's estate to renovate and he wants to offload the Uzès property. But he wants to get a FAIR deal. He is big on 'fair', and 'respect' and all, which I can understand. He listened quite well to my pitch when I explained (with proof) that houses in Uzès in need of full renovation go for 1,000€ to 1,500€/m² and that 115,000€ (equivalent to 1,850€/m²) is a very good deal under the current context.

At the end, he said he was going to make a few enquiries about the going price of small houses in Uzès, and that he would come back to me. He said I (we) would get priority. If he doesn't get any better offer, the house is ours for 115,000€ (I think I left a signed offer with him). If he gets a better offer, he will tell me, give the name of the bidder (to ensure I can trust him — remember, FAIR) and we can match the bid if we wish and get the house. He said 'you're first and I'll remember it'. A bit unusual, unexpected too. But fair, I have to say. Nothing much I could tell him to counter-act on the spot. He said a week max. I guess we have to wait . . . Tell me what you think.

Best, Pierre

Zut alors! Now I *know* Moroccans and I know how much they love intrigue and indulging in the art of *mañana, mañana*. I have written two books on Morocco and have been going there every year since 2008 to host my culinary weeks in Marrakech. Sitting in my house in Auckland surrounded by three million boxes full of my possessions, I envisaged spending the whole winter waiting for Mr Morocco as he let time pass on slippered feet. It was 7 December, the money for the sale of the house had arrived in my lawyer's account, and I was ready to rock 'n' roll. Okay, so I wasn't homeless as I had rented a lovely house in my neighbourhood, but I was still ready to rock in Uzès, even though it was long-distance. My friends were saying: 'Another brilliant move on your part, Peta — the Uzès job will take longer than you plan, it will cost more than you plan and you're doing it long-distance — it can only end in tears.' Prophetic, as it turned out.

'No, no,' said I. 'I have Gina and Pierre, whom I've known for years,

I speak fluent French, I know Uzès really well — it will be like spreading *foie gras* on *brioche* bread: smooth and sweet with a serene aftertaste.'

But it's true there was the Moroccan complication. With Moroccans, you are not just buying a house. They are very connected to home and land, even if it is foreign and even if it is only an investment property, and all transactions have to be conducted with due process, sluggishness and pointless game-playing. Needless to say, Mr Morocco did not get back to us when he said he would, and asked 'experts' to value the house as if there was room to move in his 'two-up-two-down-crappy-garden' scenario.

So, there I was, standing at my kitchen bench in Auckland, the movers walking around me in a fug of male sweat, testosterone and *eau de chaussette*. My life was disappearing into two smart boxes and I was trying not to cry. Every so often I'd scream, 'That's fragile, you know!', as I watched chandeliers, ornate *tagines* and my mother's paintings sailing out the door.

'Yes, love. We are professional movers. Don't stress, aunty.' Don't stress? I was so stressed that I drank a coffee that had been sitting on the kitchen bench since the day before. I felt sick and faint, had cramps and stress.

'Tanah made us a big feed last week when we moved her house — smoked fish and everything.' I think: Yeah, right, here we go . . . How can I compete with Mother Earth when I'm only Aunty Coffee? It was 1.30pm, very humid, with wine-dark storm clouds bubbling and thunder smacking around everywhere. Suddenly, like a bomb going off, the heavens opened and cats and dogs fell out of the sky as only they can in a city built on a rainforest. Hello — it's summer. Hello — it's December. But no, as it happens; in Hobsonville, not far from me, a tornado had struck: three people dead already and many injured. I knew this because I am so tragic that I was reading Facebook and the news was coming in from my radio-host friends.

Apparently, a tornado forms when two atmospheric bodies each with different temperatures and humidities collide and become unstable. Warm air will thrust upwards, spiralling as it goes. Suddenly at a certain point it intensifies into a thin violent funnel of wind. A tornado, by its very nature, doesn't last long but can cause an incredible amount of damage. In Hobsonville, roofs were being ripped from houses, trees uprooted, debris was flying into moving cars, and fences were crushing like dried spaghetti. Above me, a line of more thunderstorms was marching into place in the black sky, cracking loudly. All we needed was hail. Thank God I had prayed not to die in a state of mortal sin and was wearing clean snowy underwear. The sodden, heroic movers, having hefted all my stuff into the trucks, were standing on my porch looking like whalers after a kill. Now they had to go around the property and remove all Tanah and Sarah-Jane's plants, trees and flower pots. Quite quickly the property and cottage looked exactly like the day I moved in, save for the addition of my antique Spanish door grill, striped awnings and wide wooden blinds. Goodbye beauty, *bonjour tristesse* maybe.

A couple of weeks went by and Pierre had still not heard back from Mr Morocco (a week max he'd said — remember?). I stayed calm, as this was not unexpected. I was determined not to nag Pierre. I waited. Finally, he contacted me. Mr Morocco was continuing his game of poker with us, and was now saying that his price had gone from €115,000 to €165,000 because an estate agent had offered to pay this. This was quite miraculous in my opinion, as the house hadn't even been for sale when we found it, and now suddenly an estate agent was offering €165,000. Curiouser and curiouser. Neither Pierre nor I believed that the estate agent existed, and we were growing weary — Mr Morocco had already wasted a lot of Pierre's time. Pierre wanted to know why things weren't moving in a linear fashion. We are both control freaks so we like linear. We rarely get it, and Moroccans specialise in non-linear. One of my personality flaws is that I specialise in instant gratification. Having wasted half my life indulging myself, I am now in a hurry not to waste any more time in non-productiveness. Nevertheless, on this occasion I took the delicious opportunity to remind Pierre that I had told him so.

Pierre suggested we look at another house he had found around the corner. I love the street it's on, in the protected heritage sixteenth-century *quartier des Bourgades* — it's a very pretty old Provençal *rue* with recently redone paving stones (which are impossible to walk on in high heels), renovated houses and cute decorating shops. The houses of the *riverains* residents are small and high — three or four storeys — and all stuck together. I had taken an organised tour of the area and discovered fabulous gardens hidden behind houses, swimming pools, an old farm and vaulted alleyways. An elderly gentleman on the tour told me he was born and brought up in this *quartier* and remembered fetching milk from the little farm for his mother every morning. Then the cows would wander down the road to the vines and fields at the bottom of the street. This area at the bottom now has houses, and the little *place* there used to be called Place du Marché aux Cochons, where the pig market was held. It is not on the posh side of Uzès, and has traditionally been an unfavourable area to buy in, being regarded as too proletarian. This is what makes it attractive to me: lots of little secret *ruelles* and passages darting off it, and all sorts of interesting poets and writers have lived there. It's busy and cramped in a fun way.

The name of the quarter, *Bourgade,* means large village or small town. It is circled by the Boulevard des Alliés, which was part of the medieval fortified town walls, so I imagine my little street meant something like 'street leading from the town'. I look at the photos of the house Pierre has found: it is even more of a dump than Rue de la Trompe, but it looks out over a lovely garden. It is tiny, but there is also a little ruin next door and a garden I can possibly buy to expand the property. It is owned by an older couple from Nanterre who used it as a holiday home, but it would be a complicated proposition as we would be dealing with three different owners for three little parcels.

Weeks went by and nothing happened. Nobody contacted anybody. It was now Christmas, and the French, including estate agents, will absolutely not do anything in holiday time. Then it was January 2013; I had thought I was buying an Uzès apartment in September 2012, but now I was wondering what part of 'cash buyer' people didn't understand.

At last Pierre wrote to say that the recalcitrant Moroccan was still insisting on the inflated price of €160,000, so Pierre was about to move on and contact the owners of the Bourgade house and draw up a plan for the renovation. The bilingual plan arrived a few days later, with every possible permutation, configuration and outcome imaginable, including how much it would be worth if I sold it immediately after it was renovated. There were photographs, aerial views, survey maps, architectural drawings of the house on its own, the house with the ruin next door, the house with the garden next door, the house with ruin and garden, drawings with measurements, drawings of the attic. At the bottom of this 22-page novel of the story of an old house were all the costs of the renovation almost down to the last nail. This was impressive to a simple cook such as myself; I didn't understand most of it, but liked the drawings and could imagine fabulous tiles on the floor.

An offer was duly made to the agent for the owners of the house, and Pierre discovered that the owners of the ruin behind were a middle-aged local couple and the garden next door was co-owned by a family. You know all those complicated stories of how hard it is to do up a house in the south of France? *First*, you have to bloody well succeed in actually *buying* one. First, you have to talk someone into selling you their crappy house. As involved as it is to sell a house in New Zealand, it is a walk in the park next to France. It's a dream doing business in New Zealand — banking, buying, selling, opening a business and investing are very transparent and have approximately a hundred per cent less bureaucracy. The French are like the Indians: they adore officiously fiddling around with papers and taking as long as they can. All this I knew because I had owned a restaurant in Paris, and yet still I believed now that I would be the exception and that everything would move quickly and without hitches.

Meanwhile back in Auckland I was being subjected to conversations where my friends were speaking about me as if I were a mental patient or not actually in the room. I didn't understand all the things that could go wrong, I would be ripped off, I didn't know how to buy an old house and all the things to check for, I was doing it long-distance, who were these people Gina and Pierre anyway, what bank was I using, who was going to look after me when I was old, who was organising my funeral? (Okay, I made that last one up.) I was finding this lack of confidence in my competence interestingly odd, and so was my PA Rosie who said, 'This is not the impression I have of you, Peta. You are not half as la-la as people seem to think you are — you couldn't have done what you have done in life if you were that inadequate.'

My psychologist friend Gail said, 'Peta, the best way to judge a person's future behaviour is to look at their past behaviour. You do take risks, but they are calculated. You have done very well with your house buying and selling in the past, so this one will work, too. You don't run your life in a safe way, which is why people try to protect you. Just smile and keep moving.'

Pierre took Gina along to have a look at the Bourgade house and say what she thought. She didn't like it as much as the Rue de la Trompe one, but could visualise what could be done with it, especially if I was able to buy the ruin behind. I asked her to take on the site-management and interior design. I knew she would be the right person as she has a flair for the industrial look. She had done up an old barn in Saint-Laurent-la-Vernède with big steel-framed windows, polished-concrete kitchen benches and a lovely slim-line swimming pool. And, as I have said, her own home is a huge Baroque loft. My home in Auckland had been shabby-chic and I wanted something different — I was over shabby-chic. I didn't want to see another Designer's Guild pink couch.

I said, 'The challenge with this project is, of course, to have to do it within such a small budget — how to make a very ordinary little house look fabulous for very little. I would like to use recycled stuff as much as possible — I like the idea of hand basins, baths, work benches, the kitchen, doors, roofing, light fittings, etc, coming from demolition sites or whatever. I like the industrial look. As the kitchen is a teaching kitchen, I would like to buy the equipment at a restaurant second-hand place — my friend Anthony the *macaron* chef knows where to buy all this.'

We started exchanging ideas, and she set me straight on a few things and gave me a good piece of advice right away.

> *I am sure that something good is possible also in the Bourgade house. I am pretty good in this kind of finding solutions. I already gave Pierre some new ideas. But I wanted, before all, to know what at the end you will buy — only the small house or house + ruin, or house + ruin + garden or house + ruin + garden + a tiny* parcelle *behind the house which belongs to the owner of the ruin and would be useless for him. During the last 2 days I thought of some plans — but it is important to know what you will buy. Naturally the best would be if you could buy all! I hope Pierre will have the answers soon. Then — immediately — I will make drawings and send them to you.*
>
> *I didn't contact my* équipe *yet. I wait until we know to show*

them 'sur place' and ask for bids for concrete details. My 'politics', as you know, is simple solutions at the lowest cost as possible. Like in the Grange in Saint Laurent la Vernède I would make the project (naturally with your wishes and opinions), make an agreed architect do the 'démarche administrative' to have the permit (could take 2 months, même plus), get all the bids, direct the works until the end.

As we are already in mid-January 2013 I think you have to look for a house to rent when you come in June — it's not possible that everything can be finished at this time. Think also at the possibility (I spoke about this to Pierre) to buy as an SCI (Société Civile Immobilière), as owner of the house which rents it out to a cooking-school with studio or so. Doing like this (with a business behind) you could get back the TVA paid on the work-costs. I do it this way. To create a SCI needs 2 persons (for example in my case me (97%) and my mother (3%)) and cost at the notaires around 1,000€

Needless to say, the last thing I wanted to hear was that the house wouldn't be ready to live in and that I would once again be rummaging around looking for somewhere to rent. But in a way it was a good thing (once I had put the skids on my outbreaks of Instant Gratification Syndrome), because I was, after all, writing a book and it takes up a lot of time to write a book. This way, I would be supervising the reconstruction and going home to somewhere, hopefully quiet, to write. That way, I could walk onto the building site, point and scream things like 'What happened to the fireplace?', 'Where is the air-conditioner going?' and 'That wall has to go!', like they do on TV.

As I was day-dreaming about where to put the fireplace, Pierre announced that the 'desperate-to-sell' owners wouldn't be back from their holidays until the end of January and wouldn't be making any decisions until then. If I had sold an Auckland house from the jungle in India, how hard could it be for them to answer a phone call? Grrrrr. This is why the French will never rule the world but the Chinese, for example, *will*: they know about business. Why couldn't the owner be Chinese? Note to self: stop grinding teeth, drink more alcohol and stop wishing people were Chinese.

When Pierre drew the plans for the Rue de la Trompe house, all of my friends asked, 'Is there a view?' They'd contracted the view disease, endemic in New Zealand. If you want a view, go for a walk already. At the beginning of January, Pierre finally gave up on Mr Morocco and created a simple plan for the Bourgade property. All we had to do now was contact the three owners of the three bits I wanted to buy, but I suspected deep in my waters that I was looking at a protracted, patience-stretching exercise. If only I had known how protracted. I practised breathing out, as anyone can breathe in. Needless to say, by the time Pierre did make contact with the owner, someone else was already interested. They had had a lot of trouble selling this property, and now suddenly, mysteriously, there were two buyers. I could feel my teeth grinding.

CHAPTER 2

IN WHICH MY FANTASIES ARE INTERRUPTED BY NEW BABIES, PRIMARY SCHOOL AND THE MURDER HOUSE.

I was well practised at teeth-grinding, having done so from the moment they cut through my baby gums. Right now, before the blood starts clotting and the carnage becomes too cumbersome to step over, I should probably mention that my mother, Ann, and I have passed over the bridge of forgiveness, emerged on the other side and truly, honestly, get on very well now — we even make jokes about our terrible past relationship. There have been apologies for past excesses on both sides. It took a long time, but we finally achieved it.

A journalist once asked me whether my mother had had therapy to overcome the trauma of living with *me*. When I first wrote about a mother like mine in a novel years ago, my editor at the time said, 'This is quite a good story, Peta, but the mother figure is not credible — one minute she's Julie Andrews in *The Sound of Music* and the next she's Bette Davis in *What Ever Happened to Baby Jane?* You need to make up your mind about this character.' 'Welcome to my life,' I replied. The publisher at the time said, 'This novel is irredeemable.' And so it was. Ever since, I have wanted to write a book called 'Irredeemable', but here I am writing a book called *Never Put All Your Eggs In One Bastard*. I genuinely want to write a book called 'Lovely Flowers I Have Known' or 'How I Became a Little Daffodil in a Field', but it just won't come and my life hasn't been a daffodil-in-a-field kind of life.

My grandfather, Stanley Mathias, emigrated to New Zealand from a town called Cardigan in the county of Ceredigion in Mid Wales in 1910. He married a New Zealand woman in 1914 and enlisted to fight in World War I in the First New Zealand Expeditionary Force, doing service in the Middle East and France. While away, he distinguished himself by doing insane things like running from bomb crater to bomb crater with telephone lines until he had connected up the Allied troops. His specialty was communications, and this crater-hopping incident happened on 12 September 1918 in the Battle of Havrincourt Wood, up on the French–Belgian border. He was a mad, brave, runty little guy and was rewarded with the Military Medal.

Meanwhile his wife had sailed to the UK in 1916 and became an ambulance driver at New Zealand's Walton-on-Thames Hospital. Her address was given as her mother-in-law's in Cardigan. In 1919 she returned to New Zealand with a different surname! When Stanley returned home from the war, he found his wife was pregnant, and he divorced her immediately without further discussion. Clearly she was not pregnant to him, but to a certain Mr New Surname, whom she must have met in the UK — maybe she had fallen for a wounded soldier. She gave birth to a daughter. We found out only by chance that Stanley had had this first wife when I needed a copy of my grandparents' marriage certificate when applying for British patriality. There was my lovely grandmother Jessie — 'spinster from Wanganui' — and there was Stanley: 'divorced from Havelock North'. *Divorced.* What? From whom? Not even my father and his brothers knew about this divorce until we grandchildren exposed it; it had never been spoken of, ever. Eventually my cousin Chrissy tracked down this first wife; she had married someone else, not the father of her child.

Tough, short, wiry and determined, a self-made man who didn't suffer fools, Stanley came from a long line of drapers in Cardigan. He wasn't without charm, however, and was well liked. The family department store on Cardigan High Street in Wales was called Le Bon Marché. After the divorce he met a tall, lovely girl from Wanganui called Jessie Tucker — daughter of farmers in Bulls, Taranaki. They met while both were working at the DIC (Drapery and General Importing Company of New Zealand Ltd) in Wanganui. They married and opened a drapery shop there, where their first son, Ian, was born, while their second son, my father Harvey, was born in Norsewood.

The Wanganui shop burned down, but in the middle of the Great Depression in 1931 they opened a new shop, JS Mathias Limited, on Tutanekai Street in Rotorua. They drove a Model T Ford, had a third son, Graham, and were successful in spite of the tough economic times. Their entire ethos was based on service: if they didn't have it, they would secure it. Stanley was business day and night, and so was Jessie, who relieved the commitment to work with her frequent flutters at the races. They were always well dressed and had no casual or sports clothes; they just worked. I remember them as charming, lovely people. She knitted bed jackets and bed socks for the shop. They weren't exactly jackets, though — they were like short soft pink and blue capes with satin ribbons. As a child I wore these beautifully made garments in bed when I stayed at their place, which was often.

It wasn't until I grew up that I realised why I spent so much time there: to stop Mum and me from putting each other up for adoption or worse. I would go and live there for weeks, and I adored it because Grandma was calm, patient and appeared to like me. My mother, the repressed eccentric, was a different kettle of fish: I interpreted her strictness as a lack of affection. With my grandparents, I felt spoiled and loved. After they retired, they lived in a grand two-storeyed house with a big garden on Ranui Road in Remuera. Although Grandpa was hard, he had street smarts and a sense of humour. I liked him and knew where I stood with him. They drove a Humber Hawk which I was very partial to, riding around with Grandma, who always wore a fur coat, red lipstick and gloves to go shopping in Remuera and at Smith & Caughey's in town. We used to take tea in the tearooms at the top of the department store. I can still smell the leather seats in that Humber now — I think it was then that I first realised I was headed for royalty. I mean, it wasn't possible that my life was meant for suburbia, minced beef and quiet desperation. Surely I was destined for hand-made knickers, bespoke cars and opulent houses like Grandma's?

Grandma Jessie died at the age of 63 of a brain tumour. Mum had got her into Mater Hospital, with the nuns looking after her like she was their own, but Grandpa was anti-Catholic and didn't trust the friendship between Jessie and the priest who visited her. He feared she might be talked into going to the wrong heaven and had her moved to a private hospital. I was devastated by her death, and it took me years to get over. I missed her so much. She was the most beautiful, kind woman, and Grandpa never fully recovered.

Grandpa's plan had been to work hard, make money and retire early — wealthy; and that's exactly what he did. Dad and his two brothers were sent to boarding school from the age of nine, and their parents visited them once a term and took them out for a flash lunch in a posh restaurant. When they went home for holidays, they were looked after by the housekeeper, Mrs Ennis, and nannies. Their parents returned home every day for lunch. The shop was closed on Wednesday afternoon and open on Saturday morning.

The Anglican boys' boarding school they were sent to was Southwell, outside Hamilton. It was, and still is, a family-oriented school set up by Englishman Cecil Ferris and taken over by H.G. Sergel. Basically, it was a farm, and the 80 students milked cows, chopped wood, made soap from mutton fat and made jam from all the fruit trees on the property, and made their beds. It was quite rugged; they wore sandals all winter and slept on beds on the verandah. Dad's brother Ian was called Mathias Senior and Dad was called Mathias Junior. When Ian left and younger brother Graham arrived, Graham became Junior. They sang evensong to an old pump organ, and on Sunday nights the headmaster read to them in bed adventure stories like *The Thirty-Nine Steps* by John Buchan, where the hero had a stiff upper lip and a remarkable capacity for slipping out of dastardly situations. I asked Dad how he felt about being away from his mother from the tender age of nine onwards and seeing them so little, and he said it was fine — the boarding school was his family, his brothers were there, and he was happy — that was all he knew.

Dad left school at 16 and went to work in the family business in Rotorua. When Grandpa and Grandma turned the shop over to Ian and moved up to Ranui Road in Auckland, Dad had jobs at Milne & Choyce and Kirkpatrick & Stevens. He celebrated his twenty-first at Ranui Road, learned to dance at 'Johnnys' and tripped the light fantastic at the Orange Hall on Newton Road, a hotbed of repressed sexuality and city excitement. Dad didn't serve in the war due to bad eyesight, and in 1946 he decided he needed a bit of excitement, adventure and romance, so set off in an ex-hospital boat for the bright lights of Sydney. He took lodgings in a boarding house and started a job at David Jones in the fabric department. You earned your wage and a penny on a pound commission for each sale. You had to sign in and sign out for work, and Charles Lloyd Jones descended the escalator every morning to greet the staff personally. Dad wore a pepper-and-salt tweed suit to work and became friends with some staunch Irish boys who worked in the shoe department — Michael and Jimmy Long, a couple of likely lads.

My maternal grandfather, James Long, had sailed to Australia from Tipperary in 1927 to find a farm and work it. Then he sent for his family of wife, Margaret Shanahan, and nine children, and they sailed across the ocean to join him. After a horrendous journey, they arrived half-dead, but put on a brave face of it as the *Sydney Morning Herald* took their photo for its front page. My mother, Ann, and her siblings were brought up on the farm outside Sydney, and most of them moved into the city when they grew up. Her handsome father was a fantastic storyteller and what Mum calls 'a part-time drunk' who went on violent drunk rampages during which his children hid under the beds. She has no idea how her mother coped with him and all their children. Talk about tough. This is where the planets aligned when Michael and Jimmy invited Dad home for dinner. They were boarding in a Sydney house in Glebe with some of their other nine brothers and sisters — my mother, Ann (called Nancy as a pet name), Peg (real name Margaret) and Dell (short for Delia). Mum worked as a receptionist in a suntan parlour with the terrifying name of Thermoray.

During the war she was WRANS Rating No 532 (Women's Royal Australian Naval Service), her specialty being coding. Their slogan was 'Join the WRANS — free a man for the fleet'. After the war, Mum was awarded two service medals. When we were children, she used to show us how to use codes. I watched closely because you never know when you might need to decode — I could have used it to communicate with men, because sign language and interpretive dance sure as hell didn't work. Mum's initial job with the navy was delivering secret documents to the ships in Woolloomooloo Harbour. She and another girl (they were only 18) had to walk down to the wharves unescorted, through groups of drunken sailors, from where they were rowed by boat to the ship. In their sailor-girl pants, they had to shimmy up the ladder on the side of the boat, board the ship and personally deliver the secret documents to the person for whom they were intended. They soon grew sick of this and applied to train as coders, where at least they were in a safe office on the HMAS *Magnetic* in Townsville. Mum was embarrassed to tell me that these were the best days of their lives — they went to dances with the servicemen, were tattooed with beauty spots, and had butterflies painted on their fingernails. They loved the excitement, and she said that most Australians had absolutely no idea how close the Japanese ships actually were and that 18-year-olds were responsible for their security.

Dad turned up at Jimmy and Michael's house, took one look at Mum and thought 'yep'. He said they were terrible cooks and the food was awful. Mum looked at Dad and thought he was a polite, well-brought-up man. They fell in love and got married behind the altar in the sacristy of the Catholic church because Dad was Protestant, and if you married a non-Catholic in those days you were punished for it. Not only were you forbidden to be married in the church proper, but Mum couldn't wear a white wedding dress — she wore a chic violet-blue crêpe dress with chocolate-coloured shoes and hat. She was so tiny that even as a 12-year-old I couldn't fit into that dress. Also, Dad had to sign a form promising that he would bring their children up Catholic. His staunchly Protestant family was slightly horrified that he had married a Catholic, even a smart, pretty one. Soon after, they moved to Auckland and set up home in Onehunga and opened a small drapery shop, selling manchester goods, sheets, towels and shirts.

My mother was not particularly into her Irish heritage as she had 'married up', but, because I was friends with an Irish family two doors down from us, I became Irishified as I was very attracted to their free-range culture and wildness, hence the Irish dancing lessons and learning Irish songs. As Dad was a New Zealander we never knew much about the Welsh side of our heritage except to learn the song 'We'll Keep a Welcome' — possibly one of the most beautiful, emotional songs of my childhood; my grandfather taught me it. When I was writing this book I Googled it and burst into tears. You can Google it, too, though there are different versions. It uses the Welsh word '*hiraeth*', which is an untranslatable expression of longing. It's not a traditional song as I thought, but according to some sources the lyrics were written in 1940 by Lyn Joshua and James Harper, and the musician and composer was Mai Jones who worked as a variety producer for the BBC based in Cardiff. It is best sung by a Welsh male choir. I visit the Basque Country every year with my culinary tours and the Basques are very keen on saying that they have no historical relationship with anyone, and their language is completely unique in the world. But when I heard male Basque choirs, they sounded very much like Welsh choirs to me. The Basques say they are not Celts, but research shows they indeed have a common genetic heritage with the Welsh, as various different migrations during the Mesolithic and the Neolithic eras saw them leave the Iberian Peninsula. Wales is stuck on the west side of Britain down by the Celtic Sea, harsh and rugged and wet. For some reason the inhabitants have wonderful singing and speaking voices: think Dylan Thomas — 'Do not go gentle into that good night. Old age should burn and rave at close of day; Rage, rage against the dying of the light.' Then there's Richard Burton and Anthony Hopkins — they do rhetoric very well with their deep sing-song accent. Like my grandfather, Stanley, the Welsh are generally strong, independent people and ready for a stoush should you cross them, in spite of (or perhaps because of) being occupied and subdued by the English for most of their history. I can't possibly say whether any of those traits have been passed on to me.

In 1949, the year I was born, Dr Spock was all the rage — every parent used him as their guide. In 1946 this American paediatrician had published one of the all-time bestsellers, *Dr Spock's Baby and Child Care*. Up until 1998, this book was the second bestselling book after the Bible. Translated into 50 languages, it is still selling all over the world. Spock advocated using common sense, affection and instinct to raise children. He didn't recommend hitting and belting. I think my mother might have heard of it, possibly tried to take a little of it on board, but stuck to the old Victorian regime of strictness and physical discipline; it was in her blood — her own parents had been strict. My father was a gentle, sweet person disinclined to whacking, and we always felt he loved us. Everyone brought their children up the same way in those days — it was an era of accepted violence against children both at home and in school, and was completely normal. Many people still believe that if you spare the rod you spoil the child. To people who say, I was beaten and it didn't do me any harm, I say, really? Tell me about that. In my opinion the main thing you teach a child by hitting them is to be violent themselves, because they learn to resolve conflict with force and not other skills like compromise and negotiation. Physical discipline also makes it hard to develop a good relationship with the parent. When I was a child, Dr Spock's advice was seen as permissive, but I would say my nieces and nephews have been the real beneficiaries, as in their own parenting my brothers and sisters would consider his advice completely normal without ever having heard of him.

I was an unpopular child — too angry, too strong-willed, too precocious, too in-your-face — a thought would come into my head and it would go straight out of my mouth without any filter of diplomacy, politeness or social awareness. I spoke to the nuns in primer class as if they were people who were interested in my opinion. I thought I was an adult and hated being talked down to. At five I would tell adults how they should talk to me and corrected them if they were wrong. Mother would smile grimly and say, 'She's highly strung — I'll go out and beat her (that's a joke).'

When my brother David arrived I was outraged, and I punished him relentlessly for being born. David took one look at my insubordinate behaviour and lay very low from day one. He is still lying low. Then it happened again: another squawking baby insinuated itself into our household; I also punished Jonathan, who was a dear little boy, by actually trying to kill him. I started by bashing chicks then graduated to my siblings. By the time my middle sister arrived I was being worn down in the baby department, and I forgave my parents for this new outrage because she was so cute and sweet and pretty. But it didn't stop there: baby Paul turned up, and he was the first one who didn't fall under my domineering spell — he could stick up for himself against both Mum and me. Then when I was a hideous, angst-ridden teenager discovering sex, to my unmitigated horror my parents announced that ANOTHER one was on the way. This sixth baby, Desirée, was seen by us as a special gift as she was unexpected, so she was very spoiled and adored, and was sort of our mascot. She spent a childhood beguiling and charming us, and then grew up to say that she didn't feel as doted on as we thought.

Having been banned several times from kindergarten for general rabble-rousing, I was looking forward to going to the Holy Cross Convent in Epsom where I would have a broader populace for my empire. I could read, write and count quite well before I started school, but I never understood arithmetic and still don't. I was able to accomplish basic addition, subtraction, division and multiplication, but as I grew older the nuns hit us with the elusive equations of algebra, the spaciness of geometry and the limits of analysis. Please. Why anyone would choose to do arithmetic is one of the remaining mysteries of our time. My brother David, on the other hand, loved mathematics, was quite brilliant and became a design engineer.

My little natural talent lay with music, which you could say is a branch of mathematics. Although I couldn't add, I could memorise fairly complex music for my piano lessons and songs for my singing lessons. It took the nuns years to figure out that I couldn't read music — I could memorise anything I had heard once. For some reason I had innate rhythm and pitch. The really hard work came when it was noticed that I was faking it in music exams and had to start learning how to read music. I studied music, piano and singing from the age of about seven until I left school at 17, at which point I gave up classical music and singing and reincarnated myself as Joan Baez — enticed by the better hair-do than opera singers, and better-looking men to sing with.

As well as singing there was screaming. My parents bought a cheap little bach at Waiwera Beach where we all slept on top of each other. We thought it was great — swimming, living in a matchbox, lying in coffins cleverly disguised as bunks, eating outside, pulling up pipis, getting sunburnt, socialising at the Waiwera Club where they had knees-ups, singing and dancing competitions and, on every fourth Sunday morning, Mass. That little bach had a big tree behind it: the perfect venue for screaming. I was a part-time but committed screamer, and at home I normally screamed under the big pepper tree when the frustration of life and living in a straitjacket got to me. The couple who had the bach next to us were sexual screamers, and every afternoon they closed the curtains and she started screaming, so, if I was having a tantrum under the tree at the same time, it sounded like the Texas Chainsaw Massacre, and everyone in the surrounding baches went down to the beach to escape the noise. I invented the primal scream long before any American shrinks, and look at me now: I'm cured. I screamed at the head matrons during my nursing training, screamed at boyfriends, screamed at the judge when I was discharged without conviction for a drug arrest, screamed in encounter groups and screamed at abusive chefs in Paris. I can't remember the last time I screamed — you grow tired of it. Somewhere along the line you lose the anger; though it takes time. I figure by the time I am 80 I will be nice to strangers and be like my mother now is — sweet, even-tempered and accepting of life's vicissitudes. If I hadn't invented the primal scream, I would have had to march myself to the nearest Little Sisters of the Poor convent and offer myself up to Jesus. My parents always used to say they thought the child mortality rate was incredibly low in New Zealand considering how regularly children pushed their parents to the limit.

Holy Cross Convent and life as a Catholic child was tough, flamboyant, rigid and ostentatious all at the same time — the perfect breeding ground for a girl itching to break out. If you were naughty, you had to do pointless things like *lines*, where you wrote 'I must not poke Protestants' a hundred times in your little-girl handwriting. Another one was 'I must not talk in class'. Another I was given all the time was 'I must not tell lies'. If you were particularly naughty, you were strapped, even the girls. The one place you didn't get the strap was the music school, where I spent as much time as possible — somehow the musical nuns were less mad than the teaching nuns.

We had amazing freedom as children, unlike children now. From our bach at Waiwera we used to go up into the bush and spend all day building huts, finding wild things to eat and having adventures. In Auckland we spent hours in parks playing and hiding and making forts. We just had to be home for dinner at six o'clock. We were very strictly drilled in what to do if someone we didn't know approached us, but that was it — the freedom was fantastic and so much fun.

Despite the appeal of Auckland with its pohutukawa trees, glistening port, and sheep in Cornwall Park, suburban New Zealand in the 1950s was very dull and ordinary and behind the times — kind of like a colonial outpost. At this time when Sidney Holland was the Prime Minister, the population of Auckland was about 280,000 and the population of New Zealand only about 2 million. I remember some New Zealand Dutch friends receiving a package from relatives in Holland and it was full of missionary clothing, white nighties and ship biscuits. We all fell over with the hilarity of it. Europeans thought we in the tropics slept in huts and kept guns under our pillows. In truth, everyone had hedges, gardens full of flowers, vegetables and chooks, and life was so cheap that you could afford to own a house, have a car, educate six kids at private Catholic schools and take a proper holiday at Christmas. Of course there's plenty of rain in Auckland, but the upside is that it is very lush, and because of all the beaches it is very blue. It seems unbelievable now that when I left school in 1964 there was zero unemployment in New Zealand. It was truly a safe land of milk and honey. And chickens. Hence the recipe overleaf.

The fifties was a time when we lived with the seasons and, above all, ate with the seasons. There was very little imported food; an unadventurous

ROAST CHICKEN

Serves 6

1 x 1.5–2kg organic chicken
4 cloves garlic
short sprig of rosemary
good sprig of marjoram
couple of branches of parsley
few sprigs of thyme
sea salt and freshly ground pepper
extra virgin olive oil
2 onions in their skins, quartered
1 carrot, quartered
½ cup white wine
½ cup fresh chicken or vegetable stock

1. Preheat the oven to 230°C.

2. Place the chicken, untied, in a roasting dish.

3. Smash the garlic, herbs, salt, pepper and olive oil together in a mortar and pestle. With your fingers, rub this mixture all over the chicken, inside and out. Place the onion and carrot around the chicken — this is to give extra flavour to the gravy.

4. Roast for 30 minutes, remove from the oven and pour in the wine and stock. Turn the oven down to 180°C and place the chicken back in. Roast for another hour.

5. Meat always has to be rested for 15 minutes, so at this point you can remove the chicken from the roasting dish to a serving platter. Cover with a tea towel and leave in a warm place. Alternatively, you can turn the oven off, open the door and leave the chicken sitting there for 15 minutes.

6. I never add flour to the roasting juices, and, as chicken produces such good juice, you don't need to add much else to it. It will have taken on flavour from the herbs and vegetables. If you feel the gravy needs a lift, sprinkle in a few drops of good balsamic vinegar. Remove the vegetables and place the roasting pan of juices on a hot element. Bring to the boil, scraping up the bits stuck on the bottom.

татоо SERVE

Pour the hot gravy into a jug and bring the chicken to the table to be carved. To carve well, you need a sharp knife and minor knowledge of chook anatomy. With this sharp knife, you cut off the legs then cut them into smaller portions. Next you cut off the wings, then cut thick slices (I can't bear thin ones) off the breast. Serve with Agria potatoes that have been roasted in duck fat, and a crisp green salad.

selection of vegetables and fruit were sold in the Chinese shops, and if you wanted something different like artichokes, avocados or shallots you had to grow them. Breakfast was cornflakes, home-stewed fruit, toast and Marmite or marmalade, and a glass of milk. Dad had percolated coffee, which I considered the most unpalatable beverage I had ever tasted. We rose early and went to bed early. We never locked our doors when we went out or at night, and you popped in a lot to visit friends without calling first. You walked into someone's house and said, 'Cripes, I'd love a cup of tea, Ann.' As a toddler and a little girl, I was put to bed for the night at 5pm, at which hour I wasn't remotely ready for sleep. My mother put me in the cot, said goodnight, closed the door and I didn't see another human being until the next morning. I thought my father was a visiting friend of the family.

It was in these long hours alone that I started singing, talking, and telling myself stories to alleviate the loneliness and boredom. I spent hours talking to myself. My aunty Peg said the first time she met me, when Mum had brought me over to Australia to visit, I sat on the kitchen bench (I could hardly walk I was so little) and told stories for hours — to her it was quite extraordinary. She said I sang all the time.

'Does your little brother David sing, too?' she asked.

'No,' I replied, 'he doesn't talk.'

David didn't talk until he was five, mostly because he couldn't get a word in edgewise between Mother and me — the two bossiest females in the world. My quiet father didn't squeeze much of a word in either. I am still a sociable loner, and I think it originates from those days. I find it completely horrifying that strangers (fans) now shout at me from cafés, touch me and chase me down the street, because I am still that little girl in my own world who likes to control my universe. My dear friend the fabulous caterer Ruth Pretty tells me I need counselling so that I can be nicer to strangers. Other friends tell me I have improved over the years.

My first brush with royalty was when Princess Anne was born the year after me in 1950. Because of this connection I was always reminded by Mum how close we were in age, kept up to date with what she was doing, and given photos of her so that I could admire her clothes and her ponies. My mother and I were seriously into clothes and dressing up, so if Princess Anne wore a little woollen coat, so did I; if she donned black patent-leather shoes, I wanted a pair; when she displayed white gloves, so did I. My second brush with royalty was when I was about eight and my mother suggested I write a letter to the Queen, telling her about myself and asking after Princess Anne. She was always doing things like that.

'Peta, why don't you go to that wedding your friend is going to?'

'Because I haven't been invited, Mum.'

'Oh, don't worry about that — you're just a child.'

'Peta, get up on the stage and sing us a song.'

'Mum, it's a competition for professionals — you had to have registered.'

'Don't worry about that — get up there — you'll win it anyway.'

Her advice as to how to deal with Protestant children poking us Catholic kids with umbrellas on the way home from school was particularly enchanting.

'Mum, they poked me.'

'Well, Peta, you poke them right back. It's an eye for an eye and a tooth for a tooth in the Bible. If you let Protestants walk all over you, you'll never be able to stand up for yourself in the future. Remember what your name is and the good family you come from and that you are the one who is going to heaven, not them.' Mum didn't take shit from anyone, least of all a manky Protestant. To this day, my main technique for dealing with bullies is to hit back fast, then run. You've got to hit hard so they don't get back up again, then use the wild-dog technique Mum taught us: if you ignore them they'll go away.

But back to the Queen. To my astonishment, I received a letter back from the Queen's lady-in-waiting, addressed to Master Peter and thanking me for my kindness in writing. I was a bit miffed that they took me for a boy but was happy with the letter, and the story of the little girl in Epsom who'd been sent a letter from the Queen was in the paper the very next week. Little did I know I would be hearing from the Queen again many years later.

By then we had moved up in the world to the leafy, desirable suburb of Epsom. Our wooden villa in King Edward Avenue had four bedrooms, all with big sash windows, a wide, high hallway and a large sitting-room that no one ever went into. It was for special guests and was full of valuable ornaments, polished brocade-covered furniture, embossed wallpaper and flowery carpets. Out the back was a large yard with tree huts, flowers, vegetables, chickens and fruit trees. All summer we picked passionfruit, peaches, apples, oranges, lemons and plums. My siblings and I lay next to the asparagus bed and ate the tender shoots as soon as they were long enough, and we were always in trouble for doing it but couldn't stop. Sometimes I sat under the drooping pepper tree with my biscuits and milk and dreamt about pirates and princesses, and sometimes I yelled my head off. Sometimes I lay under my father's car breathing in the petrol fumes because I liked the smell. Until my mother dragged me out. Every Friday we had smoked fish pie. The recipe opposite is a flash version of Mum's pie.

Middle-class New Zealand in the 1950s was resolutely conformist, and so deathly boring you would tear your hair out just to have something to do. It was so boring that we didn't even know we were bored — we were born into this post-war universe of blandness where being bland in a bland suburb was all we knew and all that people aspired to. They wanted ordinariness after the war. My brothers and sisters and I were saved to a large extent from death by boredom because we had an exciting, pretty, artistic but slightly nutty mother. Our adorable father, Harvey, was like his mother, Jessie — easy-going, unambitious, loved a flutter at the races and dedicated to his colourful wife and loud children. He had sandy hair, a shy smile and a dry wit. He had converted to Catholicism, and they were both very staunch about it, which added to the theatricality in our household — Virgins, rosaries and crucifixes all over the place. Also ruined cartilage from kneeling on the floor to say the rosary every night after dinner. When we climbed into our car to go anywhere, our mother immediately prepared us for death by making us say a prayer, do the sign of the cross and hope to God that, if there were an accident, we would die without sin and with clean underwear. I still never wear undies I wouldn't want to die in. Imagine the shame if a doctor found your smashed body in a state of impurity.

In the early 1960s my parents bought a section on St Andrews Road, Epsom, and built a house that they designed themselves with the help of an architect, built themselves with the help of one carpenter, landscaped themselves and painted themselves. This was the first time that house design incorporated the new 'Pacific' style, unique to

SMOKED FISH PIES

Serves 4–6

1kg Agria potatoes
50g butter
sea salt and freshly ground black pepper
1 tablespoon flour
300ml milk
500g flaked smoked fish
2 tablespoons capers, washed
4 tablespoons chopped fresh dill
12 cherry tomatoes
12 hard-boiled quail eggs
Parmesan cheese for topping
4 or 6 oven-proof pie dishes

1. Preheat the oven to 200°C.

2. Cook and mash the potatoes, adding half of the butter, a little milk, and salt and pepper.

3. To make the white sauce, melt the rest of the butter with the flour in a saucepan. Turn the heat up high, add the milk, some salt and pepper, and whisk until the sauce thickens. Lower the heat and stir with a wooden spoon for 5 minutes. Remove from the heat and gently stir in the fish, capers and dill.

4. Spray the pie dishes with oil. Put some mashed potato in the bottom of the dishes, place some fish mixture on top, dot with tomatoes and eggs, put some more fish mixture on top, then a final layer of mashed potato.

5. Grate or peel Parmesan cheese on top and cook in the oven for 20 minutes, until the pies are heated through and the tops are golden.

New Zealand. Prior to that, houses were built largely along English lines, and so were suitable to anything but a Pacific climate and lifestyle: a hallway with bedrooms off it, a dining room, a separate lounge that was never used because it was too posh, and a pokey, nasty kitchen. Now, houses used more timber and glazing than before, and they featured open-plan living, and the new buzz-phrase: indoor–outdoor flow.

Our new house had a large kitchen with big windows, and it was separated from the dining room by a buffet bar. Off this was the lounge, which was much more user-friendly than the old style; all of this opening onto a long verandah, which had a fantastic view. I learned then that 'a view' was the most desirable thing in the world. I couldn't understand why adults had to see something, and why that was of such value to the upwardly mobile. Mum's friends would visit and gasp, 'Oh, Ann, the view!' and my brothers and sisters would mime behind their backs. 'Oh my God — look at the view!!!!!!' This style of house has stayed, and to this day few New Zealanders would think of buying an old villa that hadn't been opened up at the back, and no one would dream of building a house with a separate kitchen, dining room and living room; in fact, our houses now are one big kitchen with bedrooms and offices.

One cannot write about the 1950s without delving into the dark side: our innocent little lives were blighted, nay, irrevocably traumatised by our regular experiences of pain, fear, torture and ruined teeth in murder houses all over the country. I wasn't awarded one single prize at school, but I should have received a medal for surviving the murder house. A medal made of amalgam that gives an electric shock when touched. I ate apples, drank sour, warm milk at school and ate very few sweets, so why did my dear little teeth need so much twice yearly 'preventative' work? These clinics were staffed by 'drill-and-fill' dental nurses dressed in white, with white veils, white stockings, white shoes and red cardigans. We were all terrified and hated going, but our parents and teachers assured us that it was for the best and would protect our teeth. You have to suffer for the sake of beauty. I can't forget those chairs — like execution chairs with straps to hold you down. The machinery was straight out of *Dracula*, with primitive foot-pedal belt-drive machines, and tooth drills as thick as a screwdriver (slight exaggeration). Needless to say our teeth were damaged, and we spent the rest of our days paying a fortune to have the copper amalgam and mercury removed from our heads. We yelled, but mercy was not an easy thing to come by. There was gas available to control the pain, but it was expensive and I don't remember it ever being used on me. This is why New Zealanders of my age are still afraid of dentists and the sound of a drill, and why dentists have the highest suicide rate of all professionals — they feel rejected and unloved. Can't think why.

At the age of about 12 I was swimming with my friends at our bach at Waiwera and some boys were mucking around with small surfboards even though it isn't a surf beach. Suddenly I heard a loud crash like a thunder-clap and the water around me was full of blood. My head felt as though it had been lifted off, and I started screaming and spitting teeth out of my mouth. Everyone around me was screaming. A surfboard had shot out of the water very fast and hit me under the chin, snapping my head back. 'Don't spit them out, don't spit them out,' my mother shrieked. I was choking and crying and trying to climb out of the water. It was the school holidays and no dentists were working. I was taken to Auckland and began years of a chain-saw-massacre treatment at the hands of a specialist sadist in Remuera.

All the repair work — cracks, gold fillings, root canals, removal of nerves — everything was done in this dentist's chair without so much as a suggestion of anaesthetic. I cried and shook through every appointment, and stumbled home, blind with pain. When I complained, I was told not to be so ungrateful as he was the best dentist in Auckland, and how could I be so selfish when he was dying of cancer. I prayed before every appointment that this man would die before I arrived. I wondered why it was taking him so long. He was not only physically cruel but emotionally abusive as well, losing patience with my groaning, and yelling at me when I shrank from him — these days he would be sent to prison, but in those days you could do anything to children. The powerlessness of it all was depressing. By contrast, my brother David went to the same dentist and became so accustomed to the pain that to this day he doesn't require anaesthesia, not even for a root canal.

Needless to say, I didn't visit another dentist until I was 25. I was living in Vancouver and my teeth were so bad that I was forced to make a dental appointment. I walked in, sat in the swish chair, told the dentist

I was about to go into anaphylactic shock and started hyper-ventilating. Unlike the sadist, he sat next to me and quietly explained exactly what he was going to do, asked my permission before he touched me, and checked every two minutes that I was okay. I didn't feel the anaesthetic needle going into my gums, didn't feel the drilling and had no pain afterwards. Times had definitely changed in the world of dentistry.

CHAPTER 3

IN WHICH I DISCOVER UZÈS, BROCANTES AND FOOD MARKETS.

L et me tell you about the stunningly good-looking town of Uzès where everyone smiles — maybe because the sun shines 300 days a year. In fact, the sun shines so much and the skies are so unremittingly blue that it is almost monotonous . . . but not quite. When you live in a city like Auckland that's built on a rainforest, every day of perfect weather in the south of France is a gift from the universe.

I passed through Uzès, on the Languedoc-Roussillon–Provençe border, in the early 1980s when I lived in Paris, and thought it quite a dump and that no one had heard of it. But then I was introduced to a revived Uzès in the summer of 2004. I was back in France looking for a place to host my week-long culinary adventures, and planning on doing them in Burgundy, where I used to live, but when I saw elegant and fragrant Uzès I fell in love immediately, as almost everyone does. I stayed at Gina's place on Rue du Dr Blanchard in the posh part of Uzès, and immersed myself in the sunny, intoxicating lifestyle of the Languedoc. In the first three weeks, I bought a traditional lavender-picker's hat (made from straw, with a huge brim and small crown), and to cover my other extremity: pink-and-brown striped espadrilles. To further equip myself, I purchased a terrible, hopeless car to spend days driving through sleepy villages and past ancient vineyards.

'Uzès' is an unusual word, which derives from the Gallo-Roman *Ucetia*, betraying the ancient origins of the settlement. The town is also called such flattering things as 'beautiful stone' and 'jewel of the Garrigue'. It is indeed a unique town full of charm and nobility, whose architecture clearly advertises its glorious past. You can see its towers and turrets from throughout the Garrigue countryside.

At the end of the sixteenth century, the Uzège area grew rich producing serge (twilled wool), embroidery, clothing and most particularly silk. Uzès had a very illustrious bishopric, which nurtured both a saint and a pope, and it stayed powerful until the Revolution. The original noble or upper-bourgeois families also owned huge properties outside Uzès with beautiful *mas* (Provençal farmhouses), which the caretakers of their land lived in. However, with the passage of time, wars, pestilence and debt, the houses of Uzès were sold or crumbled into ruin, and during the first half of the twentieth century the town fell into a deep sleep — becoming grey and unfashionable, the basements and wells filling with putrid water. In 1958 a building in Uzès fell down, killing two people and injuring six. The same thing happened again two years later. The appearance of tap water in 1960 was seen as considerable progress, though it meant nobody used or cared for all the public fountains anymore.

As the population rose from 1,363 after the war to 6,058 by 1962, no one knew how the town was going to cope. However, Uzès was saved by the 'Malraux Law' in 1962, which released huge government funds to carefully restore it. The beautiful houses slowly got a second wind, and the arcades around the square brightened up as if they had been waiting for their illustrious history to be returned to them. With restoration money, the town decided to reinvest its wealth in top-class tourism with cultural festivals, furniture painting, ironwork and ceramics, art workshops and music. All they had to do was touch up the extraordinary beauty that was already there. In 2008 Uzès was designated as a *ville d'art*, an official status given by the Ministry of Culture and Communication in recognition of its valuable heritage.

Nowadays, this stylish, well-heeled place seduces many, and when you mention it, people seem to glaze over with dreamy smiles and sweet memories. Uzès is a town full of character due to its rich past, ancient buildings, famous Saturday market and local festivals, especially the musical ones. At the beginning of the sixteenth century, Uzès was walled, but a century later the walls were demolished and the stones were used to make the cherry-lined walks that were to become today's glorious boulevards. Inside the walls the medieval town is still evident, being full of covered walkways and shady passages. The work of eighteenth-century architects is also on show; they were influenced by Avignon, which was in turn influenced by Italy, thus bringing a grander element.

As the town became richer, often streets were realigned and neighbouring houses bought and joined together with storeys added. This was the case with Gina and Michael's house — it was originally two houses at No. 11 and is now one house at No. 17, the rest of the block being taken up by the Hôtel d'Entraigues. Today on the outside, these historic mansions look very unified, as if they were built in one period of time, but you have only to go inside to be made aware of the traces of the centuries and their complex history. Obviously the basements are the most ancient, and you can see where the builders dug into the rock to extract the stones with which to build the original foundations.

My luck in being able to stay at Gina and Michael's place on Rue du Dr Blanchard provoked me into looking into its history. In the sixteenth century this four-storey mansion in the oldest, classiest part of Uzès belonged to the de la Peyrière family of wealthy artists. It is a classified historical building called l'Hôtel l'Albiousse, written about in the book *Les Belles Demeures Familiales d'Uzès* by Jean-Christophe Galant and Mireille Olmière. By the eighteenth century it had passed into the hands of a lawyer called Antoine d'Albiousse and stayed in that family until the middle of the nineteenth century.

On the ground floor the vestibule leads to the little open courtyard where, if you look up, you can see two vaulted terraces on the first and second floors. My favourite place to write was on the first balcony, lying on the daybed, listening to the fountain. I found this dribbling water obtrusively loud when I first arrived there; soon I hardly noticed it. Off the courtyard is the vaulted living room with an alabaster fireplace. The wide, stone staircase leads upstairs to the 'noble' floor with its eighteenth-century decoration: fireplaces with ornamental stucco panels above them; tall wooden Louis XIII doors; and panelled frescos high on the walls. The floors are stone or tile, with high, exposed, wooden ceilings in some of the three bedrooms. Above this is another floor with three more bedrooms, and above this a fourth floor with two rooms. One can also go out onto the roof. In the basement there is a well dug into the rock, and a circular stone vessel for oil. Gina and Michael had left the worn and uneven stone stairs uncarpeted, which I really liked, and Persian rugs were thrown on the stone and tiled floors.

The décor in the communal areas of the house was rather masculine and traditional, but Gina's bedroom and dressing room were wonderlands of eccentric and delightful furnishings: animal-skin couches, pictures of horses and dogs everywhere, stunning collections of antique toys, and lace clothes hanging from old racks, unmade bed . . . Her natural warmth and sultriness imbued the room, and her love of horses was obvious everywhere — saddles hung over her balcony, horse rugs and chattels in the upstairs room, riding clothes in the laundry. As is common with middle-class Swiss, Michael had his own bedroom with balcony. This room, in contrast, was ordered, calm, tastefully decorated and the bed was always made. From this balcony, delicious, melancholy, heart-searing Spanish and jazz melodies poured gently into the courtyard like a river of silk.

Gina and Michael kept a very regular life, entirely dominated by their three horses, five dogs and two cats. If they could have kept the horses in the house, they would have. The horses had to be worked daily, the dogs walked four times a day, and breakfast, lunch and dinner were served like clockwork and late in the evening, often at 10pm. This was a sane, ordered life with no dramas like the other places I'd stayed, no public shedding of clothes to the accompaniment of wild music, no livid neighbours screaming abuse, and no midnight robberies. It was a retreat, a convent, a spa.

It was a house of great civility, intellectual and musical stimulation, and good conversation. When it came time for dinner, people materialised from distant corners of the mansion, cooked things together with whatever was around, and ate with wine and candles in the courtyard. With my itinerant life of the social savage, this was a rather good influence, although I suspected that Gina was more like me — if left to her own devices, she would eat bread and cheese standing up and drink sparkling water straight out of the bottle. I have a friend who tells anyone who will listen that I eat baked beans out of the tin with a fork. This is clearly made up to impress people, but I might have done it once. As Nigel Slater has said, 'There is no light so perfect as that which shines from the fridge at 2am.'

The only disgusting thing that happened in this perfect house with these ordered people concerned one of their dogs. I don't like dogs particularly, and the biggest one in the house, a Newfoundland called Gustave, fell passionately in love with me. He followed me everywhere, cried when I left the room, and drooled huge gobs of saliva all over me and my clothes. This, in spite of all the bad vibes and negative reinforcement I offered him. I think he was mentally ill. Gina and Michael adored him and were inconsolable when he died.

The first time I saw Gina she was striding across the square in riding breeches, boots and white shirt, carrying a saddle. She looked rather gorgeous and curvy, with untidy, curly chestnut hair, a little lipstick and a mysterious smile. She was very attractive in a Jessica Lange sort of way, and had the air of someone who was confident, almost regal. Subsequently I met her to discuss our arrangement regarding my lodging *chez elle*, and she was very quiet and sweet, lacking the assurance of the woman in the riding clothes. Next to her I felt like a Christmas tree; like an electrical fault looking for resolution. I was to discover that Gina is not a crowd person, and she is happiest, no, radiant, when with her horses. Talk about opposites attract.

Michael only heard of me when he returned to his house from a trip to Spain and discovered I was living there. I was wondering who could possibly be good enough for Gina as he walked into the kitchen — tall, floppy fair hair, good-looking, big nose (which is always a plus), wide smile and a charming, if reserved, manner. Must be because they're Swiss, I thought. We don't do reserved in New Zealand, particularly not me. In cases of reserve, I usually lie low and wait for further instructions or information. This tactic was to be rewarded eventually, as Gina and Michael slowly opened up to me over the months I lived there, and we were genuinely sorry to be parted when it was time for me to go back to my other life in the South Pacific.

When I moved into Gina and Michael's house, I was told there was a person missing. Gina and Michael's Swiss friend Eva was in Los Angeles, soon to return and take up her search for a house to buy in the area. Whenever there was a computer problem, the cry would go up: 'Wait for Eva — she will fix it.' One day I came downstairs and there she was — just as you imagine Swiss women to be — tall, rangy, graceful, direct stare, short hair, energetic. She was one of those women (like her mother and sisters in the photos she showed me) who effortlessly maintain the correct weight, still wear singlets and tight pants in their forties and fifties, and look like racehorses, even first thing in the morning. Strictly speaking, I should have hated her. While she jumped up and took a fast walk early in the morning, I lay languorously in bed listening to the street-cleaner and the birds; while I ate duck breast with all the fat on, she ate vegetables and pasta; while I was curvy like Gina, she was taut and coiled like a gazelle — content-ish but always vigilant to the danger of deception. Eva alerted me to all the things I could do with my laptop: cordless fast online (remember this was the mid-2000s), iChat, Skype, radio, recording music and photos, watching DVDs, and we would spend evenings iChatting each other from our bedrooms. I was enchanted. I was a modern woman in charge of my telecommunications. Sadly, I have made zero progress since then.

One of my most cherished summer pastimes in Uzès is to sit listening to a Baroque concert, which they often hold in spectacular surroundings such as the Cathédrale Saint-Théodorit or in the courtyard of the Duché (the Duke's castle). The seventeenth-century cathedral has a nineteenth-century remodelled west front and a very celebrated eighteenth-century organ. Above the tall arcades is a triforium gallery (a shallow and arched gallery within the thickness of an inner wall) with wrought-iron rails, and up against the south wall is the elegant twelfth-century Tour Fenestrelle (tower with windows). This pretty, round bell-tower is unique in France, rising to 42 metres with six storeys that recede one above the other. You can see it for miles. Outside around the back is a secret garden where little concerts are also held. It's best to go to the paying ones because the free ones are like being in a daycare centre: exhibitionist breast-feeding mothers everywhere, fidgeting children, and old people talking contentedly and loudly throughout. English tourists can be spotted in their pale meringue and biscuit linen. The evening concerts are warm, even if there's a touch of the mistral wind making the trees compete with the musicians.

If you go to a concert in the Duché, you will often see the ducal family on a balcony, entranced by the music. Dukes are a rare breed in France. You have to be a bit more dressed-up for these concerts, and your attention to the soprano is rewarded at half-time by drinks set up outside, manned by the fun degenerates from the Hôtel d'Entraigues down the road. They are so degenerate that they have now had to sell the hotel. The castle itself is a rather austere, feudal, testosterone-imbued mass, exhibiting many architectural periods stretching from the fourteenth to the nineteenth century. Now it dominates the centre of town like Gulliver in Lilliput and is partially accessible to the great unwashed. Even though the family still live in part of it, you can visit the courtyard, go up the Bermonde tower and look over the burnt-tiled roofs of Uzès and the severe, beautiful Garrigues countryside. You may also visit some of the apartments via a beautiful Renaissance main staircase, which has coffered (sunken panels), diamond-pointed vaulting. Once inside, you are surrounded by fabulous

Renaissance and Louis XIII furniture, decorative plaster-work and a Trianon cabinet gilded with gold-leaf. I thought all of these knick-knacks would look good in a house in Uzès, should I ever buy one.

Every Sunday, Uzès hosts a *puces* (flea market) in the morning in a car park off the roads leading to Avignon and Nîmes. Once I really struck it lucky: I found a specially designed silver holder for toast and *foie gras* (an instrument of my dreams), two antique wooden mandolins for slicing vegetables, an old *tagine* dish and a Moroccan vase. I've seen others make off with old beds, furniture, lamps, Dior handbags and linen. While the whole area is known for its great *puces*, the one at Uzès is particularly good — cheap and full of bargains. Antique daybeds, kitchen equipment, fountains, lace dresses, paintings, a dinner date, the latest gossip, old comics, evening shoes — all lie before you . . . with the searing sun beating down on your straw lavender-picker's hat. I once found a box full of silver-plated cutlery for €10, sadly, later stolen by the woman who squatted in my friend's apartment. It's all very relaxed and typically southern, with most of the stuff laid out on the ground on a blanket, and some artfully arranged on tables — and the best part is no one hassles you. And when you are done, it's off with your friends to the PMU betting café at the bottom of the boulevard for a restorative *crème* coffee with milk.

This was one of my favourite cafés when I first arrived in Uzès, and was not one of the chic, expensive ones where everyone goes to be seen and to see, but a little down-to-earth pinball café called Le Café de l'Hôtel, which restaurateur Paul Jack first introduced me to. It's at the lower end of the Boulevard des Alliés and is frequented by rustic workers, pregnant waitresses and people who are obviously locals and are very olive-skinned, maybe gypsies. Normally you would see gypsies further south in the Camargue, but this area of the Languedoc also has strong links from its proximity to Spain; in fact, the *abrivados* are full of Spanish dancing and singing, and there is a well-known Spanish dancing school in Nîmes. The absolute best thing about this café is the more-than-middle-aged owner. This woman is a complete knock-out — tiny, slim and brown with flashing black eyes, she is not about to take any prisoners, ever. Being on the good side of her is fun, but I wouldn't want to walk on the wild side. Upon meeting we immediately formed a mutual admiration society around our respective looks. She loved my clothes and hair and earrings, and I loved her clothes and hair and earrings. She dressed like a 25-year-old in tight short skirts, off-the-shoulder tops, high heels, with long jet-black hair tied up and shovel-loads of make-up.

She arrived at work every day in full combat gear as if she were going to a night club. It was always a pleasure to catch her in the market buying vegetables in a black frilly dress, high espadrilles and false eyelashes, or waiting tables in frou-frou earrings and hypertension-inducing leather pants. We would spy each other on the other side of the street and burst into smiles and compliments. She and her partner were not the only dashing people in the café. There was a handsome, swarthy, muscle-bound man, I guess in his thirties, with black curly hair and questionable sartorial taste, who bestowed come-to-bed smiles on the ladies and made as good a coffee as you will find in the south of France. (Italian coffee is much better.) He would say, 'I love your accent,' and I wanted to say bold things like, 'Would you run away with me?', but never did. We smiled dazzlingly at each other and didn't get any further. I found out that he was the owner's son and they live in the countryside outside Uzès.

The heart of sugar and cream in Uzès is to be found at 6 Boulevard des Alliés: the *pâtisserie* Deschamps, a tabernacle of rows of shining, refined pastries, *croissants* and hand-made chocolates. Every single pastry is *incontournable* (literally, 'unavoidable' or 'inescapable'), and there is not one single delicacy to which you would turn up your nose. Every day all the pastries are freshly made — Black Forest gâteau, *millefeuilles*, rum baba. My personal favourites are the tiny berry tartlets: raspberry, strawberry, blueberry, cassis, blackberry, gooseberry on a bed of light pastry cream.

Philippe Deschamps has been making pastries in this shop for 27 years. He is the humble, quietly spoken son of *boulangers* from Toulouse, and is married to the fragrant and always smiling Carole. He is a Compagnon du Tour de France, that organisation of craftsmen and artisans that had its origins in the Middle Ages. This provides a learning system of apprenticeships that enables the participants to travel around France learning their trade from different masters. There is not one occasion Philippe does not cater for and he loves special festivals. On Mother's Day he makes little pink handbags from chocolate, raspberries and praline. At Easter there are eggs, little characters and figurines. Saint Valentine's Day brings on an orgy of creamy coffee, caramel and hazelnut biscuits and little cakes with melting chocolate hearts. Of course he goes mad at Christmas, making many versions of the much loved *bûche de Noël* or chocolate log, chestnut pastries, preserved olives in chocolate and *panettone*.

Come New Year, everyone waits with bated breath for the famous French *galettes* and *couronnes des rois*. *Galettes* are flat flaky-pastry tarts full of frangipane, and hidden in the middle is the *fève* or tiny trinket, which can be anything from a doll to a saint to a car. The original *fève* was a broadbean, then it became porcelain, and more recently plastic. The lucky person who finds the *fève* in their slice of tart is king for the day and wears the gold paper crown that comes with the tart. The little *fèves* have become collectables and you can buy them separately. Recently Philippe collaborated with the best jeweller in Uzès, Bénédikt Aïchelé, in creating a limited-edition *fève*, which was polished porcelain in three shapes and nine colours. Two of them were actually in gold and platinum.

The Deschamps also have a chocolate shop at the other end of town at 17 Boulevard Gambetta, so if you are in chocolate crisis and are in the middle of town, you have to decide which way to run. Philippe specialises in truffles, *mendiants* (chocolate and dried fruit), pralines, nougat with preserved olives, and big sheets of dark, milk and white chocolate for eating and cooking, all made from the high-grade luxury Valrhona chocolate, the best chocolate in the world. Only a quarter of the world's chocolate comes from South America, and that's what Valrhona use, specifically the Criollo bean. Philippe says that anything made with praline walks out of the shop — it is the French favourite hands-down. One should ideally eat chocolate at 18 degrees and let it soften in the mouth before biting and slowly eating. Opposite is Philippe's recipe for hot chocolate (check out his website at patisserie-deschamps-uzes.fr).

On special days, such as Bastille Day, Uzès indulges in a grand *brocante* — a second-hand and antiques market. Up on the Avenue de la Libération, the Marronniers car park is transformed into a sparkling treasure trove of antiques, crockery, buttons, old books and mountains

PHILIPPE DESCHAMPS'S HOT CHOCOLATE

Makes 6

100ml cream
900ml full cream milk
60g sugar
250g Valrhona Guanaja 70% chocolate

1. Put the cream, milk and sugar in a pan, and bring to the boil.

2. Pour this over the chocolate in a food processor and mix until smooth.

3. Serve immediately in glasses.

CHEF'S TIP

Bring the chocolate mixture to the boil a second time for a smoother finish. You may also add spices like cardamom, Sichuan pepper, cinnamon or tonka beans.

of embroidered linen sheets, old lace, tablecloths, bedspreads, nighties and underwear. French people adore browsing the stalls or poring over old volumes, manuscripts, posters and cards. You might be loitering at an unattended stall, reaching for something interesting, when from the ether you hear, '*Quinze euros, madame.*' Looking up, you see the stall-holders close by, having lunch. They're not furtively snacking. An antique table will be set up with cutlery and glasses for a feast: roast chickens, *pâté*, *saucisson* and salads, with the wine and bread stacked up on some precious bedspreads. If you decided to buy the table in question, no doubt they would move over to the piano and keep eating.

One wonderful regular *brocante* worth a visit is held in the charming old town of Villeneuve-lès-Avignon outside Avignon. This village thinks it is still in the last century, and every Saturday Jeannot and his family are there selling the fabulously fresh Bouzigues oysters and *violets* (sea-squirts), which he grows himself. The terrifying-looking *violet* looks like a lump of rock, but is not as hard as an oyster, and you can slice them in half with a sharp knife. Inside is orange/yellow flesh, which you remove with your thumb. These things are full of iodine and look and taste a bit like kina (sea urchin) — sweet and briny — and very good. Most people take one look at them and run away.

It is worth taking the trip just to eat lunch at Jeannot's outside tables under the trees. He opens oysters with his bare hands as they are ordered, and business is brisk right from 10 in the morning. In the south of France, you become accustomed to eating oysters and drinking wine at that hour, and even earlier. The waitress takes your order, and soon you are delivered a big plate of prawns with aioli, desperately fresh, plump oysters with lemon wedges and *violets*, along with a bottle of Picpoul Blanc de Pinet — drink as much as you want and the price is worked out at the end. It is a lovely life here, and I can see why every second visitor wants to open their very own B&B and be part of that life. The southern French, on the other hand, do nothing but complain, chase foreign women, and wish they could go and live in New Zealand, *n'est-ce pas*?

When I first arrived in Uzès, I went to eat at the best restaurant the town has ever had, sadly now defunct. I will tell you about it anyway because it was so instrumental in contributing to my happiness levels and was right across the road from Gina's house on the desirable Rue du Dr Blanchard. I could actually lean out my bedroom window on the second floor and talk to the staff. It was called Les Trois Salons and was owned by New Zealanders Paul and Charmaine Jack. Of course, the problem with being a gastronomad and finding oneself in a very good restaurant is the groan situation. It is almost impossible to eat an exquisitely pink pigeon breast and then find its leg upended in a cup of *girolle* (golden mushroom) *consommé* without emitting sounds of ecstasy. Well-heeled customers strolled in with their carefully brushed canines, so I was not the only eccentric one. Where I come from, you would go straight to prison for this, but in France it is still perfectly acceptable for dogs to sit quietly at their masters' feet in posh restaurants. This and bullfighting are two of the things that make the south of France exciting and slightly naughty — you always feel you are breaking the rules and getting away with it.

Les Trois Salons was housed in the oldest mansion in Uzès (built in 1699). Paul Jack from Westport had been in the hospitality business for 20 years, and Charmaine Doyer from Christchurch had interrupted a high-profile clothes-designing career to produce their delicious daughter Scarlet, who was 15 months old when I visited. Paul had had two restaurants in London, but they were ready for a change, and the sloweddown lifestyle and beautiful countryside of Uzès was perfect. Not only that, but the town needed a really good restaurant. Having located the extraordinary, historic location of Les Trois Salons, they went on the hunt for a chef who was out of the ordinary and could interpret their vision of refined but approachable food. Their aim was to have no fixed *carte* or signature dish, but to change the evening menu each week and the lunch menu every day.

Paul and Charmaine certainly managed to find someone extraordinary in the form of Swedish chef Petter Nilsson. Already well known in Sweden and working in Paris, when Petter heard about the Trois Salons proposition he immediately jumped in his car and drove down to Uzès. The resulting cuisine has been called 50 per cent classic and 50 per cent rock 'n' roll, where no more than three ingredients found themselves on a plate at the same time, in order to preserve the flavours. It was brilliantly creative food, restrained, colourful, youthful and always full of exciting taste sensations and surprising lightness. For example: pumpkin purée, topped with fresh sardines and enveloped in a fresh lettuce heart; fingers of confit tuna on a red pepper salad with *poutargue* (air-dried mullet roe); lamb gnocchi with salted almonds and preserved lemon; and fine peach tart with pistachio purée and yoghurt ice cream.

The three rooms and garden at the back were designed by Charmaine. The cool washed-grey décor was a chic mix of old and new, with white tablecloths, contemporary chandeliers, pale embossed walls, and a lovely wooden and zinc bar. History had been kind, too, bequeathing them original floors of wood, flagstone and tiles, tall eighteenth-century multi-paned windows, gently vaulted ceilings and an enchanting walled garden with a fountain. Regular customers were particularly attached to the *maître d'*, Nacer, whose humour, knowledge and charm made him indispensable to the dining experience (not to mention his exotic good looks). The young staff were informal but always correct, obviously adored the food, and described it with great respect and joy.

Paul and Charmaine are now back in Nelson, running a very successful and stylish furniture and design business called Edito. Petter is now back cooking in Stockholm, Sweden. Les Trois Salons is now a one-star restaurant called La Maison d'Uzès.

At my first party in Uzès — the first birthday of Charmaine and Paul's daughter Scarlet in 2004 — I met a gigantic Dutchman called Rutger. We had been told about each other by Paul, because Rutger had a vineyard with a possibly suitable kitchen and I had a cooking-school idea, looking for a suitable kitchen. As is normal with someone who is interested to meet you (unless they're French), Rutger completely ignored me and proceeded to work the room, handing out huge bouquets of the sunflowers he grows on his property, kissing babies and talking loudly in various languages with the locals. I bided my time while he adjusted to the vision of an ageing guest's transparent black dress revealing ghastly haunches in a G-string, Asian-style finger-food valiantly prepared by Charmaine in the wilting heat, and people handing around joints and wine. Finally, we started talking, and he invited me around to look at his property, specifically the kitchen. In fact, why didn't I come around the following Saturday for a fire-roasted leg of *sanglier* (wild boar)? *Zut alors!* It would have been churlish to say no.

Rutger needed a wife to run his parties — he just had no idea. He invited loads of families and individuals who all dressed up and arrived at 4pm as requested. Not much was ready, and he, the master of ceremonies, was wandering around in old shorts and down-trodden shoes. His hair looked like he'd been asleep in a haystack for the past three weeks. Isn't he charming? said one of the ladies. No, I thought. I had specially pressed my little silk Marni frock for the occasion. A few hours later, the cook arrived with the leg of *sanglier*, and two hours after that it was ready to eat. Meanwhile the children were screaming, everyone was getting drunk, some old guy was looking down my front telling us that he was the last bachelor left in the area (his wife smiled pityingly and indulgently), and the old people had given up and gone home unfed. I wandered around the property and found sheds, a tasting room and a not-big-enough-kitchen for a cooking school. The house was very grand with huge rooms full of art and antiques, but it looked like the owner hadn't quite moved in yet.

The Dutch cook slapped the meat on the kitchen table, and huge amounts of cracked pepper, sea salt and olive oil were rubbed in, then it was covered in vine leaves. Next it was wrapped in tinfoil and, inexplicably, in hay, which would have had no effect whatsoever. Meat cooked in hay is utterly divine, but not through tinfoil. The thrice-enveloped haunch was carried to a fire — which had been set in the field outside the swimming pool — and left there to incinerate. Half an hour later the fire was out. The fire was relit. At 8pm we finally ate at a long table in the field, and to my complete astonishment the *sanglier* was stunningly delicious and tender. It was served with ghastly overcooked Dutch vegetables, we all got even more drunk, sang and had a lovely time. I have never waited four hours for a meal in my life, but it doesn't seem to have done me any harm.

Later that summer, Rutger invited me and friends to the winemaker's gala dinner at the Hôtel de Ville (town hall), which houses the *maire*'s office in Uzès. It is an eighteenth-century building with an elegantly laid-out courtyard, perfect for special dinners. From one side of it there is a gorgeous view of the enormous outline of the Duché and its chapel roof of varnished tiles.

We arrived gasping for non-existent refreshments in the heat, but first had to stand through the ceremonies and inductions upstairs. We faithfully paid attention as 15 winemakers filed in, dressed in long olive-green gowns printed with gold fleur-de-lis, green turbans on their heads and medals hanging from red ribbons around their necks. Not laughing proved difficult to manage in the social-behaviour department. Rutger took the vanguard, grasping a huge banner proclaiming *Compagnie Bachique du Duché d'Uzès*. Its motto was 'Wine, not water!' Smiling sheepishly (for Rutger is shy underneath the huge exterior), he looked like a schoolboy at an end-of-the-year play: slightly excruciated and at the same time thrilled. Speeches were made and new inductees bestowed with a medal, a glass of wine, a touch with the polished vine branch, and an exhortation to defend the wine of the region. The new inductees, in their turn, gave a little speech, downed the wine and shouted 'Wine, not water!'

Following this rousing ceremony, we all clomped downstairs, not avoiding the opportunity to whistle at the men removing their sweltering robes in an ante-room. We had reserved a table for 10 because we move in packs. A table for eight materialised.

'No, we asked for a table for 10.'

'Well, you can't have it,' said the Bacchus lovers who adore rules. It's odd how the Froggies stand on ceremony considering they've had a revolution.

'We're not sitting until you give us two more chairs,' said the Kiwis, who have little truck with rules.

Organisers ran up and down the beautiful courtyard, sweating, checking lists, arguing. While they were doing this, we grabbed two chairs and all sat down. This anarchic behaviour was greeted with surprisingly placid acquiescence on the part of the powers-that-be, and the meal proceeded forthwith. Subsequently, the evening proved a bit boring, so we made the Spanish musicians come to our table and incited them to play more racy tunes that we could dance to in the archways. The stuffy town burghers looked on coolly from their well-behaved tables under the stars.

On the Place aux Herbes is one of Uzès's best café/food shops, the chic Terroirs. Owned by Thomas and Corinne Graisse, it had a pretty and very funky waitress called Schumi — she's been there since I have been coming to Uzès and she's now the manager. In that time she has married and had a child. Here's her look: petite, fetching, in her twenties with a shaved head save for a long bit on top which starts off black and finishes blonde, tied in a knot; cute make-up and tiny rings in her ears and eyebrows; and a tight little black-and-white striped dress showing off the prominent tattoo on her shoulder blade. And that's not all; Schumi is a really good manager: funny, polite, efficient and anticipatory. That's what I like — anticipatory. I wish men were anticipatory. They should sense what you want and provide it immediately. Preferably, on bended knee.

Terroirs serves southern food in the way southern people eat: in small, delectable portions. The café is the perfect spot to pass an afternoon with friends, snacking on cured ham and other charcuterie, Pélardon goat cheese soaked in herbs and olive oil, *brandade* salt-cod purée, marinated sardines, *foie gras* and Provençal salads. Top it off with the *rosés*, thick fruit juices and sorbets, as you contemplate where to eat dinner. The shop stocks the best regional olive oils, local wines and produce.

The best olive oil Tom sells at Terroirs is Pierredon — I have been buying it for years in its distinctive tall, clear-glass bottles. When I was filming my television series on the area, for some reason I had decided to do a story on another olive oil producer at Montfrin; I think because he was a friend of a friend. I undertook all the research, visited the property, talked to the owner for hours and even had lunch with his family. At the last minute, as the filming crew were about to arrive from New Zealand, he changed his mind without any explanation and let me down. I went straight to Tom and asked for the contact for the fabulous, expensive Pierredon oil. My experience with Gilles Granier and his family at their ancient olive grove outside Uzès in Estézargues was wonderful — he was very reliable, polite and easy to work with. Sometimes the carpet is pulled out from under you for a good reason: there is a path of roses underneath. The unassuming pharmacist Gilles makes the best olive oil in France, and when it runs out every year, it runs out and you have to wait for next year's pressing.

The family has a dozen hectares of AOC de Nîmes olive trees producing Grand Cru oil. (AOC or *Appellation d'Origine Contrôlée* is the French certification for produce from specific regions.) They press the oil with their own press, and it is like drinking tropical butter. Gilles suggests that the oil made from Aglandau olives goes well on a salad because of its

CHOCOLATE AND OLIVE OIL MOUSSE WITH SEA SALT

Serves 6

200g 70% cocoa solids chocolate, broken into pieces
125ml extra virgin olive oil (a fruity one)
2 tablespoons cognac
80g caster sugar
4 large eggs, separated
pinch of salt
sea salt flakes to serve

1. Melt the chocolate together with the oil and cognac in a bain-marie, stirring from time to time. Leave to cool a little.

2. Stir half of the sugar into the egg yolks then stir this into the melted chocolate mixture.

3. In a clean bowl, beat the egg whites with the pinch of salt until stiff peaks form. Gradually add the remaining sugar and beat until glossy.

4. Fold the chocolate mixture into the egg whites until all of the white is incorporated.

5. Place in the fridge for at least an hour.

TO SERVE

Serve drizzled with olive oil and sprinkle with sea salt flakes.

raw artichoke taste, the fruity Picholine on tomatoes, and the herbacious Bouteillan on carpaccio. All of the olives are picked by hand, tree by tree as each one ripens, and are pressed within 12 hours to limit fermentation and oxidisation. The oil is not filtered, is kept in barrels, and is only bottled to order. Gilles says this is the only way to protect its flavour and nutritional qualities. Pierredon oil has received so many gold medals that I think they are not allowed to enter them in competitions anymore. When I was there we tasted the oils with bread and cheeses — in the south of France folk pour olive oil and sprinkle thyme on their cheese. Opposite is a recipe for olive oil chocolate mousse.

Also on the Place aux Herbes was the *boulangerie* (the bread shop), which used to make the best *croissants* in the whole of France. This is official. It was voted upon. Jérôme Dance of the Boulangerie Uzètienne had a permanent queue outside his shop from dawn until dusk, and the wait was worth every minute. His sourdough bread, *tortes*, *baguettes*, *ficelles*, *croissants*, almond pastries and candied lemon *brioches* called *citronniers* were sublime, and I've been lucky enough to go around the back to watch them making *oreillettes*, those moreish, deep-fried, paper-thin oblongs of pastry. The pastry is made with eggs and orange blossom water and rested for hours or overnight, then rolled out, cut up, deep-fried and immediately sprinkled with sugar. See the recipe overleaf. The absolute best time to turn up at the *boulangerie* was around 11am when the *oreillettes* were coming out of the fryer, then you could eat them meltingly warm. Jérôme now has a boulangerie outside Uzès in Saint-Hilaire-de-Brethmas, and in the place of the old bakery there is now a wine bar, La Famille, owned by the famous French actor Jean-Louis Trintignant's grandson.

OREILLETTES

Makes 20–30

2½ cups (300g) flour
½ teaspoon salt
3 small eggs, beaten
30g soft butter
grated rind of 1 orange and 1 lemon
1 teaspoon orange flower water
2 litres vegetable oil
frying thermometer
caster or icing sugar

1. Sift the flour and salt onto the bench and make a well in the centre. Into this put the eggs, butter, grated rinds and orange flower water.

2. Using your fingers, gradually work in the flour until all is incorporated and you have a smooth, soft ball that comes away from your fingers. Wrap in clingfilm and refrigerate for at least 4 hours.

3. Heat the oil in a deep-fryer to 190°C.

4. Divide the pastry into four and roll out each quarter very thinly. With a pastry-cutter, cut into 8x4cm rectangles.

5. Drop the pastry rectangles into the deep-fryer in batches. Fry until they are just golden, then remove them to a cake rack to drain onto paper towels.

6. Sprinkle with lots of sugar and eat immediately.

CHAPTER 4

IN WHICH TELEVISION ARRIVES, I GO TO SECONDARY SCHOOL AND THEN BECOME JOAN BAEZ.

When I talk about filming television in Uzès, it is almost commonplace to me. It's what I do . . . now. But when I think back to my first experience of television, I have to admit it's amazing that I have moved from one side of the screen to the other. Television didn't arrive in New Zealand until June 1960, but my family didn't buy a television set until a few years later because my parents disapproved of it. We kids would go to a friend's place to watch TV on Friday nights. It was a big deal — you brushed your hair and cleaned your shoes and everything.

Finally, when a television was allowed past our door, we quickly became addicted like everyone else. It was very controlled, though — we were allowed to watch only certain 'approved' programmes and only for so many hours a day. There was absolutely no question of watching TV during dinner, and we were allowed to watch movies only on Sunday. Television was black and white, the programmes always ran late, and the announcers were merely announcers, not stars like they are now. There were no make-up or hair-do people in the studio — you turned up in a nice frock, fixed your own make-up and read the news. People like Alma Johnson said it was never more than a job. They were public servants, and it didn't occur to any of them to think of themselves as 'personalities'. Initially, AKTV2 broadcast only in Auckland and only two nights a week, for three hours. This soon increased to four nights, and the TV licence fee was £4 a year.

There were wonderful presenters like the fragrant Alma Johnson with her chic beehive, the penetrating and poised Cherry Raymond, the gap-toothed, frizzy-haired Angela D'Audney with plunging necklines, Ian Watkins, Dougal Stevenson, Philip Sherry. We watched shows like *The Adventures of Robin Hood*, *In the Groove* and The Howard Morrison Quartet recorded live. In 1966 *Country Calendar* screened for the first time, and is still going to this very day. *C'mon* exploded onto the screen with the groovy Peter Sinclair, and we all danced The Twist in the lounge. The unmarried mother, who was living with us as my mother's helper, taught us how — she would give us lessons after dinner in the dining room. My parents were rock 'n' rolling to Buddy Holly up until then. The nightly magazine show *Town and Around* started in the mid-1960s and *It's in the Bag* with Selwyn Toogood in the mid-1970s ('What'll it be, customers, the money or the bag?'). Judy Bailey, the mother of the nation, came along with her rounded vowels, along with Richard Long, Jennie Goodwin and Brian Edwards. There was no auto-cue so they half-memorised and half-read the news. In 1969 the universal desire to see the first man on the moon led to the creation of a microwave link, enabling ours to be the first network to broadcast those famous pictures of Neil Armstrong walking on the moon. Colour television arrived in New Zealand in 1973, and we were treated to such salubrious imports as *The Adventures of Rin Tin Tin*, *Lassie*, *Bonanza*, *M*A*S*H*, *Soap* and *Charlie's Angels*.

Cooking shows, though, started warming up the screen quite early on, but it was with the debut of Graham Kerr in 1963 that we had found our first celebrity TV chef. 'I wish you, as always, good entertaining, and God bless you all,' said Graham at the end of every show of what was to later be called *The Galloping Gourmet*. No one had ever seen the likes of him: urbane, dapper, practically a dandy with his English accent, he actually woke people up, leaping all over the set, drinking wine on-screen, flirting with the viewers. His show was filmed in a studio, and a camera was trained on the audience, so there was an interactive conversation going on. Kerr was the first to break the dry, didactic, recipe-centred cooking show format and taught people not only how to cook but how to live, how to have fun, how to express themselves — he wasn't eating to live, he was living to eat. And he was a chef by training; his food was aspirational. Cooking until then had been domestic labour, and this was reflected in the design of the average pre-1960s kitchen: it was a place that had no reverence for the cook, being hidden away, cramped and basic.

Some people thought Graham's food was too complicated and were bothered by his posh accent, so the television executives went searching for someone who was a New Zealander, was down-to-earth and would cook ordinary home food. Alison Holst was found teaching in the School of Home Science in Dunedin. Her first TV cooking show, *Here's How*, launched in 1965. She had to perform live without stopping, cooking such comfort food as meatloaves, casseroles and muffins. There ain't nothing like a Dame and, until recently, Alison was still writing easy-to-do family cookbooks with her son, Simon. When I was filming *Taste New Zealand* in the 1990s, I interviewed Alison in her home and found her to be the most wonderful woman with a great sense of humour. One day a 'fan' came up to me and said, 'I made the *dukkah* in your cookbook and it's horrible. Alison Holst's is far better.'

'I'm so sorry to hear that,' I replied, 'I got the recipe from Alison.'

In 1976 the screen went pink with two gay chefs, Hudson and Halls. It was the first time we had seen openly gay guys on TV, and nobody made a big deal of it. Come to think of it, we have never had a gay TV chef since then, apart from a few brief appearances by wonderfully decked-out transvestites. Hudson and Halls were very entertaining and camp, and their self-named show lasted for 10 years. They were chefs, had restaurants, were partners in life, and bickered with each other and the audience. They cooked such delicacies as *crêpes* with cream chicken, peanut and carrot soup, and Italian meatballs. They moved to England and continued making cooking shows, but then Hudson died of cancer in 1992. Grief-stricken, Halls committed suicide a year later.

We didn't have competitive cooking shows then. I like cooking shows to be cultivated, have a moral core, teach you something, entertain, and show that food is love. I abhor shows where people are humiliated, burst into tears, are stressed out, and food and eating are treated disrespectfully and as a blood sport. We have now sunk to Gordon Ramsay's vulgar aggressiveness — just the sight of him makes my nose bleed.

As I watched these early presenters on television for the first time, it never entered my head that it could be a good job for me, the biggest, most opinionated talker in the universe. At that stage I wanted to be either a train driver or a fireman; in fact, I didn't want to be a girl at all. But I was living in the vice-grip my mother called an 'up-bringing'. In those days it was also called 'training'. If you saw a child misbehaving, you would sniff and say 'badly trained'. Like a performing seal.

Due to my being such a show-off, thankfully I was channelled into theatre, singing, dance and speech training. At seven, I started piano lessons at Holy Cross Convent in Epsom. My father played the piano simply, so I was used to singing with the family around the piano in the evenings until TV put an end to it. It seems unbearably quaint now to say we sang around the piano, as if it was an invented memory. In fact, you sang at parties and dinners in those days, and someone always had a guitar or a piano. And you drank beer or tea. Wine came much later, although my father was a wine buff, so our family was a bit different as Dad educated us to appreciate whisky and wine by serving it to us at dinner on Saturday nights, cut with water. God, we thought we were flash.

In 1963 I went to my secondary school, St Mary's College in Ponsonby, a renowned music school that also excelled in a healthy exchange of humiliation between the nuns (the so-called Sisters of Mercy) and us horrible teenagers. We could pick up IN AN INSTANT any weakness in a nun, and vice versa. We knew which nuns were flirting with the priests, which nuns were on the verge of a breakdown, which ones actually liked children, which ones had the most brains, which ones had a true vocation . . . and we were merciless. We reduced nuns to tears, provoked them into walking out of class, asked them impossible questions in biology and reproduction classes ('But how does the seed get in there, Sister Edith?') and had permanent periods when it came to phys-ed classes. For their part, the nuns assured me I was on the fast road to you-know-where, ridiculed my hair-dos, pointed out my stupidity, resented my time spent in the music school, and generally assured me I was a thorn in the side of Jesus, who had died an excruciating death for my sins *by the way*.

The music school was a different story. St Mary's was a school with an extremely good choir, orchestra and private music and singing tuition. Sister Leo, my singing teacher, was strict but clever and fair, and I actually learned something when under the care of the music-school nuns. I had to work hard, but the freedom and beauty of music made my life meaningful — if I couldn't be beautiful, couldn't be an A student, couldn't be sporty, couldn't win ONE SINGLE PRIZE, at least I could hold a tune. Fabulous singers walked around the music school, like Mina Foley, Kiri Te Kanawa, Malvina Major and Heather Begg. While they were a few years ahead of me, being around them was like being in Hollywood — they were glamorous and successful and fantastic role models.

Later, when I was nursing in 1971, Mina Foley, who sadly by then was resident in Oakley Psychiatric Hospital, was admitted for an operation into the medical ward where I was working. One night after dinner, another patient asked her to sing, and she stood by her bed in her nightie, opened her beautiful mouth and sang like a crystal-clear bell 'Sempre Libera' from Verdi's *La Traviata*. Everyone cried. She wasn't called the voice of the century for nothing.

Mina was a lyric coloratura, and success came very quickly for her, which was part of the problem. Her mental health was always fragile, and she was not guided in the art of handling wild success at a young age. Her troubles started in her early twenties when she went alone to study in London, then Italy and the United States. At the time, people said she should have been chaperoned. Her behaviour became more and more erratic, she attacked people occasionally, and in 1961 had a severe mental breakdown. The whole of New Zealand was in love with her and missed her voice like a huge ache. Mina made a comeback in 1978 and her voice was still heart-stopping, but she continued to be ill, and she died in 2007.

I was less of a loser in secondary school than I had been at primary school, and I made friends with girls who were unusual — it was my only option for friendship really. One of the girls in my class who was also a very good singer was Donna Awatere. She was a true subversive even then, in that she believed profoundly in overturning the status quo. She was charismatic, avant-garde and had more front than Smith & Caughey's. There was nothing she couldn't do and nothing she couldn't talk her followers into doing. This was to get her into trouble in later life. Far more intelligent than any teacher, far more capable than any of us, she was the type you could believe would perform open brain surgery on the canteen table while singing an aria, with no one thinking to question it. However, she got on the wrong side of the school law, occasionally finding herself in Mother Benedict's office, thus ensuring respect and kudos in my eyes. We sometimes crossed paths in the waiting room outside this hallowed sanctum, two heroines impersonating schoolgirls, misunderstood by society.

Donna involved 'a certain section' of the school in a spiritual philosophy called Moral Re-Armament. She got away with it by convincing the nuns that it was not a religion, and thereby was compatible with Catholicism and in fact it was probably training better soldiers for Christ. She taught us morally inspiring songs like 'Up, Up With People', which we sang in three-part harmony, as we struggled with complex philosophical tasks ahead of us, like how to extricate the boarders from the dormitory to the Beatles concert and how to bend the entire school to our will. Moral Re-Armament was in fact an important social and political movement that did have Christian roots, but people of all nationalities and faiths adhered to it. There were 'The Four Absolutes' of purity, love, honesty and unselfishness. Donna used to tell us that to change the world you had to change yourself first.

At this time, boys brave enough to pick me up from my home for a date soon regretted it. Dad would open the front door dressed in old corduroys with a pipe hanging out of his mouth. A sample conversation would go like this:

'Hello, you must be Fred.'

'Um, well actually . . .' mumbles the hapless boy.

'Oh no, sorry,' Father putting hand to mouth. 'It's George, is it? Look, there are so many boys crawling around here looking for my daughters. Not good with names. Can't remember my own children's sometimes.'

Me hissing at him from behind the door.

'I have just come to pick Peta up, Mr Mathias. My name's Willy actually.' Putting out hand.

'Pleased to meet you, Willy. What does your father do?'

'My father? He's—'

'Do you have your own teeth? Do you know what the words "eleven o'clock" mean?'

'Is Peta here, Mr Mathias?'

'No idea. She might be. Lot of girls here, you know. Have I actually seen you before? Do you know Peta is going to be a nun?'

Me behind the door going cross-eyed. Mum in the lounge weeping with the unbearable humour of it. I push Dad aside and step out to save hapless boy.

'He's always like this. My whole family is mental and that includes the new baby. I think we'd best be going.' Grabbing him, I slam the door.

Meanwhile the debutante ball was coming up and we had to learn to dance. Efforts were still continuing to turn me from an ordinary New Zealand girl into a lady. To this end, I was carted off to ballroom-dancing lessons at a dance school in Symonds Street. I got into trouble right off by refusing to wear a knee-length, gathered skirt. The mother, my sisters and I were fairly serious about fashion, and for once we agreed that I should be allowed to wear my short A-line skirts. However, any leeway that had been given me was swiftly removed when I was caught smoking out the back with some low-life boys.

'They're not even Catholics,' said my mother, as if religion were the issue rather than cigarettes. When I told my father I had been fired from dancing lessons, he laughed and snorted that he was only relieved I hadn't caught any acne from what he nasally referred to as 'youths'. I did make it to the debutante ball — photos were taken and you could go and buy them a few days later at the photography studio downtown. When I saw these photos, I realised that something truly miraculous and unexpected had happened. My looks had arrived. Finally.

In 1966 Dad was in a real-estate phase and thought it would be a brilliant idea to buy a big property, subdivide it and make some money. He accomplished this without mentioning his plan to Mum, so she woke up one morning to discover that they owned a new house and would have to sell the beautiful home she had practically built with her own hands. We moved to a rambling old villa on Coronation Road, Epsom, which had a large orchard out the back. Mum was depressed, as would be expected, had a breakdown and hated this big, dusty old house after her lovely modern, easy-to-look-after home. We must still have been there when I went nursing because I can remember nursing friends coming around and being awe-struck that we lived in this huge mansion with what seemed like a park out back. There is a photo of brother David and me sitting in the lounge all dressed up on our way to a party. A few years later my parents built a flash new house at the back, pulled the old house down and sold off the front section.

Mum, who had excelled in art at school in Australia, went back to her great love and started an art degree at the University of Auckland. This brought about profound and positive changes in her — she was happier, more broad-minded, made funky friends of all ages, started painting again and became more arty in general. This was the period of her French-polishing all her antiques, putting hessian curtains up (terribly Bohemian) and buying groovy clothes that were not her usual conservative taste.

My parents stayed in their flash new house until they moved to Australia, where they still live. We must have been left a bit of money when Grandpa Mathias died, because suddenly we had a second car and a better bach at Snells Beach. As an adult I have bought dwellings ready-made and never understood why people thought it was fun to redo an old house or build one from scratch. It seemed like a huge amount of work to me — like building a boat — and a recipe for ruining a relationship. To me, heaven was to be had in buying a house, moving in and cooking dinner that night. That was my plan in Uzès as well — it was Lucy's ready-to-go apartment I had fallen in love with; there was no way I was interested in, or capable of, a do-up. When I lost Lucy's apartment, because of my tight budget and disinclination to borrow, a do-up was thrust upon me. Thank God I had friends in Uzès to guide me or I would have bought any old tip, thrown a whole lot of Designer's Guild around, hung my mother's paintings up and called it home. I was so used to renting places in Uzès that even a student wouldn't live in, that a proper house seemed like I was rising above my station. That is, until my station changed and the Queen included me in her birthday honours list.

But going backwards, my first adventure with homemaking was when my nursing friend Marianne and I rented a little flat above the bakery in Mt Eden. I was 19. Having our own little home was absolute ecstasy and would start me on the long road to many, many rented houses and flats all over the world. I became addicted to moving because it felt so good, and was like taking drugs but lasted longer. I mean being drugged feels great, but you have to keep taking more all the time — I wanted to feel high as a permanent state of affairs (like millions of other people my age in that era). I have never understood people who like stability and say, 'Oh I'm a homebody myself.' Right from the get-go my stability came from within, I guess because, in spite of Maison Vice Grip, I had had a very stable upbringing. I loved moving digs, doing them up, acquiring fun flatmates and playing house. In those days we were a landlord's dream — we would paint every room in any colours we felt like, have parties until the police turned up, then get up in the morning, scrub the whole place and go to work, in my case, at Auckland Hospital. We made hessian curtains, picked up furniture for next to nothing at flea markets, bought a sound system, and called it the new digs. It was so easy and so cheap to rent. There were no bonds, no deposits, no questions asked. You signed the form, paid a week's rent and moved in. The landlord never ventured anywhere near you.

Our parents were horrified, needless to say, and mystified at the inexplicable turn of events. One minute life was straightforward and you were living with children you controlled and went to church with; the next minute your once-biddable offspring were living like hippies, seemingly stoned all the time and enjoying free love. Our parents stood and blinked uncomprehendingly at us. It was truly awful for them, but we were going through a cultural upheaval and nothing could stop us. Without drugs, I don't think the Seventies revolution would have been as powerful, because drugs gave insight and broke down inhibitions, the inhibitions that previously had been the glue that kept society together and, along with the Church, kept people obedient.

Opposite is one of my favourite recipes from that time, not that I ever cooked it with anything but powdered cinnamon or coriander seeds, of course. But in the interests of social history, I shall record that in these Bohemian times such recipes as these were often cooked replacing the spice with hash. The active ingredient in hashish is THC, or tetrahydrocannabinol, which cannot be dissolved in water but can be in fat or alcohol. This recipe is quite cute because it adapts the Indian method of cooking with hash where they melt it in buffalo ghee. A hash cookie could be any cookie recipe you wanted — brownie, shortbread, muffin, etc. This one is a biscuit.

Through all this madness, I went to work every day in a stiff white uniform, continued my nursing studies, graduated, got my pointy blue-and-red medal and then became Joan Baez.

HONEY AND SPICE COOKIES

Makes 12

FOR THE BISCUITS

- 125g butter
- 200g caster sugar
- 4 teaspoons honey
- 50g flour
- 50g ground almonds
- ¼ teaspoon freshly ground nutmeg
- 50g pine nuts

FOR THE SPICE BUTTER

- 4g 'spice of your choice'
- 2 tablespoons butter

1. Preheat the oven to 160°C and oil a baking tray.

2. Cream together the butter and sugar. Beat in the honey. Add the flour, ground almonds and nutmeg, and mix.

3. To make the spice butter, chop the spice finely and melt with the butter in a pan or in the microwave.

4. Generously space out teaspoons of the creamed mixture onto the oiled tray.

5. Make a small depression in each biscuit and fill with the spice butter.

PTO

6. Sprinkle with pine nuts.

7. Bake for 7 minutes or until golden.

8. Store them somewhere safe, if you haven't eaten them all immediately.

CHAPTER 5

IN WHICH I BUY THE HOUSE IN UZÈS, AND DISCOVER TRUFFLES.

I settled down in Auckland to wait for the owners of the Uzès house to return at the end of January 2013, but at 10.30pm on 16 January the telephone rang from France. Pierre told me that the owner had returned unexpectedly and was ready to do business. The other interested buyer had made his offer, which Pierre knew. Did I want to offer a sensible amount more and have it done with? I shrieked, 'Yes, offer it, offer it!'

Pierre called back five minutes later and said, 'It's done, you have the house, the owner agreed immediately.'

I had signed forms with Pierre before I left Uzès in August, so I went to sleep and woke up the next morning as the owner, bar the paperwork, of a house in the south of France. Unlike New Zealand, in France you don't get building inspections made, especially on an old house you are going to completely redo, but I asked Pierre to arrange one anyway. It was inspected the following Monday, and it came up smelling of roses. What followed was weeks of incomprehensible letters from the notary and discussions with money-moving agencies to figure out the best way to move the dosh from New Zealand.

Matthew from IFX called me from London, and I discovered how people send large amounts of money around the world. Quite fascinating and something probably even the dog next door would know, but I didn't. What happens is that the dealer buys your New Zealand dollars at the best possible moment when the exchange rate is favourable, and fixes your rate there and then. So if you decide to move your money to France a month later and the exchange rate is no longer favourable, you're sweet because you've already fixed your money. It's risk-free, cost-effective and efficient, and you get to feel like a drug dealer. Banks from this part of the world are known worldwide to be greedy, so these private exchange outfits are great as they don't charge bank fees and commissions and give you a wholesale exchange rate. As I was dealing with the longest process in the world — buying a house in France — I was not in a hurry, but the money could have been transferred the same day if required. Even if you make the deal by phone it is binding and recorded.

So now I had to try to buy the garden on one side and the little ruin at the back. I discovered the garden is called Clos de la Diligence, which I find enchanting, and decided on the spot to call my house Maison de la Diligence. A *diligence* is a stage coach; in the past the Bourgade area was full of *auberges* and dives, and the *clos de la diligence* was a coach station. The reason I needed the extra areas was because I was going to teach cooking lessons there and also rent it out when I was not in residence. The woman who knew the family who owned the garden had been contacted by Pierre, but he was going to have to go the southern French route regarding the gentleman who owned the ruin, which was of interest only to rats and cockroaches.

I said in my usual patient, relaxed way, 'For God's sake, why is it taking so long? We knew we wanted this ruin a month ago. Why don't you pick up the phone and call him?'

'No,' said Pierre, 'this is not the route to go at all, Peta. This gentleman might be sick and cantankerous, and probably hates estate agents. He's also southern French and has to be approached from the side, in a gentle southern French way. If I call him out of the blue and say I have a client who wishes to buy his ruin, he might be bad-tempered at the sound of a stranger having the cheek to call him and immediately say no and put the phone down. I can't progress from no, so I have to approach him in a softer way. Don't forget he is not selling; we are asking. My mother knows someone who knows his wife, and she will see her at the market this week and broach the subject with her.'

A week went by.

'Hi, Pierre. So what happened at the market?'

'Oh, it was cold, so they didn't go to the market.'

'Christ. So what now?'

'Be patient. I am working on it. I'm now going to bed for a few days because I'm sick.'

Honestly, you would gnaw your own bloody arm off. Another week went by. Nothing. Meanwhile Pierre was arranging for me to buy the house as an SCI or business to be called Maison de la Diligence. Another week went by. Nothing. I sent the money to the New Zealand account of IFX in London, Matthew did the sums and transferred the money in euros to my bank account in Uzès.

Suddenly at the end of February, a two-hour face-to-face audience took place between Pierre and the owners of the ruin, and needless to say they were not interested in selling because they had other plans for it. At the same time the owners of the garden also unexpectedly materialised and stated that they were willing to sell. Having started to gnaw my arm off, I now had to sit on the edge of my chair while Pierre talked the ruin owners into selling and tried to negotiate a good price for the garden. Cripes — it was like television. I wished I was filming a series on it, because I did think it would go smoothly, and of course it didn't and now it was an interesting (French for 'complicated') story.

The respective owners of the garden and ruin are wealthy old Uzès families. They didn't especially care about their little bits of property, which have sat there rotting for ages, and €10,000 here or there wasn't going to make any difference to them, but it was to me. In Uzès it is so hot that you have to have either a garden, a terrace or a little swimming pool, or you will combust. When I lived in the apartment on the boulevard, I spent half the day in a cold bath with ice-cubes, and sometimes even went to bed with towels wrapped in ice-cubes spread on top of me.

Pierre and the owners of the small ruin arranged to view it together, and agreed that I could buy the majority of it, but they would like to retain a portion of it as access to the other part of their building. Fine. We put a reasonable offer in, and predictably the owners, who didn't need the money or the space, start using the 'fair' word. The last time I had heard this word was with Mr Morocco, who whipped the price up in the interests of fairness, once he realised I was serious.

Pierre had also put forward a 'fair' offer for the garden, another bit of real estate the owners had ignored for many years, and suddenly they wanted €6,000 more than was 'fair'. I agreed, they accepted by email at the end of March, and then nothing happened. I thought of starting up a movement called 'The Slow House Movement' and giving seminars on how to buy a house slowly, how to make sure the owners and agents keep you waiting as long as possible, and how to renovate especially slowly so as not to experience the degrading effects of haste. Meanwhile the owner of the house had now 'gone away' and wouldn't be signing for the sale of the house on 23 March as had been agreed and signed by everybody. He now felt like doing it on 5 April, without any consultation with me from the notary or agents.

By April 2013 I had purchased only the house. As that had taken three months, getting the garden and ruin under my belt would take about three years, and they would have to bring the contract into my secure room in the psychiatric hospital out the back of Uzès. Mid-May, according to my pipe-dream-super-plan, I would arrive to spend four months doing up the house. At the end of April, the garden and ruin had not progressed due to laziness and incompetence, and I predicted I would spend the next four months looking at the house and doing absolutely nothing. If only I had known I wouldn't need predictions. Two weeks before I was due to arrive in Uzès, the landlord of the apartment I had rented down the road from my house let me down and gave it to his mother.

'But, Erick,' I said, 'you offered me the apartment and we have a written and confirmed agreement.'

'Sorry about the bad news,' said he, another person I would have to slowly kill — the list was growing longer; I would have to hire help.

I had rented Erick's apartment when I was still in fantasy land about doing the house up over the summer. So it turned out that I would have to live in my house anyway, which could be a good thing, as it is only by living in a building that you truly understand all its quirks — the exact spot where the neighbours can look in on you, where the light falls, how solid it is, how noisy, etc. Needless to say, I had nothing to put in this little dump of a house — no bed, no table, no fridge, nothing. Pierre assured me that it was liveable and arranged for a telephone line to be put in; Gina said she would borrow some furniture; I asked my house cleaner and friend Monique to go in and scrub it to her heart's content and beg her husband, Bernard, to check the plumbing. This is my exchange with Monique:

Hello Peta!

Hier nous sommes allés dans ta maison elle est très sympa tranquille au cœur d'Uzès le pieds. Pour le ménage j'ai noté ce qui est nécessaire elle sera toute propre à ton arrivée. La commode je te la donne on la déjà emmené. Bernard a regardé la plaque de cuisson elle fonctionne, la chasse d'eau, des wc pas de problème, la douche pareille.

Bises Monique

Wow fantastic!!!!!!!!!!! Tu sais Monique, je suis ravie que tu me dis que la maison n'est pas horrible — je ne l'ai jamais vu et je ne sait pas vraiment ce qui m'attend!!!!! Merci pour tout — grosses bises.

Peta, je t'assure qu'elle est très bien même pour y vivre tout de suite quand tu aura aménager a ton goût ce sera parfait elle est au cœur d'Uzès à côté des commerces très tranquille je vais te la briquer elle va être superbe.
    Ne t'inquiète pas!!! Bises Monique

Her words of reassurance about the house were music to my ears. All I had needed was for Monique to tell me that she liked the house and it was in a lovely quiet corner and that I would be very happy there and not to worry. Suddenly I felt excited rather than irritated at the hold-ups and let-downs.

I turned up in Uzès at the end of May to host my culinary week, expecting to move into the house. However, I was shocked at how small and unlovable it was. Fat chance: the house was not liveable at all, so I stayed at Gina's luxury loft for two weeks, pretending I was in a Baroque opera. At my house, water was leaking from the bathroom through the ceiling to the floor below, and the telephone line, recently 'connected', wasn't connected at all. It took two weeks to talk the phone company into fixing it, and in that time Gina's friend Hans furnished my house with stuff he had lying around in storage. Gina went to a *brocante* and bought me lots of fabulous linen sheets, Limoges cups and saucers, a Christian Lacroix plate, huge wine glasses and solid white dinner plates. On my first evening living there I invited her for dinner: takeaway roast chicken eaten with a shared knife and fork, aubergines fried in a cheap frying pan from Monoprix, and leftover wine from the culinary week drunk out of *brocante* wine glasses. We were in heaven.

Time went by, the weather became hotter in Uzès, nothing was moving with the ruin and the garden, and I slowly adjusted to the fact that I would be spending the summer camping in the house rather than renovating it. It was quite remarkable: nobody will talk in the south of France, not because they have anything against you but because they can't be bothered. I even grew to quite like the house, and had a hovel-warming party outside. I plugged my Bose speakers into the laptop, borrowed a big bucket from Pat to put the wine in and made all sorts of fab food, combining everything I had brought back from my recent trips to the Basque Country and Puglia. Amy turned up with lots of homemade *focaccia*; Anthony turned up with *macarons* with incredible fillings; Maïté turned up with little *vol-au-vents*; Christophe and Arnaud turned up with wine glasses. My older friends were horrified by both the house and the street, which they considered to be full of drug addicts and dangerous dogs — they actually shrunk into the stone wall as they passed the young people's house on the way to mine. Lucy, whose apartment I had almost bought, thought the house and passage enchanting, and said, 'Darling, you don't need to change a thing — I love it the way it is!'

Finally, in July, the owner of the ruin decided to accept my money. This left the garden. As nobody involved with the garden was talking — neither the owners, the notary, nor Pierre — I stomped into the notary's office and made an appointment to see him. He was charming and likeable, had no idea who I was, and assured Pierre and me that he would indeed talk to the owners of the garden to find out why they had stopped talking to us in March. But, of course, it was now almost August, and nobody will do anything in France in August. Breathing out. Anyone can breathe in.

Meanwhile the young people who were renting the other house next door had expanded their living space into the street, which is not theirs to expand into, so I now had to fight my way through rotten furniture, rubbish, washing and dope fumes. Their dog used the alley outside my kitchen window as a toilet, their cat had just had four kittens, and they played head-banging music day and night. The other neighbours had three cats whose one united desire was to enter my house, so I had to put netting on every door and window, effectively living in a cute prison. Okay, so the prison had Gina's paintings, Olivades fabric on the couch, *tagines*, *couscousières* and copper pots that I couldn't help buying, and the most expensive sage-striped linen sheets in the world from Society in Italy. It was a rich slum.

My life at the hovel was occupied with teaching cooking classes in Gina's beautiful kitchen down the road, going to bullfights and equestrian shows, discovering good restaurants in Arles and Nice, shopping in Nîmes, and doing a recce in Puglia with the view to adding this delicious and secret destination to my culinary tours. I really love teaching my half-day cooking classes in Uzès because Uzès is so enchanting that I don't have to do anything at all: I could stand there and read the phone book to my students. They are always thrilled to meet Annie the cheese lady, and have lunch at her organic farm in Collorgues. Annie's a biochemist who now makes Pélardon goat cheese, and when I say I have clients coming to see her, she strangles or slits the throat of something on the farm — a goat, a pig, a goose, a duck, whatever — and that's lunch. She makes the most delicious terrines, roast suckling goat, salads and fresh goat cheese with homemade jam. One day I asked her why there were no potatoes with the kid, and she asked me what I was talking about: 'It's summer, Peta. You don't eat potatoes in summer.'

She takes my students around her messy property, showing them all of the medicinal plants and herbs. Annie has never been sick and never been in a hospital — she cures herself, her husband, her three sons and her animals with herbal remedies. She shows the students how to make goat cheese, and introduces them to her goats, all of whom are named.

The students loved being able to go into the private homes I borrowed for teaching until my house was ready: Gina's Baroque loft; Maïté's chic apartment; the kitchen at Mas des Oules outside Uzès. I always take them to Le Tracteur, a rustic restaurant in the countryside at Argilliers. The food is fantastic and you have to reserve weeks in advance in high season. For years, chef Numa (whom I think I have seen smile once, okay so maybe twice) plates up utterly mouth-watering dishes like fresh tomato soup with salt cod fritters, watermelon with fish-stuffed courgette flowers, hand-cut beef tartare, slow-roasted lamb with pumpkin purée and mint salad. The wine list is very good, partly due to the fact that one of the owners is local winemaker Olivier Privat. My students always comment on the intense flavour of the vegetables and fruit in this area — they even think the meat is tastier. People have never eaten a homemade *brandade* of salt cod before, or a real *pissaladière* with *pissala* in the dough mix, or tasted fresh white coco beans or lavender with lamb, or thought of steaming courgette flowers rather than frying them or of putting fresh thyme and cognac into *tapenade*.

Uzès is famous for its black truffles, so I take my students to visit

LAMB WITH PÉLARDON GOAT CHEESE AND LAVENDER

Serves 4

FOR THE VINAIGRETTE

⅓ cup vinegar
1 teaspoon Dijon mustard
sea salt and freshly ground pepper
1 teaspoon honey
⅔ cup extra virgin olive oil
1 tablespoon chopped flat leaf parsley

FOR THE LAMB

400g soft Pélardon goat cheese
cream, for thinning
freshly ground black pepper
2 tablespoons chopped chives
8 small or 4 large leeks, green part cut off
sprig of thyme
4 teaspoons Dijon mustard
4 large steaks (about 180g) cut from a boned-out leg of lamb
8 sprigs lavender, leaves and flowers, chopped
olive oil for frying

1. Make the vinaigrette by whisking together the vinegar, mustard, salt, pepper and honey, then gradually add the oil. Stir in the parsley.

2. Whip up the cheese in a food processor, adding as much of the cream as necessary to obtain a thick mixture.

PTO

3. Remove from the food processor and stir in the pepper and chives.

4. Make a cross in the ends of the leeks and clean them thoroughly, then boil them in salted water with a sprig of thyme until very soft.

5. Meanwhile spread the mustard around the side of the steaks, then roll them in the chopped lavender.

6. Heat the oil in a pan and fry the lamb for 4 minutes on each side. Rest for 5 minutes.

TO SERVE

Place the leeks in the middle of 4 plates, some creamed cheese on one side, and the chops on the other. Drizzle the vinaigrette over the leeks, and garnish the dish with fresh herbs.

Michel Tournayre and his truffle grove. The heavenly truffle is an underground edible fungus that lives symbiotically with trees, particularly oak and hazel. It grows on tree roots to a depth of 20 centimetres, and has to be sniffed out and dug up by trained dogs. On Saturday mornings, from November to March, there is a truffle market in the Place aux Herbes, while on the third weekend in January there is the famous truffle fair. It wasn't until Tom of Terroirs introduced me to Michel Tournayre in 2011 that I learned the true truffle story in Uzès. I had finally met the real deal, not a pretender to the throne like some truffle shops. It seems incredible that I hadn't paid much attention to the famous Uzès black diamonds up until then, but don't forget I am there only in the summer and truffles are a winter story.

Black truffles have always grown spontaneously under oaks in the Garrigue forests in this extremely hot region, so in the 1950s Michel Tournayre's grandfather, known as 'lou Pierret', started planting oak trees on his farm, the Mas du Moulin de la Fresque, outside Uzès. The way you cultivate truffle-producing trees is to 'infect' them with the spores when they are saplings, then plant them and hope for the best — it can take eight years before you know if you've been successful. The Tournayre's fourth-generation property was originally a traditional multi-crop farm producing grapes, cereals, fruit and vegetables — in other words, market gardening. Pierret, however, decided to try to introduce truffles into the mix and it worked so well that Pierret's son René Tournayre expanded the truffle business, planting several hectares of truffle trees around the *mas* to create one of the largest truffle groves in France. He was greatly influenced by two great truffle experts — Paul Bonnet in the Vaucluse and Raoul Brunel in the Gard — and called his business Les Truffières d'Uzès. At the same time he was still also producing cereals and white asparagus.

In the early 1980s, René's son Michel took over the farm, but in 1991 tragedy stuck with an outbreak of *Fusarium*, a fungal infection, which devastated the asparagus crop and endangered the whole enterprise. Michel nevertheless continued, and in 1996 enjoyed an exceptionally large truffle harvest. Flushed with confidence, he took the decision to turn his truffle passion into the sole focus of his business, giving up the other crops and concentrating solely on the black diamonds. He extended the planting of truffle trees to a whopping 20 hectares. People now started coming from all over the world, especially Australia and New Zealand, to visit his farm, and he began opening the grove to researchers and technicians.

Grandfather lou Pierret was a charismatic local identity: so handsome, Michel told me, that people said he looked like Marlon Brando. My friend Annie, the goat farmer, remembers him well as an influential, generous man who would help anyone. His door was always open and the house always full of people. With regard to growing truffles, he said, 'It is important not only to wait, but to know how to wait.' Michel seems to have inherited his good looks, but is more a brooding George Clooney. He's very charming and loquacious and seems obsessed with truffles. Whenever I take my culinary students to Michel's place, they have a lot of trouble concentrating on the truffles.

Michel lives on the farm with his wife and daughters and can't stop expanding and making improvements. When I first met him, he had just finished building a huge conference room for functions, events and screening his truffle video, which is incredibly interesting. There is also a swish boutique where you can buy truffles, local preserved products like pâtés and olive oils, truffle books and essentials such as truffle graters and knives. At one end of this space is the glass-fronted sorting and brushing room, where, in the season, one can watch these activities. Another part of the space is devoted to an exhibition of family photos, historic photos of famous truffle-growers and groves, and old sales documents and objects.

When Michel takes you on a tour of the truffle grove, you visit the different plantations (he even has a grove of bonsais producing truffles), meet the dogs who are all in love with him, observe the bare circle around the base of the trees that betrays the presence of truffles beneath the surface, and watch the dog sniff one out and dig it up (*le cavage*). In the winter season, the aroma is so strong that you can put your nose to the ground and smell their musky pungency. Obviously the dog has to be trained not to eat the truffle he has found, which was the main problem with the traditional method of using pigs — you had to jump in quickly and grab the diamonds before they disappeared down their throats. Michel has also excavated down into a part of his land to show visitors the history of the sweet limestone alkaline soil in the area, the oak roots, fossilised truffles, and roots and layers of soil through the centuries — absolutely fascinating.

Obviously you can only buy the *Tuber melanosporum* (fresh black truffle) in winter, from December to March, but you can buy them preserved or what Michel calls 'extra first-boiled' all year round. The expression 'first boiling' is like 'first pressing' with olive oil and, like olive oil, any second-boil truffle product will be very inferior. First-boil preserved truffles will last for up to two years, but once the jar has been opened they must be consumed within two weeks at the most. No rubbish such as products imbued with artificial truffle aromas will be found at Michel's place; that kind of thing makes him go cross-eyed. For example, most truffle oil has never been near a truffle in its life: the flavour (which I can't stand) comes from a synthetic agent such as 2,4-dithiapentane.

A preserved truffle is cooked differently from a fresh truffle. Never take it out of the jar and eat it: it will taste of nothing. Remove it from the jar and gently pat it dry with a tea towel. Slice with a truffle slicer, then softly and briefly sauté it in any fat you like — extra virgin olive oil, lard or butter. Now you can add it to your dish of cooked pasta, scrambled or soft-boiled eggs, mashed potatoes, risotto, hot buttered toast or whatever.

A fresh black truffle can vary widely in size from that of a pea to a tennis ball or even bigger. It is black, roundish, irregular in shape, and has a warty surface. When you cut it open you will find it is black and marbled with thin white veins. The aroma is strong and absolutely unmistakable — a pungent mix of earth, dampness, cockles, hazelnuts . . . so powerful, in fact, that if you put a truffle in a basket with eggs for a few hours the eggs will smell and taste of truffle. A black truffle is often eaten fresh and uncooked: you slice it onto whatever you are eating. There are many recipes for using truffles — from terrines to *foie gras* to baked inside bread to poached in Champagne. Truffles love fat, so they are very good with duck fat, cream, lard and bone marrow. They also like holding hands with seafood: scallops, oysters, langoustines. You can even make truffle ice cream.

There is another product, the white summer truffle *Tuber aestivum*, which appears from May to July. If you visit the grove with Michel in the summer, his dog will dig up a white truffle for you. Michel considers them not worth bothering with because the taste is so inferior, but I quite like them as for me they are better than no truffle at all and a lot cheaper than the black one. Also, a white truffle is another one of the little joys of a Languedoc summer, like black figs and white asparagus. You cook with them the same way as the black truffles, but don't expect the same stunning result.

The ancient Greeks and Romans ate truffles, and in medieval times there were so many that anybody could eat them. A lot didn't, though, because they considered them to be evil as they were black, hidden secretly underground, loved by wild boars (which were hated by the peasants), and the *brûlure* or burn mark around the oak tree signifying the presence of truffles was thought to be a witches' circle. The first-ever truffle grove in France was eventually planted in the Vaucluse in 1808 by Joseph Talon. Later in the nineteenth century, France was digging up a massive 1,000 tons of them a year, but now only 40 tons or less are harvested. How did this dramatic decline come about? Wars, that's how. After World War I there was huge socio-economic change, meaning less land was cultivated (with the peasants moving to the cities), the death in battle of the men who cultivated truffle groves, and the wartime destruction of trees and deforestation.

But Michel is doing his best to keep up the tradition, and the rewards aren't too shabby. Right now, the price for the most expensive truffle in the world, the exceptional Italian white truffle, is €3,000–€5,000 a kilo, French black truffles are €1,000 a kilo, €100 for white summer truffles, and €20 a kilo for Chinese truffles, which are worthless (they are a counterfeit, but a natural one).

As soon as Michel realised I was a New Zealander, he smiled and said, 'I know about your truffles and I know about Alan Hall.' In 1987 Alan and his wife, Lynley, planted half a hectare of English oaks and hazels impregnated with black truffle spores. The Froggies said it couldn't be done in our fair land, and even if it could the fungus would taste like some impoverished bush-pig mushroom, bearing no relationship to the noble Perigord black truffle, one of the most expensive foods in the world, along with caviar and *foie gras*. But this was New Zealand and what we can't do with some No 8 wire doesn't bear scrutiny, so when Dr Ian Hall of the Crop and Food Research Institute at Mosgiel and his

TASTOU

cloves garlic
slices of sourdough (*pain au levain*)
goose or duck fat
fresh black truffles
black pepper

1. Preheat the oven to the highest it will go.

2. Rub garlic onto the sourdough slices. Spread as much fat on the bread as you like. Cover with fine truffle slices, and top with a bit of fat to stop it drying out.

3. Place the truffled bread slices in the oven for a few minutes to heat through. Cut into slices and grind the pepper over the top.

brother Alan decided they wanted truffles in their very own back yard, they went forth and planted.

Since Alan's *truffière* was established, many more have been planted all over the country. Before long, nine *truffières* were in production in New Zealand, from the Bay of Plenty to Canterbury. More trees have been planted and infected with the fungus both north and south of those regions, but whether their climates suit truffles has yet to be discovered. In July 2012, at a Waipara truffle farm, Rosie the beagle found New Zealand's first Burgundy truffle, weighing in at 330 grams. Sadly, it is practically impossible to buy a fresh New Zealand truffle, as they all go to restaurants and lodges and the demand far exceeds supply. So desperate are Asians for them that a Korean businessman turned up on Alan's doorstep with a suitcase full of money, demanding to be supplied with 100 kilograms a day. The typical price for a New Zealand truffle is NZ$3,700 per kilo, but to date the highest price paid for a locally grown truffle was a mammoth NZ$9,000 per kilo. Believe it or not, you can actually find native truffles or parekoko in New Zealand under manuka shrubs if you are very lucky.

When I left Uzès for India in September, absolutely nothing had moved with the house. The owners of the ruin had invented more delays, obliging me to pay to have the ruin measured again, so I closed the door on the hovel having not actually paid for the ruin yet. I won't even mention the garden . . .

of convent life, I incurred a personality change, wherein I became slightly more happy and agreeable. This improvement coincided with the seemingly overnight ugly-duckling story that happened at the debutante ball. Out of the blue, or so it appeared, I was no longer shapeless, ugly and unfeminine. My looks, such as they would ever be, had turned up, and boys were suddenly noticing me. This was so abrupt a transformation that it took much adjusting to — it was like having been a cripple and then suddenly standing up and walking. I had been given a reprieve from the social death row I had always assumed would be my lot. My former ugliness was all imaginary: years later, when I was in therapy in Canada, the therapist asked me to find photos of myself as a child and teenager so we could get to the bottom of my self-image complex. My parents sent them over from New Zealand and nowhere was there an ugly girl — nowhere. I had invented her. There were just photos of an averagely pretty girl in a check dress with waist-length black hair, a girl in bikini, a girl with flicked-up hair in the school photo . . . no fat girl, no ugly girl.

Trainee nurses had to be in by 11 o'clock, or midnight if it was a special occasion like a ball. Once again I was drawn to the girls who stood out for some reason — the naughty ones, the exotic ones, the fun ones — and we became a gang. Most of them had come from similar backgrounds of private schools, middle-class households and fairly strict parents, and all of them like me went completely berserk on the powerful aphrodisiac of relative freedom. We played practical jokes and games like hide-and-seek from the childhoods we had barely left behind.

Nurse Ruth was a short, bob-haired girl with cupid lips and a tomboyish character. One evening for fun, she climbed up into the ceiling of the nurses' home, but fell through it into the hallway so patched the damaged panel up with Sellotape. A week later it fell on the home sister's head as she was taking her rounds. Ruth also unwound the huge fire hose in the hall in order to help someone hide in it, ravelled it up again and forgot about the occupant. When the home sister discovered the unfortunate individual, the poor girl could hardly walk or talk.

The old buildings of the nurses' home were plagued with cockroaches, a ready source of torture for the faint-hearted. Nurse Janine was terrified of them, so of course we collected a whole bunch and locked her in her bedroom with them. We also convinced her that as part of the training you had to perform a cold spoon round. Every evening before retiring, the patients on bed rest had their backs washed and massaged. We explained to the desperately innocent Janine that during the back round, male patients frequently got hard-ons, making it difficult for the nurse to perform her duty, so you had to take a cold spoon with you to whack any erring parts of anatomy into submission. Janine screamed and screamed. We insisted and insisted. She said she was leaving nursing. We said we were sorry but she would have to face it. Finally Nurse Sharlene released her from our grip.

Sharlene was a voluptuous half-Polynesian beauty with long, dark, wavy hair who flaunted her sexuality and carnal knowledge. Being much more mature, she humoured me and patiently answered all my questions about life and sex. Where I wore jeans, a hand-made sweater and my hair in a ponytail, Sharlene wore push-up bras and breathtakingly tight white slacks, and was seriously into big-hair. She was very bright, passing her exams easily, and was way beyond locking people in water closets while we were all prostrate over the hilarity of it. Then, in her first year at the top of her class, the inexplicable happened: she fell pregnant to her boyfriend and left nursing to get married. Far from being envious that Sharlene had found herself a husband, I mourned the loss of a bright student and her career, and prayed fervently for her at Mass. This was the first indication in my mind that maybe finding a husband was not such a brilliant idea after all. It was very clear to me that pregnancy and marriage had wiped Sharlene out as a successful woman. I was surprised that I felt this way, that I now saw her as a flawed heroine who had fallen into the first trap in the jungle. I shouldn't have worried about her, though, as she did very well in life.

Nurse Sarah was also one out of the bag. One day, she emerged from her room with her mousy hair peroxided white, then went out and bought some leathers and a motorbike. At the time she was working on the TB ward, and one fine evening, on the way to a party, decided to visit her 'boys'. She drove her motorbike through the main doors into the ward and sat down to a meal of pork and puha, which one of the patients' families had sent from down the line. Not being one to bother with crash helmets, she had several accidents, one of which permanently left her mildly paralysed on one side of her face. In the lounge of the nurses' home, she organised séances wherein a lot of table-shaking went on, due either to nerves, laughter or spirits, no one was sure which. Sarah grew up to be a bourgeois paragon of wife- and motherhood, reluctant to be reminded of her delinquent youth.

Formal balls were the order of the day and petals were the hair-do. I was good at sewing, so made myself a gown of navy blue organza with tiny white dots on it, empire line with a white ruffle around the low neck. Pearls, wrapped five times around my throat, completed the look. Black eyeliner, brown arcs of eye-shadow, false eyelashes and pale pink lipstick were a minimum requirement.

The father said, 'Careful you don't lose your balance girl.'

The mother said, 'You look much better without make-up, Peta.'

Mothers. What did they know? Better without make-up! By this time I wouldn't have considered even going to the toilet in the morning without make-up. False eyelashes were only for big dos; the rest of the time three layers of mascara plastered on with tiny brushes and spit sufficed. All the balls were held down on the marina, and guess what else you find at marinas? Launches, yachts and water. After one ball, my escort drunkenly insisted on taking our group out on his father's launch at two in the morning. My girlfriends and I were dared to jump overboard, so naturally we did, practically drowning in a sea of gin, eyelashes and hair spray. I can tell you that if you spend more than 10 minutes in a harbour at night wrapped in four yards of organza, chances are you may never breathe again, let alone dance. This was the start of my efforts to sabotage my chances of surviving long enough to find a husband. These balls always had to be dragged out until dawn. We went to someone's house for breakfast, then went home, had a shower, got changed, ate a whole handful of glucose lollies and turned up for work at 7am, where we held people's lives in our hands.

Of course, entering the nurses' home after curfew was another exciting part of a nurse's life. The maids' quarters were not supervised and were connected to ours. Apparently maids had the innate ability to go to bed whenever they liked because they hadn't gone to private schools and didn't have impure thoughts. Eighteen-year-old nurses, however, were capable of doing night duty on their own, cutting gangrene out of festering wounds and laying out the dead, but were not capable of going to bed on time or saying no to the marauding men waiting on every corner to use them as receptacles for their sperm.

To sneak in, we removed our shoes, hitched up our ball gowns, and either climbed through a friendly maid's window or slid tipsily along the maids' corridor. Danger lurked at every turn, the way strewn with traps and home sisters. The most frightening trial was trying to recognise your own room in the blackness to avoid losing consciousness in a bed that was, technically speaking, not your own. You might end up unconscious on the floor of a room of a nurse you wouldn't normally give the time of day, but you didn't find that out until the next morning. The punishment for breaking curfew if you got caught was being grounded, which was a joke to us — the rest only served to enhance our reputation and give us more energy for the next escapade.

I had quite a few beaux, but the nuns and my parents had said save it, so I kept saving it. I did everything BUT you-know-what, having fully recovered from my first kiss, which had felt like a snail going into my mouth. I was under the impression that what I had to sell was of great value: the education, the virginity, the good family stock and, of course, the probability that I was undiscovered royalty and my body a golden temple. In 1967 in New Zealand you couldn't go wrong with those credentials, all of which my friends and I took as our given right. It was razor-clear in my mind that, if I blew it, I would lose every advantage in life that I had been born with. I would go to hell in more ways than one. Even if I went out until two in the morning and played strip poker with Italian waiters, I still went to Mass every Sunday and confessed my now more dangerous sins.

Our beaux were law students, medical students and, if you were desperate, engineering students. They were 'nice' boys from good families who had been educated at schools like King's College, where they underwent transmutation and had their pelvises realigned so that they could sit comfortably in law offices for the rest of their lives. They engaged in extremely rugged sports, which involved beer, permanent joint damage and 'scoring chicks'. One of my nursing friends was in love with an engineering student who made marks on the bedroom wall to keep count of their carnal encounters. She grew up to marry him, have multiple children and live on Valium. He grew up to cross-dress in her clothes, ruin her make-up and beat her. She finally ran off with the rubbish collector, who proceeded to do the same thing but without the lipstick.

Three months after entering nursing, I failed my prelim exam, which genuinely came as a shock to me. I had done approximately zero study and gone out almost every night, but still seriously wanted to be a nurse. At this point I sat up and pulled myself together. Once again the mother found herself pleading for the defence, this time in the matron's office. The matron was a starched, be-medalled apparition with huge white wings on her head, the awe-inspiring Amazon chieftainess of the nursing matriarchy. Mother wore her best suit from America and Chanel No 5 perfume to plea-bargain a deal wherein I transferred to the 18-month community nursing course instead of the three-year general course whose prelim I had just failed. The promise was that, if I did well, I would be placed back in the general nursing programme with a year taken off. That was the first lie the matron told, but I was blindly determined to be a fully qualified nurse come hell, high water or deception. The shock and humiliation of failing made me determined not to blow any more exams, even if it meant I had to study, something I said I would never do again when I left school. If God had meant a girl to waste hours in a small room studying, why had He invented cramming?

I tried to fit into the nursing world, but it stuck out a mile that I was an outsider. I determined, however, to rise to the challenge and conquer this new world. As time went by, the harsh reality of what being a nurse actually meant revealed itself to me. The shifts that necessitated working until 11pm then starting again at 7am the next day left me desperately tired; the lifting of patients three times my weight damaged my back permanently; the sordidness and debasement of scrubbing bedpans and cleaning liquid excrement off the bodies, beds and walls of colostomy patients deeply shocked me. Where was the romance? Where were the handsome doctors? Where were the grateful patients whose lives I had saved?

I wasn't a normal nurse, being hard to discipline and too interested in the patient's psychological welfare. What I got was bad posture, bad ward reports, doctors behaving like gods, and ward sisters behaving like angels from hell. The sister on the medical ward was a most diabolic, foul-mouthed dictator who instilled terror wide and far. These dysfunctional, middle-aged harridans ruled totalitarian states cleverly disguised as hospital wards. They were in love with the doctors, considered the patients their children, and the nurses slave labour and foils for their malignancy. Just before my training ended, this sister was admitted with terminal cancer. In great pain, she talked fondly of the good old days in her ward. Now she was the victim; I the boss. Some of the nurses refused to tend her, but I wasn't one to hold a grudge. Maybe there was a God after all.

While at Greenlane Hospital, I performed my first layout on night duty, an event that gave me nightmares for three months. It was the only thing that had happened to me so far that was worse than the *Ben-Hur* and *Ten Commandments* films to which the nuns had taken our class of 10-year-olds. Night after night, I and my classmates had been tortured by visions of bloody, screaming men broken by chariot wheels, people disfigured by gangrenous, suppurating leprosy, and, worst of all, Jesus on the cross, pierced, beaten, broken and dislocated. But Greenlane Hospital was worse. The patient had died of liver cancer, so his skin was a grey-yellow colour. Only the bedside light was on because it was night. I begged the senior nurse not to ask me to do it, not at night, not that colour.

'Are you absolutely sure he's dead?' I asked nervously.

'Don't be ridiculous,' replied the senior nurse, 'of course he's dead. Hurry up and bring the bowl of water and we'll wash him.'

'You said he was dead.'

'He is.'

'So why are you washing him? Isn't it too late for personal hygiene?'

'Don't be smart and get the layout kit. Don't forget the plugs.'

I at this point was devoting all my energy to epiglottis and sphincter control, but didn't feel the need for plugs yet, and said so.

'The plugs are for the corpse's orifices, stupid.'

'I would scream if my mouth wasn't full of vomit.'

'Don't be pathetic: this is life, kiddo.'

'This is life, kiddo' is probably the leading cause of mental illness in this country and maybe the world. Green with fear and loathing, I began washing the vile-smelling corpse. As we turned the body over to wash the back, air was expelled from the lungs and a long, loud sigh was emitted. I screamed, dropped the body, ran to the sluice room and locked the door where I sat on the cold floor and sobbed. For months afterwards I couldn't sleep by myself, couldn't sleep with the light off, and couldn't be alone anywhere at night.

I was not cut out for nursing and would not admit it. Okay, so I was going to get married and never nurse again, but, considering there wasn't a queue of suitors lined up before me, I had to have that piece of paper that proved I had achieved *something*. I had to show the parents and the nuns that I wasn't useless. The parents had wasted all that money on an artistic education for me and for what? Well, they certainly weren't going to waste that kind of education on the other five children in the family. I wasn't an opera singer, I wasn't a ballerina, I wasn't an actress and I wasn't a wife. The least I could be was a nurse with a medal to prove it, for God's sake. The least.

Within the year, the nurses' home was too small for me, so I announced my desire to go flatting. You would have thought I had announced a wish to hang upside-down in hell or tear strips off newborn babies. The matron acted like I was a crime wave waiting to happen, and my family took it as a personal insult. I persisted and moved into a dream flat above the bakery in the Mt Eden shopping centre with Nurse Marianne. The dining room had rustic-coloured curtains and an oak table with flaps, the living room had red check curtains and old armchairs, the twin beds in the bedroom had orange candlewick bedspreads. We were in ecstasy, we were playing house, we were grown-ups, we cooked and entertained and did housework. This was true happiness.

It was at this time that I met Jonathan. He was slim and dark-haired, with a sly smile and confident manner. Jonathan was a departure from the sort of boys I had been going out with so far, in that he was a bit devil-may-care, wasn't in a profession, and came from a rather wonderfully eccentric family. He was dangerous, sexy and fun, though I found him a little controlling and chauvinistic. He said things like 'Keep your voice down and don't call me "lover".' If anyone else told me to lower my voice I knew exactly what to do, but coming from a boy or man (Jonathan was 21) made me stop in my tracks momentarily. He didn't want me to be too forward, I had to know my place, I had to wait to be seduced. There were seducers and seducees and let's not get mixed up, and let's remember who's the boy and who's the girl. My father had never so much as raised his voice to me, let alone anything else, so I didn't quite know how to deal with a man telling me how to behave. I suspected I was being a sook, but was powerless in the embrace of carnal desire. We went out together for about six months. I wouldn't let him go all the way, but he was my boyfriend and I quite liked him and I was happy with the way things were. He was the sort of man who anyone in the universe except those in love with him could see was bad news.

I was so taken with him, and he looked so good in his stovepipe pants and pointy shoes, that I decided to introduce him to my friend Nurse Lily, who was tall, slim and striking, with a fantastic personality. She wore her tallness like a badge and stood very straight with perfect posture, being possessed of both cheek and wit. And you'll never guess what happened. As it transpired, she did me a big favour by stealing Jonathan, because he turned out to be what I would call a faithless sod. I went to their wedding in a yellow linen dress, three kilos of make-up and a black velvet ribbon in my hair. The wedding photo shows me with my legs crossed and a cigarette dangling in my fingers. I wasn't *that* bothered by the betrayal, once I got over the initial shock — there would be other boys and, who could tell, maybe I didn't want to be stuck with just one man. Maybe I wanted them all?

The fortuitous thing about my life is that I was born so that my teenage and young womanhood years coincided with several medical and social revolutions. The first revolution was the invention of the birth-control pill, which happened 10 years after the introduction of television into New Zealand. Television and Pond's beauty cream had up until then been the chief forms of birth control. Women slapped buckets of thick face cream on their faces before going to bed to keep their husbands off them. Families who had previously talked to each other, sung around the piano or read in the evenings, were relieved of that burden by THE BOX. However, I was now starting to view my state of virtue as a liability rather than an asset. What if Jonathan had found Lily more attractive because she didn't have my qualms about sex?

To this end, I took myself off to the doctor (not the family doctor, obviously), explained that I wished to be disencumbered of my liability, and asked what he was going to do about it. In those days, doctors didn't talk about sex, emotional problems or thick ankles. Nor did anybody else. You didn't confide in your parents, there were no psychologists, psychiatrists were only used for psychopaths and schizophrenics (mostly Catholics), and priests were hopeless because they gave you more and more Hail Marys to say. The doctor was horrified by my request and told me that the pill was for married women who had already proved their fertility to the State, thank you very much, not wanton 18-year-olds. Not an 18-year-old who couldn't even have a boyfriend without him being nicked, for God's sake. But 'no' was a word that held magical properties for me. 'No' meant that even if I hadn't particularly wanted it before, I now badly wanted it.

So I, who had been blessed with easy, relatively painless menstruation, then invented the myth of my irregular, harrowing periods. To another, younger doctor I, ashen-faced, recounted my trials. He prescribed a new hormone drug to control matters: the pill. The whole business was starting to irritate me anyway. Boys didn't have to go through this. They didn't have to be examined by total strangers in the worst parts, they didn't have to fear pregnancy or muck around taking pills, they didn't have to behave like a lady. I had always wanted to be a boy, realising quite early on how many more advantages boys had intellectually. It was expected that they should think for themselves, be assertive and take what was their due. It was nothing flagrant, but they seemed freer, less burdened. In the get-a-life department, being a boy would definitely have made things easier. Later on, I revised my reason for wanting to be a boy, realising that men's main assets in life were their wives.

The community nursing course finally ended; I passed easily, and applied to be transferred to the second year of the general course, as agreed. There had never been any question for me that I wouldn't continue nursing or that the matron wouldn't keep her word. When the time came, however, the deal wasn't honoured and I had to turn around and start all over again and undergo three more years. I was so disgusted, I left Greenlane and transferred myself to Auckland Hospital.

To my new class, I had status because I was two years older than they were, I 'lived out' and was already a nurse. I refused to wear the bullet-proof lisle stockings, wearing instead stylish cream pantyhose, which was the next revolution to arrive in New Zealand. Mini-skirts were in, and the arrival of pantyhose meant that you didn't have to have your hands surgically attached to the hem of your dress anymore. I was also a role model to the younger nurses because I wore a red petticoat under the wall of white starch, behaviour considered by the matron to be one slippery step away from communism. Nurses were so straight — it took only a red petticoat to impress them.

Within a few months, a core group of girlfriends had been established. I moved out of the little gingerbread flat above the bakery into a pretty little wooden house across the road from Auckland Hospital with Nurse Anne and two other nurses. Anne woke up in the morning, lit a cigarette, and had a cough and a coffee for breakfast in bed. Short blonde hair framed a striking elfin face that always had a derisory smirk on it. She had the attribute of true natural beauty and even emerged from sleep looking good. This was hard to forgive when I caught a horror glance of myself in the matinal mirror. Sleep or lack of it had no effect on Anne's flawless skin and green eyes.

'Pete, bring me a gin and tonic, please,' she would call from her bed.

'It's only 11 in the morning, Anne.'

'Haven't you ever heard of elevenses? I thought Irish Catholics drank themselves stupid. My parents always had their first drink at 11 after tennis and before reading the stock market, and they were C of E — hardly rabid by any standards.'

'What's the stock market?'

'It's not a soup kitchen and you don't find it on the fashion page. How could you not know what a stock market is?'

'Here's your drink. Our family never discussed money. We were too busy singing around the piano and going to Mass,' I said, leaning over the hurricane zone she called a bed. 'What are you reading?'

'The *Kama Sutra*.'

'Wow! You dirty dog. A girl got expelled from my school for having that book in her room. Let me see it.'

She pulled me onto the bed and read aloud. Soon the flat was full of shrieks and screams. We lay exhausted from laughing.

'Pete, why are men like lino?'

'Why?'

'Because if you lay them right you can walk over them forever.'

The phone rang. 'It's for you, Anne.'

'Who is it?'

'A boy.'

'Tell him I'm busy.'

'Anne, it's Scottie. His family is loaded, he's marginally good-looking, and this is the third time he's called this morning.'

'If he wants me, he'll call back,' she shouted through a smoke-screen, putting her fingers down her throat. I admired her cavalier, cool attitude to men, which rendered her a great object of desire. They always called back no matter how she treated them.

Anne, too, was the eldest girl from a large family, always doing well in exams, always wearing the skimpiest of outfits that seemed to be held together only by her not inconsiderable will. We were bright sparks, funny and tough, our constant joking masking whatever private sense of alienation we carried around inside. We had lots of friends, a great social life and kept each other motivated in our studies. After one year of general nursing and vomiting while assisting a tonsillectomy, my determination to be a nurse whatever the cost was fading. Although we had been at it a whole year, it seemed to me as though no progress had been made.

'I can't stand it anymore already,' I groaned to Anne. 'What I had wanted so badly is being beaten out of me by hard work, bad pay and, I suspect, a lack of any talent for nursing.'

'Oh, Pete, that's not true. The problem for you is that with community nursing you have in fact done a year and a half of drudgery instead of the usual one. Don't give up now, you've only done a year. Give yourself a chance, don't let them break you. I'll stand by you.'

'Okay,' I sighed, being a warrior. 'I'll plough on. Maybe something deep and meaningful will happen to make it all worthwhile. Maybe sainthood or royalty still awaits me.'

Sainthood would not be my destiny, however, as I lost my faith overnight. One Sunday evening at Mass in St Patrick's Cathedral, I experienced a religious catharsis. I had returned to my seat from receiving communion and had knelt to pray. In a blinding revelation of pure truth, I was suddenly aware that I didn't believe anymore. I didn't believe any of it. I had spontaneously decommissioned. I didn't believe that the host I had just swallowed was the body and blood of Christ, didn't believe in heaven or hell, didn't believe that it was a sin to miss Mass on Sunday.

I must have been thinking about faith subconsciously for years, because all catharses have a build-up, but it came as a surprise to me. I felt profound relief, a strange sort of lightness, and was aware that I was looking at myself from above. To say I was relieved to be free of a belief system that no longer had any relevance to me would be overstating the fact. It was like the day I lost my ugliness — I looked on it more with wonderment than joy. I sat in the pew in the cathedral for hours, reflecting on what had occurred and what it would mean. I had lost my ugliness; lost my faith; now all I had to do was lose my virginity. The next step would be to find myself.

There was no going back. With my dumping of Catholicism, I relieved myself of the threat of hell, meat sticking in my throat on Friday, and any vestiges of goodness. I decided to travel light from thereon in — no husbands (maybe), no guilt, no possessions, no ambitious career. I was slowly starting to rethink things. Up until then, I had been very centred, knowing exactly where I was going and how my life would eventuate, but giving up guilt proved to be a joke. How could you stop being guilty when it was genetic? I was a guilt machine. I manufactured it like a hormone. I enjoyed the rush and negativity of it. The secret pleasure of guilt has never fully been acknowledged by psychiatrists. It's like heroin. You know it is destructive, but it's exciting to be able to manipulate other people's emotions. Reading the *Kama Sutra* would have been boring if it hadn't been forbidden. If it wasn't for guilt, I would never turn up to work on time. Fear is an upper, and guilt is fear. To become fearless I had to ditch guilt and its control.

My spare time with Anne was spent on such important tasks as procuring daffodils from parks, learning how to remove grilled cheese from sheets and squeezing into jeans two sizes too small for us. I had stopped classical singing lessons with Sister Leo and reincarnated myself as Joan Baez. With my long black hair parted down the centre, I sang folk and bluegrass with my guitar at a folk club on Symonds Street and at the Poles Apart in Newmarket. It was at this point that I discovered black stockings, boots and baggy jumpers. I was bored with the straight world I moved in, and the attraction of the underworld of folk singers and pot-smoking inexorably worked on me.

Through the folk-singing world, I met a wild woman called Bubbles. Honey-blonde hair, flawless skin, and a deceptively open angelic face hid a siren. Bubbles talked me into a trip to Wellington and Christchurch that was to change my life forever. It transpired I was a cover for her real motive, which was to visit her lover. For some reason, I ended up alone in Wellington for four days before meeting up with the siren in Christchurch. I had been given an address to stay at in Wellington, a huge house of many flats where everyone was interconnected.

Ron was to be my host. Bubble's husband said, 'You can't let her stay with Ron — he'll be awful to her.' But she said, 'No, no, it'll be okay. I'll ask someone to keep an eye on her.' Ron was repulsive to me as predicted, gave me a bottle of whisky and left me alone in the flat to entertain myself. What have I done? I thought, bewildered. I'm alone in a city I don't know in the custody of a madman when I could be having a good time with just about anyone else in the universe. What to do? Why, drink the bottle of whisky of course. Sometime in the middle of the night, a man broke into the flat, turned the bath tap off just as I was about to sink unconscious under the water, and dragged me out of the tub. He dried me, wrapped me in a bathrobe, walked me up and down the room, helped me to vomit, walked me up and down some more, then put me on the bed. The room spun uncontrollably, the vertiginous walls closed in. I knew I was either dead or heading that way, and I welcomed obliteration as a respite from the agony of alcohol poisoning. The man then cleaned up the bathroom and left.

To my surprise, I didn't die, but I woke up in the morning wishing I had. Hair still clinging damply to my back, I pulled the bathrobe around myself and lurched downstairs to the communal telephone in the hallway. Weeping, I called Anne to say I was having a horrible time and would be on the first coach out of town. As I turned to crawl upstairs, an Adonis poked his head around the door of one of the other flats.

'Hi,' he said, 'you must be Peta. Are you okay?'

'No,' I groaned. 'Who are you?'

'I'm the person who saved your life last night. Johnny.'

'What are you talking about?'

'You flooded Ron's bathroom, thus irrigating my kitchen. I pulled you out of the bathtub. Ron's still out.'

I put my hands over my face. He'd seen me naked. Oh God. What else happened? Leaning against the wall, I couldn't quite think what to say next aside from 'Do you have a stomach pump?'

'I think you had better come in and have a cup of coffee and some aspirin.'

I sat down in Johnny's lounge, looking like a corpse, drank his coffee, and fell in love with him. Could this be the man I was going to marry? Built like an outdoor brick shit-house, he was a muscle-bound departure from the skinny, folkie intellectuals I hung out with. In the sex appeal and personal magnetism department, I had to admit that Johnny rocked. Sitting across from me in nothing but a pair of cut-off jeans, golden skin warm in the summer morning heat, languid smile mesmerising me, he proceeded to revolutionise my tedious little life. Johnny had long blond hair, soft eyes and a gentle touch.

I didn't leave his side for four days. I had met my soulmate, my teacher, my lover, my spiritual and intellectual guide — in short, my muse. Okay, so it was only four days, but life was intense in those days. He was already separated from his Catholic wife and child at the tender age of 22, was living a hippy lifestyle and had just dropped out of university. I lived in Auckland, hundreds of miles away, yet the bond was so strong between us that time, distance and circumstance only served to make our hearts grow fonder.

As arranged, I dutifully continued on down to Christchurch to rendezvous with the siren, who I found in the missionary position at the beach house with her lover. Unfortunately, her suspicious husband had followed her down and also found her in the self-same position. Great drama ensued, with me asking everybody why he wanted to keep her anyway. A man under the influence of love. A woman under the influence of hormones. The couple we were staying with were hippies and into free love and sharing. This was a new concept to me and very radical. We talked for hours about Allen Ginsberg, who said drop acid and you'll understand the meaning of the universe; Jerry Rubin, who said don't trust anyone over 30; and Henry Miller, who said don't save it man, give it away.

Johnny and I defied the odds and continued our long-distance relationship, visiting each other often, but mostly conducting our romance by mail. He wrote me long, rambling, almost daily letters on coloured paper and posted them in coloured envelopes with *GUESS WHO?* written on the back. I received these epistles as if they were packets of gold, which of course they were. They contained invaluable treasures like love, advice, political propaganda, theology, book reviews, birth-control information, career guidance and the state of his marijuana crop. With gentle patience he steered me from the right to the left path, from black to white, from believing to non-believing, from sleep to wakefulness, from dream-walker to thinker. I flew to his side in planes, raced to his arms in trains, thirstily drank his elixir of peace, love and freedom.

Johnny's mind was as complex as his life was simple. In love with the poetry of his writing, I didn't think of the future, only the present. He wasn't even mortal to me, so the idea that he would eventually disappoint me didn't come into the equation. I didn't stop to wonder what he saw in me, an immature, straight (but bending), middle-class nurse with a big nose and freckles. Maybe he saw a willing pupil, a person who would have tied up the family roast with a clothesline had he willed it, a person who would have sewn him a duvet out of tea bags, a person who was, quite frankly, a rebel without a cause. I had that ungovernable tongue, but I was becoming transformed into who I thought I really was, under his influence. He got me reading books like *Orlando*, *Women in Love* and *Crime and Punishment* — complete eye-openers for me.

This was the era of spiritual and mystical awakening, and Johnny was nothing if not a preacher. We read from *The Rubáiyát of Omar Khayyám* and Hermann Hesse's *Siddhartha* when we were together. I was careful not to be too gluttonous in my literary awakening, not wishing to find myself suffering from acute aesthetic indigestion. My palate, stimulated by unaccustomed ideas, painlessly developed a new sensitivity. My life was becoming a banquet that not even the drudgery of nursing could poison. My parents loathed Johnny, his scandalous hippy appearance and his influence on their daughter, who was sliding faster and faster on the downward slope to you-know-where. I made the mistake of introducing the three of them, who immediately began a battle for my morals. Any letters that were sent to the parental household were thrown away, any phone messages were ignored, any mention of his name started a slanging match. If the other swains were to be ridiculed by my parents, this one was to be feared.

One terrible day, not suspecting why I hadn't had a letter from Johnny in a while, I received one from Brenda, his ex-wife, whom I had never met. The letter said, 'Obviously Johnny can't find the courage to tell you, but we have got back together again to give our marriage another try. The reason I have taken the liberty to write is because I know how important you are to him and how much he respects you. As one Catholic to another I would like us all to remain in touch and be friends.'

My grief at losing Johnny was strangely tempered by Brenda's understanding and Christian attitude. I forgave him for not telling me himself, I forgave him for two-timing me, I forgave him for having met Brenda before me. Brenda invited me down to Wellington to visit them, but regretted it when she saw me. Anyone can write a noble letter, but having the living, pulsating woman in your own home produced feelings of discomfort she wasn't quite prepared for. But the bond between Johnny and me was too strong to break, so we all three of us worked hard to have the friendship work, and it did. Brenda and Johnny bought land on the West Coast, lived the hippy commune life with their idealistic friends and had another child. I visited them, sent their children presents, and continued my intellectual relationship with Johnny by the usual long letters. I was still in love with him and remained so for many years. Needless to say, when I met him again 20 years later, I was disappointed. The main problem was I had stopped smoking dope years ago and he hadn't.

CHAPTER 7

IN WHICH THE UZÈS HOUSE SAGA CONTINUES.

My own attempts to settle down have never been as easy as it seems to have been for others, particularly as I have become the specialist in the unplanned life. It was now October 2013, and I had been camping in the Uzès hovel-house all summer, waiting to buy the garden. The notary had not talked to the owner of the garden as promised in August. He had done nothing, as far as I could see. Pierre refused to push him for political reasons — he's too important! So I tried to find out why the notary hadn't talked to the owner, and what was going on, using my usual calm system of four-letter-word problem resolution. The owner had agreed in an email to sell me the garden and agreed on the price for which I could now sue him, but I knew deep within my now very suspicious brain that I was not going to bother suing someone for a garden. I jumped on the plane to India, and by November had released myself from wanting the garden, washed my hands of it and instructed Gina from the mountains of Darjeeling to draw up plans for just the house and the ruin.

Being a patient, never-give-up sort of gal, Gina said, 'Wait, let me try one more time with the owners. Maybe they will respond to a woman rather than a man, you never know.'

I said, 'Okay, but it has to be fast as a lot of my time has already been wasted.'

It turned out that the garden was technically owned by a 17-year-old boy, so Gina found out his mother's number and called her. She gave Gina the number of the father, as he looked after the property. He refused to return her calls as per usual, so she found out where he worked and went back several times until his office gave her his mobile number. Astonishingly, he answered it, and they set up a meeting at which he said one of his tenants in his apartment that partially looks out over my garden had recently re-signed a three-year lease with the garden in it. This he had done after agreeing to sell it to me. So, it was up to Gina to ask the agency looking after this apartment to change the tenant's lease so that the garden was no longer in it. The agent promised to resolve the situation. Months went by, and they did nothing, so I spat the dummy again and asked Gina to give up on it, so she did.

At the end of November, the owners of the ruin finally accepted my money, plus another €968 for the surveyor to change the measurements by 1 centimetre. So, now I had two little properties, and Gina went ahead and brought in the architect to measure up and confirm her design. Nobody does anything in France in December because it's leading up to Christmas, and January is out because it's after Christmas, so in February 2014 the architect finally turned up and drew her plans for the union and reconstruction of the two buildings.

Time passed while the builder, the plumber, the carpenter, the electrician and the gutter-maker wrote up their quotes. At the end of March, the dossier was submitted to the *mairie* (council) seeking permission to build. Gina was convinced that, when I turned up in Uzès in June, she would have started the renovation, so advised me to rent an apartment down the road. Needless to say, that was incredibly complicated and required a lot of running around from Gina and Pierre, and needless to say I didn't think for one minute that the renovation would be underway in June. True to my prediction, in April the *mairie* said there were problems with the building proposal because of the ruin, the windows, the house, the façade — everything. This was a proposal I had paid the architect a lot of money for, but because the property is in a protected neighbourhood the *mairie* is extremely particular. Everything would be delayed once again. Teeth-grinding ensued.

As it turned out, I didn't need to rent the apartment down the road because absolutely nothing was done on the house all summer, but I had already rented it so I had to live in it, and it was nice not to be living in a hovel. During that summer, I was invited to a friend's house outside Uzès, and she casually fried up some sage leaves from her garden to go with our drinks. This turned out to be one of the most moreish things I have ever eaten. See overleaf for the recipe.

At the end of summer 2014, as I was girding my loins to leave Uzès for my culinary tour in Puglia, we finally received permission to build. We put a big notice up on my house that had to stay there for two months so that neighbours could object if they so chose. Now the design of the new house had changed because, unbelievably, the *mairie* had agreed to industrial-style glass and steel on the entire three levels of the front façade. The whole ground floor would be an open teaching kitchen, the whole middle floor would be an open living room, and the top floor would be bedroom and big terrace.

ANCHOVIES AND SAGE LEAVES IN TEMPURA BATTER

Serves 6

> lots of large fresh sage leaves, washed
> lots of top-quality anchovies (Ortiz is a good brand)
> 1 litre vegetable oil for deep frying
> 1 cup flour
> ½ cup cornflour
> 1 teaspoon baking powder
> 1 cup iced sparkling water

1. Stick 2 leaves of sage together with an anchovy inside. Continue doing this until you have used up as many leaves and anchovies as you like.

2. Heat the oil to 160°C. If you don't have a cooking thermometer, test the heat by dropping some batter in (see below). It should bubble and fry immediately.

3. Make the batter by mixing the flour, cornflour, baking powder and water together. It doesn't matter if there are lumps in it. This can't be made in advance.

4. Dip the sandwiched sage leaves in the batter and deep-fry for about 5 minutes or until turning golden. You will have to do it in batches.

5. Drain on kitchen paper, then eat immediately.

The other change was that the reconstruction was now going to cost twice what was originally quoted, and I couldn't afford it. For a start, the demolition bill alone, which hadn't been included in the very first quote, was going to be one of the biggest costs. The master plan at the beginning had been to sell the house in Grey Lynn, and with the proceeds buy and renovate a house in Uzès without a mortgage. At the age of 65, I didn't feel like looking for a loan and being in debt again — being free felt quite good. I asked around anyway and made contact with a French loan-broker. You will be astounded to read that, in spite of all her charming talk, she achieved absolutely nothing. From my own enquiries, it turned out that neither French nor New Zealand banks would lend to me, so I was faced with doing exactly what my soothsayer Charlie had suggested — work more, and earn more money to pay for it myself.

He read my cards and said, 'Oh, there is a sleeping card lying over your garden.'

I said, 'You're not kidding — the whole bloody south of France is under a sleeping card.'

He told me it would take a long time but it would happen, and I would have to exercise super-human patience.

He also said, 'Keep earning lots of money, because you're going to need it for this house.'

I hosted my culinary tour in India, then arrived back in Auckland at the end of October 2014. Before I decided that I wouldn't seek a loan, I had made myself sick with worry, and my blood pressure, which is always on the low side of normal, went up so high for a month that my doctor gave me a blood-pressure machine so I could check it four times a day. Once I had released myself from the prospect of a loan, the blood pressure went from 161/86 to 118/70 almost overnight. At the same time, in one month, I released the book on India, *Hot Pink Spice Saga*, with Julie Le Clerc, with all the attendant television appearances and magazine and radio interviews, learned new songs and toured the South Island with my roadshow, I taught cooking classes, performed at public-speaking events, and continued organising my new New Zealand culinary tour for February with my wonderful PA Rosie.

When Christmas came, I lay on the couch at my sister's place in

Hawke's Bay and did nothing; Keriann and her family did everything: cooked non-stop heavenly meals and ran around after chooks, cats and dogs. The salad was pulled from the back garden, the strawberries were picked from the front garden, the new potatoes were harvested from their plastic growing bags, the ham was delivered from Havoc Pork, the smoked salmon from Stewart Island, the turkey was brined, and chocolate log, Christmas cake, plum pudding and gooseberry fool whipped up by Keriann. My sister is the domestic goddess that everyone thinks I am. She is into upcycling, permaculture and letting her hair go pewter. I am into running the world, keeping planes up in the air with the power of my will, and dyeing my hair red. This is what happens when you teach a child to be a high-achiever from day one — it's my parents' fault. From the couch, I spoke to my big family in foreign climes, worked on my New Year's resolutions to be a better person, and avoided any contact with dish washing.

In the middle of my horror November in Auckland, the deconstruction of the house in Uzès was supposed to start on the 19th. You will be gob-smacked to read that on the *very* day the work was supposed to start, the puller-aparter had *both* of his trucks break down — can you believe that?! Later in the month he did turn up with his tractor, which was very hard to fit into my narrow street, but he managed it. And, by December 2014, he had started the BIG BASH. Gina took photos of the bash, and I put them up on Facebook to be flooded by concerned friends saying, *OMG this is going to be a HUGE job!!!* It was only at this point that I realised I was, in fact, building a new house, not doing up an old one. Needless to say, at some point in the middle of the night there was a small fire in the ruins, fortunately noticed by the neighbour, who called the *pompiers* to put it out.

I can't tell you how many times I have watched those nightmare-house-do-up-in-France TV shows and thought, 'That wouldn't happen to me, those people are stupid.' Now that Gina could see the foundations of the original house, it turned out that they were much older than we thought: late seventeenth-century. My building was a part of other buildings and goes back to the fortifications of Uzès, built by the Protestants. She also checked my beautiful second-floor chimney with the Monuments de

France and discovered that it is a real Louis XIV chimney, which is quite stupendous.

When I need comfort, I turn to potatoes, and overleaf is one of my favourite recipes as it involves spuds, fat and garlic — how can that be wrong? You slice some sourdough bread, open a bottle of Syrah and, along with the following recipe, that's a comforting dinner.

POTATOES IN DUCK FAT

Serves 6

1kg waxy potatoes like Désirée, Draga or Jersey Benne
8 tablespoons duck fat
sea salt and freshly ground black pepper
2 cloves garlic, finely chopped
3 tablespoons chopped flat leaf parsley

1. Peel the potatoes and slice them very thinly. Dry with a tea towel.

2. Melt half the duck fat, pour it into a bowl, add salt and pepper, and toss the potato slices in it.

3. Heat the rest of the duck fat in a large heavy-based frying pan. Tip the potatoes in and cook them on medium heat for about 10 minutes to create a golden base.

4. Now start moving the slices around so that other layers can take on some colour.

5. When the potato slices are all golden and cooked through, you can either stir in the garlic and parsley or scatter the garlic and parsley over the top before serving.

CHAPTER 8

IN WHICH I EMBRACE THE SOCIAL REVOLUTION, ENDURE THE FIRST SEXUAL ATTACK AND DUMP NURSING.

My second year of general nursing terminated in the usual identity crisis:

'I can't stand it,' I said to Anne, throwing my white nursing shoes against the wall.

'Oh, Pete. You've already done two years and there's only a year to go. You can't stop now — it would be such a waste. I'll stick by you.'

'Okay. I love you. If I get that medal, I'll give it to you and you can wear one on each breast.'

I was casting off my middle-class clothes, values and friends, Satan was no longer an issue, nor was God, and I was extremely relieved to be free of purity and the obligation to pretend to enjoy rugby games. In fact, being a hippy meant I could quit trying to fit into New Zealand's all-pervasive sporting culture altogether. Unfortunately, I wasn't entirely cured and was talked into going on a skiing trip. To this day I am the only person in New Zealand to actually succeed in injuring themselves while cross-country skiing.

'CROSS-COUNTRY?!' screamed my brother Jonney rolling about in agony. 'No one in the entire universe has hurt themselves cross-country skiing. All you have to bloody well do is walk straight ahead on flat terrain, for God's sake.'

Nevertheless I defied the laws of gravity and fell on my posterior so many times that I bent my coccyx out of shape. Skiing seemed easy, but that was a trick. I was given a total of two skis, or more or less one per foot, and two poles to prevent me from forming synthesis with a bush. What a joke. There was absolutely nothing to prevent me from rearranging my skeletal structure, getting lost and not being found until the clean-up at the end of the season. This was the most subversive sport of all because it made you wish you were at home watching rugby and drinking beer out of a bottle.

My brother used innocent words like 'powder snow' to lull me into a false sense of security. Powder snow is actually a millimetre of white gauze covering a foot of solid granite cleverly disguised as snow.

'Tell me why I am doing this?' I asked him. 'Give me one good reason why I can't progress to the lazy-school-of-skiing handbook, which clearly stipulates that it is unsafe to spend more than 20 minutes outdoors without a glass of wine.'

'Come on, Pete, it's easy — you put one foot in front of the other.'

As it turned out, the pain of falling on my butt 37 times was nothing compared to the pain and humiliation of the chiropractic treatments that followed. Let's just say that there was digital manipulation, unusual positions (I won't mention dogs) and a lot of undignified yelling involved.

My life of travelling and moving actually started the moment I left my parents' home, for thereafter I never lived in a house for more than six months. Anne and I were still close but it was time to move on, and I moved into a house on Scarborough Terrace in Parnell. The mother turned up periodically on a Sunday morning to drag me out of bed and march me off to Mass, but it was way too late: I had already been turned. Next door a woman called Jill and her straggly brood of kids lived in anarchy and chaos. Jill was a hippy who had relationships with artists and writers and knew everyone in the art scene. When she applied for a sales position that had been advertised in a local art gallery, the owners looked her up and down, not managing to conceal the snobbery and élitism that had got them where they were. Her kids waited outside and half her lovers' work lined the walls.

'But, madam,' they sniffled viscidly, 'do you know anything about the local art scene?'

'Madams,' replied Jill, opening her eyes very wide and flaring her nostrils, 'I *am* the local art scene.'

'What happened, Mum?' asked the kids, ducking as Jill furiously slammed out of the gallery.

'Who cares what happened?' she snapped. 'They're a bunch of fuckwits.'

'Okay, Mum.'

Although I was straight by Jill's standards, we became friends. She was easy-going, flamboyant and generous, sharing ideas, clothes and men. She loaned me a ribald poet called Connor, who wrote love poems on my sheets in ballpoint pen, on my mirror in lipstick and on the kitchen wall in tomato sauce. The flatmates were very entertained by his grandiose gestures and loud, laughing *joie de vivre*. He was in love with everybody, especially women, and seemed to be my mirror twin. He was like a Bacchus at a Rabelaisian picnic. I asked him how he had met Jill, and he told the story of seeing her prancing across the pedestrian crossing followed by all her little children: 'It was such a wonderful scene, how could I not fall in love with her?'

Men like Connor and Johnny were so much more interesting to me than the registrars and lawyers my friends and I were surrounded by as nice little nurses. They were intellectuals, anarchists (a word meaning 'no dress sense', which included wearing jeans so tight it is a wonder their sperm count ever reached above 1,000), and creators. They made something from nothing, they enriched the world, they preached free love, they revolutionised my safe little life, dancing me onto a joyous, empirical path from which I was never to digress. Where once there was nothing, there would be a poem; where once there was silence, there would be a song; where once there was space, suddenly there was colour, art and experience in paint. Surely this was more worthy and made more sense than counting money, irrigating kidneys or defending corrupt corporations?

One afternoon, I borrowed without asking a white linen dress from my cousin Nurse Lee to wear to the annual meeting with the matron, an occasion when I had to look respectable. Afterwards, time was running short so I took a short-cut through the park that bordered my house instead of walking around it. Hurrying along the path in Lee's sparkling white dress, humming to myself in the sunshine, nothing about the waving trees made me feel on guard. I was like a lamb to the slaughter, except they say that lambs know somewhere deep down in all that fuzz what's going to happen to them.

Out of the blue, strong arms immobilised me from behind and I was thrown to the ground. I didn't react immediately because it crossed my mind that it was a joke. Boys could be quite rough in their games, and I had already suffered fractured ribs at the hands of an enthusiastic massage-giver. All I could hear was heavy wheezing, and all I could think of as my face was rammed into the grass was that Lee would kill me when she saw the grass stains and mud all over her white dress.

When I twisted my head and saw that my attacker was a huge dark man I didn't know, who was trying to pull my pants off, I snapped into the horror of the situation and opened my mouth. The screaming didn't stop till the man was halfway across Auckland, and it continued until someone found me, helped me up and took me home. To Lee's credit, the last thing on her mind was the dress. She turned out to be helpful, supportive and very good with the police, taking everything under control. I felt ridiculous telling the police about these things after the event. At 19, who can find the words for terror, nausea, loss and fury? They didn't ask about your spiritual or soul damage, they asked only about the physical. They didn't ask how it felt to realise that from then on you would always have to be wary and watchful, that people would *take* what they couldn't have by asking nicely. They didn't ask why you should want to marry one of this gender that attacked you. Was this love or war? I certainly couldn't answer that question. Now, in either love or war, I knew what could happen if vigilance slipped.

By my third year of nursing, I was leading a truly double life. I moved once again to a communal house in Ponsonby; communal meaning men and women, a scandal the parents considered second only to World War II. There was no use pretending that this house was not about drugs, sex and rock 'n' roll; you had only to take a look at the people sitting on the front porch to get that. Anyone who sits on a porch smoking dope and listening to Jethro Tull must necessarily be having sex or worse. I drove to work at the hospital on my motorbike in bare feet, with no crash helmet but flowing Indian skirts flapping suicidally in my wake. Upon arrival at the hospital, the long black hair would be scraped back into subservience and the tie-dyed T-shirts (without a bra, of course, because bras were now a symbol of enslavement and our breasts longed for liberation) replaced by white starch. This is when it really started annoying my parents that we were related — they certainly had no wish to be associated with this left-wing, ridiculous clown who didn't even appear to know a decent marriage offer when she saw one.

Life in Ponsonby consolidated the direction I was going in, and I embraced it with open, bangle-laden arms. I was the only one in the house who worked full-time and had such an uncool, straight job. Paul was an arts student, a lovely girl called Sarah worked in television, Peter was a full-time student, and Tom could fix any machine in the universe. Doing shift-work had always suited me. I liked the freedom and flexibility, having long ago lost track of the concept of weekends. We were happy and enjoyed non-prescription substances and ate vegetarian food, alfalfa sprouts, mung beans and things made from bran, something we had never heard of until we rejected the devil that was white flour. Smoking joints and living unknowingly with junkies also led to my finding out what the inside of a police cell looked like. Or maybe it was eating all those mung beans.

Unbelievably, I didn't realise that Peter and Tom were junkies until the day I returned home from the hospital early and found syringes and needles boiling in a pot on the stove. I stared at the pot, my nurse's uniform trailing on the floor, trying to get my mind around what it meant. Everyone smoked marijuana, but that was benign — to us it was no different from smoking cigarettes and drinking wine. Also cannabis had cultural attachments like music, literature and art. Needles meant hospitals and dangerous drugs, but this was not a hospital, this was my home.

Needles boiling in a pot on my stove meant that there was heroin and morphine in the house, and that was malignant. Having something called a will to live, it was absolutely clear to me that needles meant death or worse — living death. Needles were for losers. I had never countenanced for one second injecting destruction into my veins, and could not understand the crossing of that border through the badlands and into the rivers of hell. I stared at the cooking pot, then picked it up and threw the whole lot out the window into the giant rubbish container of the supermarket next door.

The following day, while I was at the hospital bringing light into people's lives, the house was raided by the drug squad. Nurses are the only people in the world who get up earlier than the squad, so I was well on my way to work when they bashed the door down at dawn (the drug squad and immigration police never knock). They trashed the house. I was told all about it upon arriving home. With stoned eyes like pools of mud, Tom and Paul had stuffed handfuls of LSD down the cover of a Doors record and chucked the rest out the window into the supermarket delivery area next door. We spent that afternoon crawling around on our hands and knees trying to retrieve tiny bits of blotting paper. Peter and Tom were always very careful of their stash and equipment, so nothing was found, and in the drama they never asked me about the syringes. The next day I was at home alone reading in the back yard when two police officers stood over me.

SARAH'S BRAN MUFFINS

This recipe is supersonically simple but inexplicably delicious, especially slathered with butter.

Makes 12

> 1 tablespoon butter
> 2 tablespoons golden syrup
> 1 teaspoon baking soda
> 1 cup milk
> 1 cup bran
> 1 cup flour
> 1 teaspoon baking powder

1. Preheat the oven to 180°C.

2. Melt together the butter and golden syrup.

3. Dissolve the baking soda in a little of the milk, and add this to the butter and golden syrup.

4. Sift the dry ingredients into the milk mixture, add the rest of the milk and stir well.

5. Grease small muffin tins and divide the mixture up among them.

6. Bake for 15–20 minutes, until golden-brown.

'We found drugs in your room and we're arresting you for possession of narcotics and prescription poisons,' they said. I had no idea what they were talking about. They watched me get dressed, watched me use the toilet, didn't allow me to make any phone calls and didn't show a search warrant. I was so surprised and terrified that I didn't speak.

At the central police station, I was interrogated and, as I knew nothing, said nothing. The 'narcotics' turned out to be a chillum I had never used, and the 'prescription poison' some Mogadon tablets I had been given by the night sister to help me sleep during the day while I was on night duty. It became obvious that I was there to snitch on the others. It was just as well they had hidden their usage from me because I would have said my grandmother had sex with fire hydrants I was so scared. I was given my first-ever body search and left in a cell overnight, like a child facing the punishment wall, to weep and contemplate the ruination of my life.

The next day, my lawyer made a plea bargain that was very much in my favour. I was discharged without conviction and assured that, because of the good standing of my family, my name would be suppressed in the newspaper. Chance would be a fine thing. In the *Herald* the next day, the parents read over their cornflakes that their daughter had been doing more than sitting at home making jam. Well, at least it wasn't Class A. My father gave me a stern talking to, my mother threatened to have me committed and forbade my brothers and sisters from having anything to do with me. This edict made me much more interesting to them, and our visits had to be clandestine, which was very exciting for all concerned.

Soon after that, the beautiful, brainy, tortured Peter drove to the top of Mt Eden and died of an overdose. Tom eventually stopped using. Paul and I got together for a while, but I made him cry by leaving him for another. He wore flamboyant clothes like purple crushed-velvet flares, flowing psychedelic shirts and black velvet jackets, which later in life translated itself into cross-dressing. He read Jeeves stories to me as I cooked. When I made contact with him many years later, I opened my door to find him a visual symphony of blue lamé, black stilettos and blood-red lipstick — an outfit even a peacock would give a double-take. Every time he got drunk at a party, he would tell everybody how I had thrown him out of bed for not being good enough when he was young and tender, which had ruined him forever and turned him into a crossdresser. This is what is called urban myth, because I didn't have a clue what I was doing myself.

It was *de rigueur* to be vegetarian if you were a hippy. To my discredit, and flushed with the arrogance of youth, I called my parents and thanked them for ruining my health with white flour, cream and red meat. Thousands of New Zealanders ate cows because they were good-natured, simple and easily killed, and that went for the cows too. When I realised how chickens lived, I was so grossed out I decided never to let putrid flesh pass my lips again. Until . . . until the day a year later when I returned home to find someone frying bacon. The smell of cooking piglet was my vegan downfall, but I turned out to be much more intelligent because of this change of heart. Scientists say that the move away from our prehistoric vegetable diet triggered the growth of the human intellect. About 1.8 million years ago, give or take a few days, *Homo erectus* started to climb down and eat meat, fat and bone marrow. Such easy-to-digest foods required smaller stomachs and intestines, which used up less energy. That surplus energy fed our brains, which grew significantly. The moral of the story is: you can't have a big brain *and* big guts, which is why we eat cows and they don't eat us.

At this point, I was going out with lovely, interesting men. Graham was a tall, striking-looking young man studying the arts, English and Italian. He was blessed with a head of soft, dark curls, large brown eyes, a broken nose and a gorgeous smile. In love with literature, he turned me on to the writers he studied by day, reading *Brave New World* to me by night. I was a voracious reader as was everyone in my circle — these readings and our long, penetrating talks together were bliss. We went to poetry readings, university plays, folk-singing sessions, and sat around the fire listening to music, toasting marshmallows and talking literature.

My fiery temper was beginning to show itself to men, something that had not happened before. Up until then I had passively accepted shoddy behaviour, but that all went out the window with my new-found alternative principles. If anyone 'sailed too close to the wind' — a marvellously evocative expression I learned from my mother, having frequently done so in her company — my reaction was swift and demonstrative. After one bout of criminal activity, Graham presented himself at the front door protected by a bunch of carnations. A rolling pin hurled down the long hallway didn't wipe the smile off his face. He ducked, kept walking and presented his token of appeasement. I said, 'How dare you think a measly bunch of hospital weeds can wipe clean your slate?' and grabbed the carnations, shoved them down the toilet and flushed. Unfortunately for the show, the toilet was not designed to process plant life. The carnations would not go down, no matter how many times I flushed nor how much I shoved. Yelling at them didn't seem to help either. I sat down on the floor and burst into laughter, which led to the first kiss, which led to the second . . .

There was another boyfriend, Tony, whose sense of style included long blond hair, a cowboy hat, and a mad sense of humour. Being crazy about baseball, he formed the famous Allison Allstars team, which consisted of his friends, their girlfriends, anyone who turned up and wasn't too stoned, and various other serious athletes. His seduction attempts were sweet, fake, bumbling and patient. When I made it clear I expected a bit of an effort, he gathered up every candle he could find in the house and slowly lit them in my room, put on soft music, gave me a massage and asked what the hell other hoops I would like him to jump through.

Tony lived in a communal house around the corner from us that was up for sale, and the inhabitants were constantly being disturbed by real-estate agents and prospective buyers. One sunny Sunday morning, the doorbell rang — agents.

'Right,' roared Tony, 'I've bloody had enough of this!'

He leapt out of bed and opened the front door wearing nothing but a sock on his cock, smiled politely and said to the agent, 'Good morning. Has anyone seen my other sock?'

Like everyone else, he was in revolt against the assumed conformities, the bland hypocrisies and comfortable conceits of society. As hippies and refugees from the middle class, we felt that only the present held meaning. The past turned out to be valueless, but we could still possess the moment. Not only did Catholicism not mean anything, but marriage was now seen by me as slavery at worst and very uncool at best. Who needed a piece of paper anyway? Who needed to tie themselves to one person anyway? We saw ourselves as heroes, revolutionaries; there was a fantastic sense of belonging, community, us against them. We felt very powerful and utterly convinced that we could change the world. In fact, the world did change. Things like vegetarianism, grunge fashion, care for the environment, yoga, meditation, etc, which are a normal part of life now, were initiated by the hippy generation.

In the 1970s in New Zealand, one didn't lock the doors except maybe at night if one remembered. It was the smell and the sense that I was not alone that awakened me. How does this penetrate your dreams? I was lying in bed asleep when my eyes snapped open to see a dark man emerging through the window behind me onto my bed. Incomprehension and shock paralysed me for an instant and the taste of bile in my mouth was overwhelming. Then chemicals called 'over-my-dead-body hormones' took over and I leapt up stark-naked to confront my attacker. I had been assaulted before and my reactions were quicker this time. Without waiting for him to speak or move, I grabbed my dressing gown and launched into a discourse on the mores in New Zealand regarding courtship.

'Look,' I said, faking calmness, 'in New Zealand if you want a woman, first of all you ask her name, then you ask her to go to the pictures with you, then you hold her hand, then you wait and see. Climbing in people's bedroom windows is not how it happens here.'

On and on I raved, almost vomiting with impotence and confusion in my still half-asleep state. The man stared at me in rapt fascination, not moving. All was quiet as dark clouds filled the room and polluted my head. I pointed commandingly to the window and stood back while he climbed out and ran off into the night. It was then that I realised he hadn't understood a word I had said. Feeling sick with fury, I stomped around the house locking the doors and windows, especially my own bedroom one. My flatmates slept on like the disciples in the Garden of Gethsemane.

As I was drifting off to sleep again, my window was suddenly flung open and he was on top of me. I couldn't move with the weight of him, so I opened my throttle to full power and screamed and yelled for help. He sat up with fright and I slid out, running and shrieking into Tom and Sarah's room. The man had again disappeared into the night through his chosen point of entry, like a fox through a barn door. Tom was grumpy at being woken up, made a half-hearted attempt to look around the street outside, and went back to bed.

I realised that night that I was going to have to make improvements in the looking-after-myself department as no one else was going to take on the job. I got dressed, made a cup of tea, turned on all the lights and sat rigid at the dining-room table for the rest of the night. I meditated long and hard on whether I was at war with, or in love with, men, and how I could reconcile the violence with the need to be loved. If this was a lesson to me, what was I supposed to be learning? One of the worst things about sexual attacks is the aftermath. It takes a long time to recover, lose the fear, sleep, be alone anywhere. I wouldn't sleep alone, wouldn't be in the house alone day or night and had to have the bedroom light on all night. For months. The flat became a day-care centre for Peta.

As well as being fairly useless in an attempted rape situation, Tom could also be frightening. Anger management had not been invented then, but jumping out the window had. A few weeks after my dark-man-through-the-window drama, I was vacuuming what I thought was an empty house on a dirty, shady day at 10 in the morning. One major hangover from my bourgeois-pig past was my propensity to cleanliness and tidiness — I couldn't overcome it and was ridiculed and humiliated for this perversion many times in my Bohemian life. Tom said people who wash and clean too much are sexually hung-up at worst and not getting enough at best. Peter said they were into power and control. I turned Van Morrison up to top volume and threw myself into the vacuuming with religious zeal. Having heard nothing, I only realised Tom had an axe in his hands when I turned to move to the next room.

Six foot three of unbridled rage inflamed the lounge, and in one slow, powerful ark he swung the axe high, bringing the blade down onto the leads connecting the stereo and the vacuum cleaner, approximately three-point-five inches from my hands. A frenzied howl preceded the next blow, which split the speakers. Call it instinct, but I didn't wait to find out about the next strike, but cleared the window in one adrenalin-powered leap and ran to a nearby church. There in the front pew I shook, blanched with shock for an hour or so.

Christ, life is a battle, I thought. I buy a pot and in my own kitchen they boil syringes instead of eggs in it; I go to bed in my own home and am attacked; I vacuum in my own lounge room and get axed. If I survive to find a husband without a police protection programme, I'll be bloody lucky. After a few phone calls to check out the lie of the land, I eventually put my shoulders back and marched home. Tom was in the kitchen, hunched over a cup of tea. He looked up sheepishly.

'Sorry about that, old girl,' he smiled, 'but I was trying to sleep. The moral of the story is: don't worry about the carpets when I have a smack hangover.'

'Oh, okay.'

Sarah was beautiful in an ethereal way, with a sweet rosebud mouth, a wan complexion and fine blonde hair. She was as gentle as Tom was full-on, and her influence tempered him to some extent. She and I sang folk songs together and listened to The Rolling Stones and Cat Stevens and Carole King and Rod Stewart. We loved Leonard Cohen, Julie Driscoll, Bob Dylan, The Band. We lay on the floor with joints hanging out of our mouths listening to Mahler and Mozart and Wagner through headphones. Paul used me as his model for his photography thesis. Many years later, he turned up to my house dressed in a crimson evening dress and showed me the photos of me from this old thesis. They were of a girl wearing purple crushed-velvet bell-bottoms and a smocked blouse. She had long black hair hanging like thick hessian curtains from a central parting. I didn't recognise her.

I continued my house travelling, creating beautiful oases wherever I went. Like a perfect wife and home-maker, I painted and decorated entire houses every six months, taught hopeless male flatmates to cook and clean, threw huge dinner parties, cooked and cooked and cooked. The perfect wife with no husband. Cooking and eating made me happy and was a form of therapy — all that shopping, chopping, stirring, slurping. My latest abode was a huge house on Mt Eden Road across the road from the Crystal Palace picture theatre, where I had watched Tarzan movies as a child with my brothers and sisters. The house was large with a lounge the size of a ballroom, which I talked the other flatmates into painting Mediterranean blue. I painted the huge split-level kitchen canary yellow, and my bedroom white with burgundy trimmings.

One day Anne dropped in with a girlfriend. We were all sitting on my big four-poster bed when I stood up and squeezed past them to retrieve something. Out of the corner of my eye, I saw a tiny gesture pass between them. It was unmistakably the intimate touch of a lover — muted, automatic, imperceptible. I stared at them as if I had just noticed they were Siamese twins, put my hands on my hips and said, 'Oh my God, are you two, you know, in love or something?' Anne had visited especially to tell me, but I had deduced it way before the intended announcement. I was thrilled to see her so happy. But there was more to come. Another nursing friend had recently got married in a black suit to a family friend who had long been besotted with her. It was beyond me (a) why she felt the need to marry and (b) why she had married such a dull (but rich) man.

'Peta, there is something I have to tell you about that marriage,' said Anne, blowing cigarette smoke.

'No! I don't believe you!'

'I am telling you, yes.'

'Since when?'

'Since always. She has never liked men. Remember how she and Shandy magnanimously agreed to share the only double bed in their flat?'

'No!' I gasped again. 'They were doing it right under my nose? So why did she get married to that guy?'

'Her rich grandfather said she would be cut out of the will if she didn't. Zilcho. Nulissima.'

But really, it wasn't so much the money as an attempt to be 'normal' and fulfil the expectations of her social parents — this was the early 1970s! Needless to say, the marriage was annulled not long after.

At the end of my final year of nursing, I told Anne I really truly couldn't stand it, walked out, sat my finals from home and passed. Now I was a registered nurse for no other reason than to have succeeded at something; a registered nurse who would never darken the doors of a hospital again. Ever. After that I was gainfully employed sewing and selling beautiful clothes like the ones I made for myself. Love for my nursing friends and determination to graduate had not been enough to help me slot into the alien environment of hospitals and matriarchies.

Playing the guitar, singing in folk clubs, and selling the white, ribbon-bedecked dresses I produced from my sewing machine at the Cook Street Market was much more fun than dressing patients' suppurating abdominal wounds.

The following nut loaf recipe is from my vegetarian past. Because nut loaf is possibly the least sexy recipe in the world, I have sexed it up a bit with an intense roasted tomato sauce.

NUT LOAF WITH ROASTED TOMATO SAUCE

Serves 8

FOR THE NUT LOAF

- 400g mixed nuts (eg, cashews, walnuts, hazelnuts, almonds, pine nuts)
- 2 tablespoons extra virgin olive oil
- 1 medium onion, finely chopped
- 2 large cloves garlic, finely chopped
- 2 tablespoons fresh French tarragon
- 2 tablespoons fresh lemon thyme
- 2 tablespoons fresh sage
- 1 tablespoon grated lemon rind
- 1 teaspoon sea salt
- freshly ground black pepper to taste
- 1 tablespoon sherry or cognac
- 150g fresh breadcrumbs
- 2 organic eggs, beaten
- extra whole nuts for decoration

1. Preheat the oven to 180°C.

2. Chop the nuts coarsely in the food processor.

3. Heat the oil in a frying pan and sauté the onion and garlic until golden.

4. Stir in the herbs, lemon rind, salt, pepper, sherry or cognac and breadcrumbs.

5. Place the mixture in a bowl, and stir in the beaten eggs and chopped nuts.

6. Line a 23cm terrine with baking paper and spoon in the mixture. Decorate the top with whole nuts.

7. Bake for about an hour or until the loaf is firm.

FOR THE ROASTED TOMATO SAUCE

Makes 4 cups or 1 litre

2kg Roma or acid-free tomatoes
sea salt and freshly ground black pepper
¼ teaspoon sugar
4 cloves garlic, finely chopped
chilli sauce, to taste (I recommend Espelette: read Chapter 15 to know why)
¼ cup chopped fresh mint
1 tablespoon fresh chopped thyme
2 tablespoons orange juice (or lemon juice)
2 tablespoons grated orange rind (or lemon zest)
¼ cup extra virgin olive oil

1. Preheat the oven to 150°C. Spray an oven tray with olive oil.

2. Wash the tomatoes, slice them in half, core them and lay them out on the tray.

3. Sprinkle with salt, pepper and sugar. Spray again with olive oil.

4. Roast for about 2 hours until the tomatoes are semi-dried and a little browned. Remove from the oven and cool.

5. Chop roughly, and mix in a bowl with all of the other ingredients.

PTO

TO SERVE

Lift the loaf out of the terrine with the baking paper and serve on a platter surrounded by the tomato sauce, which is bursting with sunshine.

CHAPTER 9

IN WHICH I EMIGRATE TO CANADA, MOVE TO LONDON, THEN ON TO PARIS.

After I left nursing, I fell in love with 'the man who ruined my life', the man I wrote about in my book *Just In Time To Be Too Late*. In a normal life, I would have married Screw and had little babies with him, but he was a philanderer. Although I was in love with him for many, many years, deep down I didn't want to be tied to a man I couldn't trust. My parents didn't think he was good enough for me, and, looking back, they might have been right. In any case I would probably have been a restless wife, always wanting something more exciting. He was going to be a lawyer, but probably not a really rich one. As it turned out, I became a much higher achiever, and would that have happened if I had married him?

I told Screw I wanted to travel on my own for a while to see how I felt, then might return to him, but I was lying — I knew profoundly that marriage was not the right thing for me at that time. You would have thought the fact that I applied for immigration status in Canada might have been a hint. I had been bitten by feminism, a good education, contraception and confidence, and felt I had choices.

So I left New Zealand in 1974 with nothing but a suitcase and my immigration papers, flew to Canada and lived there for six years. At the age of 24, I had escaped phlegmatic New Zealand, a man, and a destiny of marriage, children, possible murder, mayhem and gin. I ran with open arms to a place not so different from Auckland, but thought that anywhere would be better than an island at the bottom of the Earth. It was a good idea to remove myself from Screw, but I didn't go far enough, as he followed me a year later; I realised I should have gone to the moon.

During my six years in Canada, I lived in Vancouver and Toronto, but Montréal was the city I loved best. As soon as I arrived there, I could see that the people were different and mixed: olive-skinned and dark-haired, golden-skinned and fair-haired, and they spoke Italian, Portuguese, Chinese, Lebanese, French and Hungarian. The pace was faster than Vancouver, more nervous, noisier. This was more like it — this was what I had in mind in the quest for adventure, excitement and romance. I wanted a sea change, and Montréal provided instant colour, stimulation and fabulous food. I loved all of these foreign people instantly, and far from feeling *dépaysée*, I felt much less like a foreigner and misfit than I did in New Zealand. For once I was the least different-looking, for

Montréalers not only looked different, they dressed differently. They were fashionable and chic, making me take a second look at my antipodean, hippy, bra-less, long-tressed style.

The men proved to be *very* different. The Italians called out to me in the street, whistled, tooted and stared. Being a staunch hippy feminist, I was horrified and yelled 'sexist, chauvinist, Roman pig-dogs' while giving them international finger signals. They were enchanted. I could have slightly eased up on that, because when I hit 50 I started whistling back, grateful for the attention. The English Protestant Montréalers were similar to New Zealanders, but that was only a visual trick because they didn't understand me when I spoke. Having a great sense of humour, Montréalers fell over themselves to make fun not only of my incomprehensible New Zealand vowels but also my general naïveté.

'Say "sex"!' they would scream.

'Sucks,' I would say.

'Say "dance"!' they would scream.

'Dahnce.'

'Say "fish"!'

'Fush.'

Half of Québec was French Catholic, but in Montréal when I arrived in the mid-1970s they all spoke English and a bit of French. Now they mostly speak French with a bit of English, but it was a good way to start learning French, and within 10 years I would not only be speaking it fluently but be married to a Frenchman.

I loved the city's wide, leafy streets, extreme muggy-hot and freezing-cold climate, terraced houses with steps up the front, and the open, friendly people. I enjoyed Arctic cold and central heating in the winter, and stifling heat and air-conditioning for the first time in my life, and used to go into the underground *métro* to keep warm. I didn't drive then, so I took the bus everywhere, thus experiencing the city at much closer range than most people would ever want to. Montréal is full of chic boutiques, sidewalk cafés with menus in foreign languages, endless discos, bars, great dress shops, international restaurants and beautiful old buildings. I visited art galleries, bought French clothes from the sublime shops on Saint Catherine Street, and went to McGarrigle Sisters folk concerts with my new friends.

I initially stayed with friends in their rather grand apartment that had wide corridors, lots of light and large white rooms. Their kids were as sharp as razors and talked non-stop in French, telling dirty jokes that their nanny taught them. I didn't understand their jokes, but laughed because I was happy. This was the first time I had ever lived in a home without a backyard and lemon trees. In fact, it was the first time I had ever paid for a lemon. The kids made up for the lack of outdoors by throwing themselves up and down the stairs and chucking pot plants at each other. The nanny taught me how to cook a steak the French way, which necessitated heating butter in an iron frying pan until no one could see the kitchen anymore.

'*Bon*, is perfect. Now, Peta, you can put 'er in. Ze steak. Put 'er in.'

I followed her voice and threw the steaks in from a safe distance, then ran out.

'Where you go? You 'ave to turn 'er over . . . *Viens-là, viens.*'

'But Lucette, *I* put them in,' I spluttered, waving smoke out of my eyes. '*You* take them out.'

The kids screamed with delight at the cooking lesson. I had tears streaming down my face, and the steaks were black on the outside and red everywhere else. With pride, Lucette removed them from the pan, poured the black butter over them and served them up: a symphony of black and red oozing all over the plate. Now I knew how to cook a steak French-style. This recipe (opposite) always reminds me of my first steak-cooking lesson.

My money lasted a few months, and then I had to find a job. All I was qualified for was nursing, but I was loath to sink to that level unless an emergency presented itself. One night at a bar (wearing an op-shop dress and chopsticks in my long black hair), I met a woman who was a counsellor. This woman was as mad as a cut snake and couldn't have helped an amoeba, so, as is totally standard in these professions, she had a senior position in a youth-counselling agency. When I looked at the mess she called a life, it was obvious I could do a better job with my eyelids sewn together. As I was still suffering from my missionary complex, I took her advice and applied for a position as child-care counsellor at a drop-in centre funded by local government, called The House.

STEAK AND CHIPS

Serves 4

FOR THE CHIPS

> 4 cups lard or soya oil
> 1kg floury potatoes like Agria or Darwina
> frying thermometer
> sea salt

1. Heat the lard or oil in a deep frying pan or a pot to 140°C.

2. Peel the potatoes and cut them into even, long chips about 1cm thick.

3. Wash the chips and dry them with a tea towel.

4. Place the chips in a frying basket and lower into the hot oil.

5. Cook until the temperature has gone back up to 140°C. Maintain that temperature for about 10 minutes, stirring the chips occasionally.

6. Lift the basket out, drain the chips and leave them for about 20 minutes. Turn the oil down low while you wait. (This stage can be done well in advance if you want.)

7. For the second fry, reheat the oil up to 190°C. Lower the basket of chips into the oil and cook for 3 minutes.

8. Remove the basket, allow it to drain, then tip the chips onto a cake rack covered with kitchen paper. Salt to taste.

PTO

FOR THE STEAK

2kg T-bone steak in 1 piece
4 big garlic cloves, cut into splinters
sea salt and freshly ground pepper
olive oil

1. Preheat the oven to 200°C.

2. Make slits in the meat with a kitchen knife, and stick in the bits of garlic. Sprinkle salt and pepper on both sides. Rub the olive oil into the meat.

3. Brown on both sides for 5 minutes each, in a very hot frying pan.

4. Place the T-bone in a roasting dish and cook in the oven for half an hour.

5. Remove from the oven and allow to rest, covered, for 10 minutes.

6. Cut the meat off both sides of the bone with a sharp knife, then slice those pieces to any thickness you like.

TO SERVE

Eat the steak and chips with homemade mayonnaise or Dijon mustard.

The position required someone with a medical background, because the youths kept slitting their necks shaving and suffering all sorts of damage such as pregnancies, bad breath and mistaken identity due to excessive pimples. Having never applied for a job in my life, I discovered I had quite a flair for the interview game. The person who has the most confidence in spite of the fact that they may have the least qualification is the person who wins the job. Thirty years later, research shows that this is absolutely true. Also, even though I was a fully paid-up feminist, I saw no reason why I should not smile nicely, slap on a bit of lipstick and throw in a few womanly wiles. As it turned out in subsequent years, this interview technique rarely failed. I took great pleasure in manipulating the game so that I was doing the interviewing.

This is how I entered the world of 14-year-old alcoholics, child-mothers, and curing by camping. I could barely stand normal children, so I wasn't sure how I was going to cope with disturbed ones. I had to teach the boys to spell well enough for graffiti, after coming into my office to find *I HATE GRILS* spray-canned all over my walls.

'Oh, for fuck's sake,' I said. 'What a bunch of losers — you can't even spell.'

I went on camping trips, where the staff got up to more tricks than the hooligans, the tent ropes were eaten through by beavers and foxes, and Québec almost burnt down as a result of my creative campfire techniques. But, hey, at least God's misunderstood children were receiving personality tips and not trying to have sex with anything that moved, this last leading to my decision to initiate sex-education classes. These were met with mild hysteria from the kids, and resulted in an increase in my sexual vocabulary of 80 per cent. I called the classes 'relationship management', which was rather ambitious, as no adult had ever suggested the concept of responsibility or choice to these teenagers and I wasn't exactly sure of the details myself. They gasped when I told them about the clitoris and that women can have orgasms indefinitely, the only thing stopping them being tiredness. Men, on the other hand, are to be pitied as they can only have one or two, then die. At this information they all lay down on the floor and screamed.

At the same time that I started the counselling job at The House, I left my friend's apartment and moved into a communal dwelling on Rue

Saint-François-Xavier. I found this apartment on the bulletin board of the nearby health-food shop. The announcement read:

wanted woman to join three wild, feminist, hedonistic, gorgeous women in beautiful two-storeyed apartment.

How did they know I was there? Bonny, Beth, Shelley and I took one look at each other and fell instantly in love. The apartment had a kitchen, dining room, lounge, bathroom, two bedrooms downstairs, and two bedrooms up. It was an old, funky brick building full of comfy furniture and books. Living with only women was so easy. In a household of all women, the housework always gets done, the food is great, the toilet seat is always down, and there are never any scenes.

Bonny, who was a filmmaker and artist, had the real Jewish look of olive skin, dark curly hair, almond eyes and generous mouth. Beth, the actress, was not beautiful but had that thing that tall, dramatic women have: carriage and great vowels — like Vanessa Redgrave. Shelley, with the long dark hair and cat-like eyes, had been around and was a late student of medicine. Bonny sharpened up my feminist principles; Beth had been to France as an exchange student and introduced me to buttery *croissants* and *brioche*; Shelley changed forever my teeth-cleaning habits. Her bedroom was next to the bathroom and it was devilishly hard to concentrate on scrubbing while she loudly made love next door.

Near the apartment was a lovely little park, the centre of civilisation for the neighbourhood. And of course, as with everywhere in Montréal, most of the neighbours were Portuguese and Eastern Europeans thrown in with artists, writers and musicians, all living in gaudy houses. In the street, the kids played and bashed each other up with big pieces of wood called hockey sticks. McGill University was nearby and teemed with colourful students, the proletariat and immigrants. At the end of the block was a plant shop, two second-hand clothing shops, a leather shop, a weaving shop and a quilt shop. Also, there were two Chinese, one Greek, one Italian, one Lebanese and one Polish restaurant. It is there that I learned to eat *borscht*, *blinis*, *pierogi* and *bigos*. Also lining the streets were pastry shops and delicatessens, the best of which was Schwartz's on the Boulevard Saint-Laurent (which still makes the most succulent smoked-meat sandwiches in the world). You went in at two in the morning for a sandwich, and people were there in ball gowns — it was fabulous. The cheap stores on Saint-Laurent were palaces of delight for the flamboyant such as *moi*, overflowing with peasant scarves, coloured pantyhose, tin bowls with flowers in them, lace curtains and ethnic rugs for my floors.

The new flatmates and I enjoyed each other's company so much that men felt they were almost intruding when they came visiting. We lay in the sun on the roof reading passages from *The Second Sex* and *Fear of Flying* to each other, and discussed our relationships in graphic detail. Bonny of the huge smile and raven curls was seeing the boy across the road, who was a doctor. Beth had two boyfriends and was rather earnest and dramatic but not beyond a little flippancy. Shelley had various boyfriends, one of whom she dumped because she didn't like the way he turned his jeans up.

Leonard Cohen lived down the road. We had the best parties in the neighbourhood, cooked the best food, and were intoxicated with the power of being young, free and loving our lives. For my part, ambivalence was the order of the day in my half-hearted attempts to communicate with the opposite sex. I had affairs, but my flight from the philanderer in New Zealand was too recent, and I hadn't entirely left him in my heart or head. I should have cut him out of my heart with an oyster knife and then had a lobotomy, because we continued torturing each other for many years. Our relationship became so famous for its toxicity that my friends changed his name to The-Man-Who-Ruined-Peta's-Life, and still introduce him as such at parties.

We ate in Greek restaurants opened by expatriates. These restaurants were by and large cheap, but some were very chic, upmarket and served beautiful food rarely seen in Greece, I later found out. Gorgeous, sophisticated, dark-haired men played backgammon at the bar and at low tables, smoking diminutive Greek cigarettes and drinking endless tiny cups of thick, sweet coffee. Greek men and women were warm and charming in an openly fervent way that to a girl like me, brought up in an emotional vice grip, seemed almost perverted. I was hopeless at card games and gambling because I'm not very competitive and don't care whether I win or lose. But I did have a flair for backgammon, playing with my new Greek friends all night, sipping gloopy ouzo, eating baklava, and learning how to be passionate about tiny round discs. My friends and I also indulged in breakfast crawls in the winter on Sunday mornings, during which we ate different courses in different restaurants, interspersed with walks in Mount Royal Park and classical concerts at the Cathédrale Marie-Reine-du-Monde. It took all day — I wept into my Jewish poppy-seed cake, so happy was I in my new home, Montréal.

Another time Bonny and I decided to hop on a plane and visit friends in California. San Francisco in the mid-1970s was exploding with colour, the inhabitants were relaxed and spilling out onto the footpaths from coffee shops and corner bars, and the Victorian houses were slashes of yellow, brown, pink, blue and black. Every corner we turned revealed fabulous shops, pottery, foreign food, street music, flower power and little neighbourhood hangouts. Reggae music had just hit America, and we danced all night in our flowing dresses to its intoxicating rhythm.

The West Coast of America was spearheading the fledgling therapy industry. Everyone was smiley-sharey and into 'getting in touch with their feelings', which was new stuff to me, but I thought 'What the hell, go with the flow, man, and get in touch.' It turned out to be a repulsive experience and almost turned Bonny and me off each other for life. Nevertheless, I was a counsellor and I wanted to save the world, so I persisted with feelings. It makes me weep to think of all the years I wasted as a nurse and counsellor in the realms of ill-health and as a cook in the hot, hard kitchens of the world. My missionary complex unfortunately negated using the abilities I had actually been born with — writing, entertaining and drama-making. It wasn't until I was 45 that I finally became who I was supposed to be from the beginning: a writer and television presenter. Talk about being in the wrong life. At eight years old, I was directing, producing, acting and singing in my own productions, not to mention designing the wardrobe, negotiating funding and running the neighbourhood. The counsellor in me would diagnose arrested development.

I had been in Canada for a year to the day when I received a letter from the philanderer in New Zealand, saying that he was coming to see me with the intention of reuniting. He missed me. My blood ran cold (but not cold enough), and I stared at the pages as if they had

CHOCOLATE BAKLAVA

Makes approx. 50 little 'cigars'

FOR THE SYRUP

    2 cups sugar
    1 cup water
    ½ cup Muscat wine

FOR THE STUFFING

    200g hazelnuts, chopped
    ½ cup dried breadcrumbs
    ¼ cup sugar
    ½ teaspoon ground cinnamon
    ½ teaspoon ground cloves
    ½ cup currants
    70g dark Valrhona chocolate
    1 packet filo pastry
    ¾ cup melted butter
    pastry brush

1. To make the syrup, boil the sugar and water together for 15 minutes or until syrupy.

2. Remove from the heat and add the Muscat. Cool.

3. Preheat the oven to 180°C.

4. Mix all the stuffing ingredients except the filo and butter together in a bowl.

PTO

5. On a dry surface, lay 1 sheet of filo, brush with the melted butter, then on top of that lay another sheet and brush with the butter.

6. Sprinkle 2 tablespoons of the mixture along the short edge, fold the long edges in by 1cm, then starting from the short edge with the mixture on it tightly roll the filo up to the end.

7. Continue with the other sheets until all of the mixture is used up.

8. Place the rolls in a greased, shallow roasting pan and bake for half an hour or until golden.

9. Remove from the oven and pour over the syrup.

10. Leave for at least 1 hour, or overnight, and then cut into short cigar lengths.

come from a coffin. My response to his destruction of my love, trust and romantic illusions had been surprisingly decisive: I had made such an effort to become hardened in the battle against betrayal, and forced myself with an iron will to erase him from my new world. But now here he was again, looking for more punishment. I had convinced myself of my own invulnerability, but felt waves of the eviscerating loss of the love that had so wounded me. On and off in the past year, I had felt the longing for what I thought had been the good times: the hours of lovemaking, the complacency of partnership. Sometimes your body betrays you in the sexual memories department, but on the outside I was staunch. So, as is entirely appropriate for someone whose past is catching up with them, I started an affair with a guy from work, more to relieve tension and diffuse my fear of seeing the philanderer than anything else. Rick was a nice, simple boy and far too good and normal for my scarred heart, and the lure of the bad boy was still strong — Screw arrived right on cue.

There he was a few weeks later in the lounge room on Boulevard Saint-François-Xavier, impressing Bonny, Beth and Shelley with his sexy smile, tight jeans and high-heeled boots. Oh, God, I thought with loathing and panic, they like him. We'll soon bloody fix that. I dragged them up to the roof, lit a joint and said, 'Stop being so nice to him.'

'But he is perfectly charming and so good-looking,' they chorused.

'Of course he's charming. So was Dracula.'

'Oh, really, Peta, give the guy a break.'

We went back into the apartment where the girls' boyfriends were amiably chatting away and sharing beers with the philanderer, the King of Cool. Eventually I had to be alone with him. He slung his things into my bedroom and sat on the bed.

'At least kiss me.'

'I can't.'

'Okay, but you know you're the only woman in the world for me. I've had lots of time to think and I've got other women out of my system.'

'Is that right?'

'Look, I've come all this way. We have to give it a try.'

'I'm seeing someone else.'

'That's all right. I didn't expect to find you in a hair shirt.'

'Look, you can stay here for a while if you want, but then you'll have to move on.'

'We'll see. If you really don't want me, I'll go to London.'

Every day, he told me he loved me and that I was the one, and every day I felt myself vaguely weakening. He probably did believe he loved me and that I was the one, because it seemed like the right thing to feel at the time.

We were invited to a friend's farm for the weekend. In the bucolic setting with the hosts' relaxed hospitality and no pressure being laid on, the philanderer and I got along well and I managed to modify my rigid stance towards him, while still maintaining a healthy mistrust. We ate huge meals and went for walks and talked. I told him I believed I wasn't in love with him anymore but that I would always love him and maybe in time something could happen. I needed time to think and feel again, and having sweet Rick didn't help. But dark clouds were scudding, and I didn't see them until it was too late. I never found out what it would be like to make love to the philanderer in a feather bed in the farmhouse because he trumped me. The first night in the country, we all went to the pub then crashed in various bedrooms in the house.

'Where have you been?' I asked Screw the next morning when I wandered down for breakfast, assuming he had drunkenly slept in another room.

'I met a girl at the pub and spent the best night in a woman's bed I've had in a long time.'

Everyone put their spoons down and stared at me. I instantly snapped back into what it felt like to be caught up with him again. I slammed my fist down on the table. 'How could you do this to me after coming all this way to find me?'

'Well, *you* didn't want me darlin', so I considered myself a free agent.'

'Just because I don't want you absolutely *does not* mean that someone else can have you, you bastard.'

'You're being unreasonable, Peta. You can't have your cake and eat it, too.'

'Since when? Where does it say that I can't love you and not love you at the same time? Where? Oh, why did I fall for your tricks?'

'But you have Rick, whom you parade around in front of me.'

'That is *no* excuse. None whatsoever, and I don't parade him. This isn't about Rick and you know it.'

I went for a long solitary walk while they had breakfast, made my decision, quietly packed my bag and jumped on the first bus back to Montréal. I stared unseeing out the window in a rancid rage that I had allowed myself to be fooled. Again.

Back at home, the consensus of the wimmin on the rooftop with glasses of wine was that I had no rights over him, but that he had been insensitive, to say the least. There was a bit of feminist hair-splitting over that one. Normally the rule was that men are bastards, have no rights and, whatever happens, it is their fault and they are bloody lucky to be alive. However, Bonny felt for the philanderer, probably because she fancied him, and they agreed that I should forgive him, so I did on the surface to please them. Mustn't hold a grudge. Needless to say, he hopped on a plane to London quite smartly.

I'm very sorry to tell you that I saw him again and he did something even worse — we continued visiting each other from time to time between London and Canada, simultaneously having relationships with other people, and after six years he asked me to come to London and give our relationship one last try with a view to marriage. I gave up my job, my life, my friends, my apartment and my boyfriend and moved to London to be with him. I found him living with another woman. You'll be pleased to know I was permanently cured after that, but unfortunately never able to trust another man again.

During my six years in Canada, I had relationships with other men that didn't work out for various reasons — mainly because we simply weren't well matched and I had turned into a bit of a bolter, suffering from the early signs of marital dyslexia. Having tried so hard and for so long with Screw, if a man became difficult, I could see the road ahead and cut my losses fast before too much damage was done. I have remained friends with most of the men I loved.

I turned 27 in Canada and had a catharsis about it just like the crisis of faith I had experienced in church when I was 19 and realised I didn't believe in God or Catholicism anymore. I was standing in the bathroom, looking at myself in the mirror, when I realised I was no longer a girl and couldn't keep wandering around enjoying excitement, adventure and romance forever.

Well I *could*, but I had to do something constructive at the same time. It took a few more years for me to achieve something constructive due to my being a late developer, but I did eventually in Paris.

I stayed in London for a year in 1979 and found a job in Neal Street, Covent Garden. Neal Street in 1979 was fun, and there were still kitsch little 'coffee shops', and the cheese shop in Neal's Yard was still small and homey. I was chief sandwich-maker at Olive's Pantry, Olive being a working-class gal done good. She was exquisitely proud of being a true Cockney, having been born within hearing distance of the Bow Bells in the East End.

Blonde and blousy, Olive worked hard and never stopped telling stories about her poor but colourful childhood and wild youth. She was suffused with romantic nostalgia for her large family and gambling father. One of her many sisters once told me that their life had been harsh and bittersweet, but Olive's eyes glistened with relish when she described it. The dishes were washed by Olive's Aunt Kate, a tiny, aged, sparrow-like creature who went to Stopitam (stop at home) for her holidays. It crossed my mind that I would be better off at the Ritz than at Olive's Pantry, but it was a start. As it turned out, I knew more about food than they did, but they taught me Cockney rhyming slang and I laughed so much in the year I worked there that my jaw ached constantly. Olive 'gave it' to her obese husband, Pat, once a week on a Sunday, and I heard all about it on the following Monday. What I didn't learn about cooking, I learned about marital sex. That Christmas I was invited to spend a long weekend in Paris.

'Don't go,' pleaded Olive and Aunt Kate, 'you'll never come back.'

'Don't be silly, it's just a weekend.'

I went to Paris for three days and stayed for 10 years.

CHAPTER 10

IN WHICH I LIVE IN PARIS, GET MARRIED, GET REAL AND OPEN MY FIRST RESTAURANT.

I arrived in Paris is 1980, and my life over that 10 years in France is covered in my book *Fête Accomplie*. More stories on French life appeared in *French Toast*, *Beat Till Stiff* and *Just In Time To Be Too Late*. Following, is the story of my one and only marriage, and this is the last time I'm telling it. As it turned out, I never married any of the men I loved and didn't love the man I married. You know how some people are dyslexic around language? I have marital dyslexia. I married a very beautiful young gay man called Alexy Zabiego so I could remain working in France. At that time, I was in a relationship with an American oil engineer who took my attraction to inappropriate but exciting people to new heights (or depths), and I think we both felt it entirely correct that I marry someone else.

'*Franchement*,' Alexy moaned in 1984, 'you're not seriously going to wear a black wedding dress, are you?'

I decided that as nobody wanted to be the one who wore white at the wedding, we should both wear black, no arguments. 'Yeah I am, and what's more I'm considering wearing a big feather necklace. I've bought a second-hand designer gown made in Milan and — guess what? — the *pièce de résistance*: Margaret is loaning me a red veil with red roses on it. She found it.'

'*Ça va pas la tête?*'

Alexy and I were sitting in the writing corner of the spacious Montparnasse *atelier* I lived in with the well-known, elderly gay German photographer Willy Maywald, marinating in the sunshine that filtered through the huge skylight, a skylight that was in fact the entire south wall of the house. The writing corner was downstairs, hidden behind the front door, and the best time to sit in it was late morning. The best place to sit was on the white, sheepskin-covered seat, looking out at the sitting room and curved stairs going up to the second floor. Alexy made some Lapsang Souchong tea in a white china teapot and poured it into white china tea cups. He never used a sieve on the pretext that the leaves falling into the cup keep the flavour intense, *n'est-ce pas*? This morning, in my egalitarian New Zealand way, I lost my head and thoughtlessly made up a Moroccan mint tea.

'*Mais enfin*, what are you thinking of, Peta? Mint tea at 9am? Some tea is drunk with milk, some with lemon and some at certain times of the day. It is only 10 in the morning. Mint tea is drunk in the afternoon, *nom de Dieu.*'

'But why? If I feel like it now, why can't I have it now?'

'Because, *petite sauvage*, it is a light, refreshing tea to be taken in the afternoon when one wishes to be calm and relaxed. That's why God invented English Breakfast tea, because it is a stimulant and full of caffeine to make you ambulant.'

'Look, *cher*, if you're going to be my husband, I'm going to have to spend far too much time looking at you anyway, but I am prepared just this once to stay open on this important topic. It seems to me this is very similar to our earlier roast-lamb discussion wherein you maintained that lamb is always served with beans, not with sweet potato, peas, *gratin dauphinois* or any other bit of reinvention of history that I care to impose.'

'*Exactement*. It is vulgar colonialism to tamper with old recipes and ancient tea ceremonies, because they are not thus *comme par hasard*, they are thus for solid gastronomic, geographical and historical reasons.'

'What gastronomic reasons?'

'In the old days when *gigot* was served, the only vegetables available were dried flageolet beans and they go well with it. They don't drown out the delicate flavour of the lamb, unlike that English abomination mint sauce. *Quelle horreur.*'

'But you need the acidity of the vinegar to cut the fat of the lamb.'

'So, roast the lamb with rosemary and preserved lemons.'

'Oh, yes, that's quite good.'

This was Alexy to a T, this willingness to discuss in detail the cultural and social *raison d'être* of a cup of tea.

Alexy — future husband, handsome model — carried his slim frame and medium height as if he were modelling an Yves Saint Laurent suit, which actually he was in his head. He walked in that slightly stylised, stiff but liquid way some male models do. Alexy was too discreet, well-bred and fundamentally shy for overt displays of sexuality. His rigid Catholic private-school upbringing had seen to it that he never expressed himself openly. Also, he never fully recovered from his mother's death in his early childhood, always feeling an outcast even in his own family. Being the youngest of seven boys was bad enough, but having been ripped away from the breast at such a vulnerable age, he remained vulnerable into adulthood. His homosexuality effectively alienated him from his straight siblings, strict father and unsympathetic step-mother, cementing his profound insecurity. Nature, however, had blessed him with a perfectly proportioned face. Everything fell into place on this face as it had never done in life: full lips, large eyes like wine-dark rivers at night, high cheekbones and a classic square jaw. A French Rupert Everett.

He thought that if he was polite, moved quietly without taking up much space and didn't rock the boat, someone would eventually love him for something other than his beautiful face. I was prepared to put his beauty to one side and love him for his ability to turn me into an honest woman by marrying me. I shared his complex but had an inverted personality. I spent my childhood as an ordinary, freckled, big-nosed eldest child in a family of six children. Even though it all evened out in the end and ordinary turned into passably pretty, I was still surprised when men fell under my spell. I was a woman longing for someone to bypass my personality and fall for my looks alone — this five-foot-four, mouthy person with black hair.

'Let's discuss what's going to happen at this wedding, Peta. What do you want me to wear? Who's on the invitation list? What about catering?'

'Okay, come back this afternoon and we'll have a beer in the garden.'

When he arrived wearing his matinée-idol smile, olive skin and open-necked shirt, I ushered him out into the garden, where we sat at the weather-worn white iron table. It was late winter in Paris, so there was little to shade us from the pale blue French light, so different from the light I had grown up with. Years ago, when I stood in front of a Manet painting in Melbourne for the first time, I had wept, and now living in France I could see that the muted soft light he painted so often was exactly as it is.

Willy, who loved to surround himself with young people and often said that his door was closed to no one, had agreed to be Alexy's witness at the civil ceremony. Lulu, my boss at L'Assiette restaurant where I worked, offered to provide the wine at cost from a winemaker she knew in the Touraine. As we both lived for feasting and loved the therapy of preparing food, Alexy and I decided to do the catering ourselves.

We sorted all the paperwork that French bureaucracy demands for even such a simple thing as two people getting married. If one tiny piece of information is wrong or missing on any paper, a mental note is made by the power-hungry reject-from-hell behind the desk. The knowledge of the mistake is deliberately withheld from the victim and saved for the next time they crawl into the office, begging for what is already theirs. Thus a potentially brief encounter could be stretched out indefinitely, each time a fresh missing bit being discovered. For example, Alexy's father was Russian and had slightly changed the spelling of his name upon arrival in France, so his birth and wedding certificates had different names on them. Major diplomatic drama! They almost had to close the airports. My birth certificate said I was born in Mt Albert, but on my application form I wrote Auckland. Triumphant, wall-eyed with passive-aggressiveness, the clerk pointed out quietly that now everything had to be done again. Not any old birth certificate, *n'est-ce pas*, but a long birth certificate, one that includes the births, deaths and marriages of relatives back to the Inquisition.

But all was finally arranged, the hell-hag at the *mairie* had been subdued, a gold wedding ring had been procured, Lulu gave me her sapphire engagement ring, and everyone was ready for better or for worse. The big day arrived on 12 March 1984. Lulu was my witness and arrived at the *atelier* in a cowboy hat and boots and three metres of rawhide tassel. She visited Texas every so often, was impressed by the style of dress, and assimilated it into her French uniform of jeans and leather jacket. Alexy strolled in looking thrilling in a black smoking-jacket and white silk scarf, and Willy descended the stairs in his sharp pin-striped suit. I stalked down nervously in my black wedding dress and black patent-leather shoes with red stiletto heels.

At this precise moment, Margaret swept in the door, all six foot and red hair. She was there in her capacity as official wedding photographer.

'*Bonjour, chéris*, I have brought your veil, Peta.'

Everyone crowded around as she drew out of her handbag a splendid crown of red silk roses holding a long red veil. I asked her to pin it onto my hair. Alexy remained expressionless to camouflage the thought that if his father ever caught wind of this he would be dead meat. It was thus we swept up the garden path and around the corner to the Vavin *métro* stop on Boulevard du Montparnasse. Sitting on the *métro* in my black wedding dress and red veil, I pondered on what the Sisters of Mercy would say if they could see me now. Bold and brassy would be the least of it.

Our Fellini-esque party of black bride, cowgirl, six-foot lady photographer and two men who resembled undertakers exited from the *métro* at Saint-Sulpice and made our way up to the mayor's office. Other friends joined us, similarly attired, mostly in black. The clerk from hell saw us go past her office, saw me brazenly on the arm of a 24-year-old matinée idol — *moi, Mademoiselle*: big-nosed, ordinary and foreign, dressed in a radiant smile and a few metres of raven *crêpe*. I curled my lips in a triumphant smile. Alexy wore an expression that said, see how normal I am?

We all stood in a row in front of the mayor, whose immaculate manners were exceeded only by his charm. Chatting and giggling continued throughout the short ceremony, though Alexy was very formal and my mind started to wander.

At 35 I was finally going through this rite of passage that had long ceased to mean anything to me, suffering as I was from marital dyslexia. Women interviewed in studies say that their wedding day is the most wonderful and important day in their whole lives, the only day when they are truly honoured, celebrated and treated like they have done something worthwhile. They never feel like that again in their lives; in fact, from thereon in they become invisible. They have horrid, ungrateful children who grow up to tell them they are responsible for all their problems, and husbands who betray them. No wonder they have mental breakdowns and facelifts. Not me, thought I, I'm safe now.

There are persons in my family who say that my '*mariage blanc*' is immoral and dishonest and I have no values. There are persons in my head, like the Sisters of Mercy, who say, 'You are on the fast track to hell, girl,' and persons like the French secret service who say, 'You have broken the law because you are not in love, you are not going to populate Mother France with your little babies and for this you will go to prison or be expelled.' The thoughts behind Alexy's black eyes went like this: 'If I marry her, my father might find out and cut me out of the family permanently, and if I don't marry her, my father will eventually find out I'm gay and cut me out of the family permanently. If I keep a low profile, maybe nothing will happen and I'll get away with it permanently.'

What did happen was much sadder.

'Mais où est le gâteau?' gasped Alexy's friends as they perused the food department at the wedding party, by then in full swing upstairs and down. Six stunning young men all in formal dress, all models, all with their hands outstretched, all directed at Alexy and me — like a herringbone suit. They looked tipsily at each other.

'*Mon Dieu, le gâteau,*' said the husband.

'*Zut alors,* the cake. It never entered my mind. What are we going to do?'

'*On se calme,*' chanted the herringbones, 'leave it to us — we will create something, *n'est-ce pas. Vite, vite,* to the shops.'

At least a hundred people were crowded into the *atelier,* dancing, singing, falling up and down the stairs, shouting. The real romance of the evening happened outside in the garden between Lulu's huge dog Boules and the dog of another guest. The earthy Lulu was out there in the thick of it, loudly choreographing their coupling, inciting Boules to greater heights of performance. She absolutely wanted the bitch to be sired to further her empire of ridgebacks and thus eventually rule the world. She spoke to him in an extraordinary gobbledygook language that meant nothing and was conveyed uniquely by the tone of the voice. If Boules wasn't getting the message, the gathering crowd certainly was, volunteering their versions of how it should be done. Willy came out, tipped his cigarette-holder back and sneered, '*Quelle vulgarité.* Can't you give zem some privacy on zere vedding night?'

Back in the house, the noise level was suddenly raised by screams and clapping. The herringbones had created a wedding cake from *langue de chat* biscuits and whipped cream, the result resembled either the Eiffel Tower or a phallic symbol, depending on your orientation. Alexy was very calm and relaxed at the wedding party, taking care of business, changing the music from Bruce Springsteen to Les Rita Mitsouko to Les Négresses Vertes to Sting.

I didn't like being in the position of having a hundred people all wanting to talk to me — I felt slightly hysterical and overwhelmed, so collapsed with a cigarette into my favourite corner under the skylight. The temporary relief masked the fact that the smoking actually raised my stress levels, but it prevented me from doing something worse with my mouth, like telling everyone to go home.

My Parisian friend Michèle, a serious literary translator, sat next to me. She was a vision of unmitigated perfectness: small, slim, feline, elegant. There were no uneconomical movements in Michèle, no loud talking, no superfluous smiling beyond what was appropriate, no lapses in taste. She was dressed in black with a leopard-skin scarf wrapped twice around her neck the way Frenchwomen do, Stephane Kélian snakeskin shoes and a narrow snakeskin belt. Her hair was in a dark brown bob, and her lips were matt aubergine. She wore little other make-up on her olive skin except for a kind of mustard-coloured eye-shadow and a flicker of mascara. Her thin lips were usually tightly clamped around a cigarette.

'*Alors*, so how do you feel?' she asked through a screen of smoke.

'I feel like finding one of those Mills and Boon romance novels and going to bed with it,' I replied.

Michèle permitted herself to raise an eyebrow. 'You are kidding. *Mais enfin*, Peta, it's not real life. No one could possibly relate to anyone in these stories. I mean, how many rich, handsome, masculine sheep-station owners can there be?'

'Who cares? What's so great about real life? The station owners behave like no man has ever behaved towards the readers in their lives. It is socially accepted female pornography, I tell you. You can buy it in the supermarket like toilet paper. Contrary to their husbands, the hero in the book has a fabulous body, is a sexual paragon, is polite, is romantic and is completely and utterly besotted with the heroine.'

'Not unlike your husband.'

'Not unlike my husband.'

After the traditional onion soup at 5am, the party diehards suddenly felt sleepy. Some of them went upstairs to various beds and couches, and the rest wandered off up the garden path as the first soft suggestion of light was dawning. Willy, the most senior member of the wedding, was the last to go to bed. Alexy kissed his wife goodnight and went off with his young man. I wandered around the house switching the lights off, sat down at the dining-room table, poured a cognac and thought, 'So now I am married. *Et vogue le navire.*'

After working in various restaurants in Paris, in 1985 I opened my own, called Rose Blues in the fifth *arrondissement*. It was a friendly cosmopolitan bistro where people swapped tables, started up conversations with strangers, and wandered into the kitchen to gossip. My clients were left-wing intellectuals, arms dealers, local artists and philandering husbands. We had sing-songs, punch-ups, melt-downs, run-ins and very good food, such as molten-cheese fritters, marinated herrings, *navarin printanier*, *andouillette*, charlottes, chocolate mousse and homemade ice cream.

I had lots of fun but worked 12 to 15 hours a day, my weight went down to 55 kilos, I fell ill frequently and stopped sleeping: classic signs of stress, but I didn't know that then. I lived on chocolates and cigarettes and was in a relationship with an abusive Frenchman. I succeeded against all the odds to make Rose Blues work in the toughest food city in the world, but was dying in the process. After three years, I sold the business and the doors closed on an era of eclectic eating, riotous parties and hard lessons learned. Selling up gave me the strength to dump the French boyfriend, get my looks back and resume eating. Sadly, I never learned how to sleep properly again.

As I also described in *Fête Accomplie*, I fled south to work as a chef on luxury barges on the Loire and other rivers, mainly in the Burgundy region. In some ways barges are the perfect home for a nomad. I fell in love with the local food, the local villages and the local men, but after a blissful time had to escape from the tantrums of yet another man and ended back up to Paris.

Alexy and I remained friends, and then a terrible day dawned and he discovered he had AIDS. I couldn't believe he wasn't having safe sex, but in those days the French thought that AIDS would stop at the border. In 1990, I returned to New Zealand to live, and we kept in touch by letters and telephone. Eventually he went to live in a hospice because it was obvious he was too fragile to survive.

In 1995 I received a very kind letter from his eldest brother, Jacques, saying that the family didn't know that Alexy was married — they had found letters from me among his possessions. Alexy had died, and Jacques and his wife, Aline, were inviting me to visit them at Cordes-sur-Ciel, where they lived in the southwest of France. I went to see them and stayed for a week — they were adorable and we talked and ate and talked and ate. While I was there, the father died, the father who had alienated Alexy, refusing to visit him even as he lay dying. But this same father, on his own deathbed, asked to be buried next to Alexy. What you can't achieve in life, you try to achieve in death — there's nothing like being just in time to be too late.

CHAPTER 11

IN WHICH MY PARISIAN LIFE CONTINUES, MY MOTHER VISITS AND I ENDURE MORE SEXUAL ASSAULTS.

I had arrived in Paris in 1980 from London, and a year later François Mitterrand was voted in with his socialist government, which was a cause for riotous celebration in the streets. I and thousands of delirious *Français* stood outside the Élysée Palace waving red roses and weeping with political hope. The newspaper *Libération* was permeated with rose perfume and dyed pink, and all the restaurants were overflowing with huge bowls of red roses. I loved living in Paris because of this emotionality. The architecture seemed so dramatic to me: every corner I turned I found beauty, especially when I looked up — a rewarding exercise in cultural terms, but you could get trapped in dog excrement. Paris is a city that lends itself to self-indulgence and a certain intellectual hanging out. I always began conversations that I simply couldn't end, and why would I end them? For what? To go home and knit, to work, to do badly needed shopping? Inconceivable. In Paris you talk. I had the feeling that the meaning of life was to be had and enjoyed there and then, and to be a slave to schedules was a *petit-bourgeois* habit and anti-life. These thoughts were not new to me, to tell the truth.

Marriage changed nothing in my life, which, it struck me, was how it should be. The only thing that changed was I now had a big fat wedding ring, a legally bound friend and a flash new name. Being Madame Zabiego has an appeal, so I kept the poetic name — it was so close to Dr Zhivago that I felt myself turning into Julie Christie. Peta Zabiego would be a smashing name if I became rich and famous — I couldn't have invented it if I had tried. No one could look at me with my freckled skin and hazel eyes, hear that name and succeed in placing me. The fact that it was Russian and not French only added more poetry in my eyes, and my friends wittily insisted on calling Alexy 'Mr Mathias'. I also now had a natural immunity to catching a real husband, so was practising safe marriage, which is even safer than safe sex. I had pioneered a spontaneous cure for marital dyslexia.

My mother turned up from Australia at Rue de la Grande Chaumière to visit for Christmas. She entered my realm with bizarre presents that explained to my friends how exotic and alien my background really was. These are the presents: a Christmas cake; a tape of a haka; a book of Maori mythology; a hand-knitted pink cardie; a jar of Marmite; 37 packets of tiny raisins; and a card stating that she and my aunty

Peg were saying (and paying for) an endless stream of novenas for me. I turned on the tape and listened to the haka, then took it in to the restaurant where I couldn't induce Lulu to stop playing it. Every time a customer came in, she played it and banged on about native spirituality and noble savages. Willy liked having Mum visit, and made a big fuss about how ladylike she was in comparison to me. They were both artists: Willy dabbled with collages and Mum watercolours and drawings, so they had a lot to talk about over endless cups of tea in the dark dining room. Also she was a new ear for his war stories.

We went sight-seeing, which to Mum meant visiting every church and every art gallery ever built. Each church we visited happened to have a Mass going on, and she always had to stay and get holy. Quite aside from the trauma of having to sit in all these churches when I was a recovered Catholic, it was very boring following her around all these monuments to excess. As it was Christmas, she asked to be taken to midnight Mass. I was prepared to make a concession to my rabid anti-Catholicism as both Alexy and I loved pomp and ceremony. In fact, it was the one thing we missed about our religious upbringings. It is difficult to replace the sensual incense, the dramatic costumes and the ostentatious ritual of organised religion. So, we all wrapped ourselves in warm coats and scarves and tramped off in the light snow to Notre Dame Cathedral on the Île de la Cité. We invited Willy to come with us, but he refused point-blank to go anywhere near a church.

'Vere vas ze church ven ze Jews and gypsies vere being incinerated in Germany?'

I knew early arrival was essential, so we turned up at 10pm, even then totally underestimating the popularity of this particular venue. We couldn't get anywhere near the front portals, let alone the altar. The faithful, which in France means those who never go to Mass except on Christmas Eve, begin their vigil hours in advance. People filled every seat, every inch of the aisles, every centimetre of floor space in the ornate medieval wedding-cake of a cathedral. They sat cross-legged, stood glued back to back, and even sat on each other's knees in the confessionals, which I thought was pretty borderline behaviour (considering how many hours I had spent in those boxes inventing sins). I tried to imagine what would happen if they all started spontaneously confessing unthinkable things to total strangers, then remembered that's what happens with priests anyway. The concept of sharing your problems with a stranger who can't see you but has the power to forgive you is, in principle, a very clever one. Unfortunately it doesn't matter how often you confess, you still feel guilty.

The next day, we had a French Christmas lunch and invited Willy, Lulu, Michèle and other friends to join us *chez nous* on Rue de la Grande Chaumière. Everyone screamed at Lulu's dog Boules all day, laughed themselves hoarse and told ribald jokes. My mother wasn't used to this European worldliness and didn't have the taste for it, but managed to smile indulgently as we fell about full of oysters, *foie gras*, smoked salmon and intellectual self-abuse. She found French food intolerably rich, however. For days I cooked her special meals, spending hours over miraculous sauces and showing off my new culinary knowledge. She perched on a stool in the kitchen, dressed in slacks and a nice Fairisle jumper with her hair neatly combed, and said things like, 'There's too many fancy things in that salad, Peta' or 'That's very nice and I appreciate your efforts, but do you have any boiled potatoes?' Then she discovered succulent French black pudding and ate it for breakfast, lunch and dinner with dry toast.

Mum read me letters from home, and we sat around giggling at the hilarity of them. My family refrain from telling news of any sort in letters, sticking instead to descriptions of the minutiae of the personality quirks of the neighbours, how people were dressed at Mass and the clinginess of my brother's girlfriends. We were visited by freezing rain during this week, which turned to ice the minute it hit the pavement, but Mum went out fearlessly in it every day, trawling the streets for art and gothic buttresses. Three days were spent in the Rodin Museum, not counting toilet breaks.

Mum became very adept at sign language, and insisted on speaking to people in New Zealand/French even though not one person in Paris understood what she was saying. I find that application and enthusiasm bear no relationship to ability in languages. It's like painting — either you've got it or you ain't. She would return from her street-trawling bearing bizarre gifts like dried mangoes, which I had to admit were a slight disappointment. We soaked them as instructed, expecting them to regain their original splendour and swell into fat luscious morsels, fully anticipating the appearance of tropical sunshine and a general feeling of exotic sensuality to invade our persons. None of the above happened, but we were grateful for the fantasies they provided us, and, in this valley of tears that is life, I suppose it was a minor disappointment. My mother left Paris in tears, maintaining that she, too, was meant to be living there.

Paris is a romantic and exciting city except for the *métro* at night, which can be violent and scary, but I refused to bow to the fear of the underground, refused to learn the body language of the endangered, despite previous sexual attacks. I still walked in a typically New Zealand way, with long steps, swinging hips, head up. Michèle often told me that if you have blonde or long hair in Paris you have to wear a scarf if you are out alone at night. I suppose I should have listened to her. It was a balmy summer's night and I was on my way home from the restaurant, having stayed late to do the accounts with Lulu. She and I took the last *métro* home, she disembarked at Saint-Sulpice and I continued on to Vavin alone. I was wearing a yellow cotton dress, no make-up save for red lipstick, and had my long dark hair piled on top of my head. In Paris, most apartment buildings have huge heavy outside doors with a code on them for security. Sometimes there is even another door inside that, with a concealed button. I pushed the street door open, and walked through the garden to the front door. I heard the heavy outside door click closed behind me. No one was around and the *atelier* was in darkness. What happened next was yet another sexual assault. This time, I negotiated my way out of a rape by agreeing to let the attacker masturbate.

Gentle reader, this wretched slice of humanity then buttoned himself up and backed slowly towards the exit, all the while apologising, begging my forgiveness, and agreeing with each new insult I hurled at him. Why do men confuse sex with aggression? Are love and hate two sides of the same coin? I went inside, vomited and called the police. They were quite good but not overly so, and I told them I would go to the station in the morning to fill out the report.

Next I removed my clothes and had a very long shower, scrubbing the filth of the incident off me. I threw all my clothes in the bathtub and washed them, too, then got in the shower again. I called Alexy to come over, and we sat on my bed, smoking and talking about it. He was touchingly concerned, but all I could feel was sadness and tiredness. The main problem with sexual attacks is that they change you and change your attitude to men whether you want them to or not. It takes a long time to stop being afraid, to sleep properly and to understand why women's lives have to be blighted in this way. There's no point in asking why you can't walk home at night from work. The fact of life is, for a woman, that you can't. And most good men like Alexy, who would never dream of attacking anyone, honestly have no idea how it feels to live a life like that.

My birthday arrived and my French friends were as usual fascinated when brown packages arrived for me from New Zealand. They asked why there was so much wrapping paper for a gift so small, or why such elaborate wrapping for a gift so cheap like jelly babies. I explained it was a joke, that my siblings thought it was funny. People came and went and we all settled into winter in our various ways. For me it meant quiet evenings reading and listening to music. I devoured Lawrence Durrell's *The Alexandria Quartet*, Marcel Proust's *Swann in Love*, Paul Bowles's *The Sheltering Sky*, and reread Anaïs Nin's diaries. For Alexy winter meant chasing boys interminably — the same routine as summer but with the addition of a fur-lined leather jacket. For Michèle it meant virtual hibernation in her sixteenth-*arrondissement* flat with cognac and esoteric books. Michèle denied this, but she was taught to be irascible and isolationist by her father. Like her, he was intellectual and demanding, fuelling their love-hate relationship. They fought constantly, and ever since birth she has been trying to control men. She got very irritated with my colonial openness, something she would never permit herself. In life as in fashion as in ideas: she had to have the last word.

For Lulu winter meant more workaholic cheffing and walking around the streets at three in the morning with Boules. She talked to the mad people of the night — male prostitutes, cleaners, *clochards*, lost souls. Lulu covered up her soft heart with a tough exterior. I found out by chance that she supported and fed an ailing *mamie* lodged in a room in the same building as the restaurant, and gave clothes and money to street kids. Her peasant upbringing and her Pau accent made it impossible not to place her. In France, accent and family name are everything. They can help or prevent you from getting a job. So, although Lulu (secretly) aspired to be bourgeois, she understood very clearly that would never be possible.

For Willy winter meant business travel to New York, a city he adored, always returning with layers of stories. He was exhibiting a huge retrospective of his fashion photos at the Fashion Institute of Technology, and left his portfolio worth thousands and thousands of dollars in a cheap restaurant on 77th Street. The photos turned up the next day in a garbage can across the road from the restaurant. He loved stories like this, and told them over and over again. The part that amused him the most was that anyone could have such a monumental lack of imagination as to give streets numbers instead of names.

To Willy's astonishment, photos that he had always considered merely the livelihood of a capable craftsman were now being revealed as the work of the great artist he was. He was also interviewed at length by the oral History Library of the International Centre of Photography in New York, and laughed that they paid such court to him. Willy was a modest, serene man who took composed photos of subtle opulence even when they were in arcades, or on footpaths or stairways. He not only photographed models but also painters and writers like Cocteau, Chagall, Utrillo, Simone de Beauvoir, Picasso ('Picasso vos a terrible man. He 'ate vomen, vas very mean and often bad-tempered'). These photographs were all in the house on Rue de la Grande Chaumière, and I was always horrified that he kept his work in old envelopes in drawers in his office simply marked dior, fath, piguet, etc.

Many, many evenings were spent in the dining room of the *atelier* in Montparnasse, sipping mulled wine and listening to his stories. His Nordic-blue eyes always seemed to be laughing, even when he wept describing the war (*le temps*) and how his parents had died of grief.

'You know, darling,' he said, 'ze bloody French put us German artists in an internment camp in ze south of France. Everyvon vas there — Max Ernst, ze writer Hasenclever (who committed suicide), ze journalist Alexander Alexander.'

'But what did you eat, how did you live?'

'Ve made bags and shoes out of raffia and sold them in ze village. One day I vas sitting outside a café. Of course ve had no money to buy anyzing but ve liked ze smell of ze coffee. A voman came up to me and said, "Vy don't you put a coat on, it's so cold?" You know, darling, she had no idea zat ve vere starving and didn't even have coats. On ze vay home ve collected mossy stones and boiled zem up for soup.'

The conversation could turn from morbid to indiscreet very quickly. Another sip of wine, another Rothmans in the holder, and he gently ridiculed an old spinster friend who'd had only one man in her whole life.

'She and our old friends vere gossiping about ze problems of lovers. Suddenly she said slowly and knowingly "*À qui tu le dis?*" In ozer vords — I know better zan anyvon. Everyvon turned to her. She who had had ze sum total of von man in 80 years, she who had ze experience of an amoeba, she who vould have been so lucky to have had problems viz lovers.' Willy had tears of merriment in his eyes. It became a catch-phrase in our circle. Whenever someone confided something about which the other knew nothing, we all shouted '*À qui tu le dis!*'

I often went into the kitchen and found Willy hunched over the stove, which was at a level much too low for him. The wine would be open, the candles lit and the kitchen smelling of garlic.

'*Ah, te voilà*, Peta,' he would say, throwing me his sparkling, blue-eyed smile. I would perch myself on one of the barstools at the counter, fill my glass and luxuriate in the culinary smells and the pleasure of watching someone prepare food. I would feel the tension of the day draining from my shoulders while observing Willy moving confidently around his kitchen.

'How utterly divine it smells in here, Willy.'

'*Merci, Madame*,' he'd say, with a flourish of his tongs. 'It is ze simplest of ze simple but von of my favourites — boiled Bresse chicken viz *béchamel*.' Opposite is how you make it, in all its delicious simplicity.

It is thus we all spent the winter, seducing each other with words, telling stories, exchanging ideas and enjoying the present, with no thought for the future.

BOILED CHICKEN WITH BÉCHAMEL SAUCE

Serves 6

FOR THE CHICKEN

good handful of fresh tarragon
1 large organic chicken
1 stick of celery
1 small carrot
1 medium onion, halved and studded with 4 cloves
6 cloves garlic
bouquet garni (bay leaf or kaffir lime leaf, thyme, parsley stalks)
1 cup dry white wine
sea salt and freshly ground pepper

FOR THE *BÉCHAMEL*

4 tablespoons butter
4 tablespoons flour
sea salt and freshly ground white pepper
¼ teaspoon freshly ground nutmeg
1 little onion, whole
2 cloves garlic, whole
sprig of fresh tarragon
2 cups milk
2 egg yolks, beaten

1. Stuff the tarragon into the cavity of the chicken, saving a sprig for the cooking liquid. Truss the chicken by tying the legs and wings with kitchen string.

PTO

2. Place the chicken and all of the other ingredients for the chicken in a large pot, cover with water.

3. Bring to the boil, cover and simmer gently for 1½ hours. You might need to add water occasionally to make sure the chook stays under the liquid.

4. Remove the chicken from the broth and keep warm. Strain the broth and keep to use in the *béchamel* but discard the solids.

5. To make the *béchamel*, melt the butter in a saucepan, then stir in the flour with a wooden spoon. Keep stirring over a gentle heat for a few minutes to cook the flour (you don't want to brown the *roux* as that would colour the final sauce, which must remain white). Add the salt, pepper, nutmeg, unchopped onion, garlic and tarragon.

6. Grab a whisk, pour in 1 cup of the chicken broth and all of the milk. Turn the heat up high and whisk continuously until the *béchamel* has thickened.

7. Remove from the heat and strain through a wide-meshed strainer to eliminate the solids. Now take the wooden spoon and stir in the egg yolks. This gives the sauce a wonderful richness and sheen.

TO SERVE

Place the chicken on a large serving platter, cut the string off and pour over the *béchamel*. Garnish with little sprigs of tarragon.

This would be good served with steamed waxy potatoes or *tagliatelle*.

CHAPTER 12

IN WHICH I RETURN TO NEW ZEALAND TO BECOME A WRITER BUT ONLY BECAUSE I INSISTED.

I didn't deliberately move back to New Zealand from France in 1990 — I flew over for my brother Paul's wedding in Sydney and decided to spend a year in Auckland, catching up with family and friends. I had absolutely nothing — no job, no money, no home, a dying husband and the feeling I had to reinvent myself. A few years went by, there was an economic depression holding New Zealand by the throat and, in spite of all my flash ideas, absolutely nothing was happening. I had various ghastly jobs as a chef, working in kitchenware shops, corporate catering (the most boring, ridiculous job in the world), making cakes for sale from home, etc, but I was lucky to have a job at all — lots of people didn't. I was flatting with friends and developing my plan for world domination or being able to pay the rent, whichever came first.

Here's how the plan for world domination went from my desk in Ardmore Road, Ponsonby: I drew a circle with various doors — one door said culinary tours to France, one said television cooking programme, one said book writing, and another said singing. I had fulfilled the dream of becoming a chef and owning a restaurant in France, but I knew that my cheffing days were coming to an end — it was too hard, too stressful and too limiting. Lots of people can cook; it wasn't my only skill and I didn't want to be trapped in the chef role forever.

I always knew that if one of the doors in the circle opened, all of the others would flip open as a result of the first one — like a house of cards but inverted. I knew no one in Auckland (except friends and family), had no contacts and absolutely no qualifications in hosting tours, television, business or writing. I had been trained how to nurse, cook and sing, that's all. I hawked my carefully constructed culinary tour of Burgundy around to many, many travel agencies; no one wanted to know, no one had any money, and no one could place me. If I went to a travel agency now with that idea, people would be falling all over me, but then I was a complete unknown.

During my period in the desert of the early 1990s in Auckland, I started teaching cooking and telling stories of my life in Paris. My students asked me to put the recipes and stories into a book, so I wrote it all down on pieces of paper and in exercise books. I took the manuscript, called 'Fête Accomplie' to various agents like Ray Richards, who said things like, 'This is a good start, I can see what you're getting at, but it needs to be completely rewritten.' Other agents said, 'Well, there's nothing original about a New Zealand woman going to Paris to learn to cook, and there are more than enough French recipe books in the world. There is no market for this book — maybe it could be serialised in a women's magazine?' Not knowing any better, I took it to *Cuisine* magazine; not interested. When I went into their office, I found them so dismissive I almost choked. So I put the book in a drawer and forgot about it. What did I know? I had never written anything before and assumed they were right.

When I was in Paris, I had learned lots of Édith Piaf songs for my own pleasure, and this was one thing there *was* a market for in Auckland, so I started singing in restaurants. I sang, along with cheffing, for a few years, but my voice was being affected by the smoke in restaurants, and the mystifying fact that the diners considered me background noise, when there I was pouring my heart out about love, loss, betrayal and addiction and thinking I was one step from Carnegie Hall. I felt that my heroine Mina Foley would never have prostituted her voice by throwing her pearls before swine. I remembered her standing by her bed in her nightie with her long hair flowing down her back in that hospital ward and, believe me, no one would have blown smoke in *her* face. I figured there had to be a more respectful and respectable way to make a living than being a singer.

By this stage, I was tearing my hair out that my plan for world domination was not working — why could no one see that even one of my ideas was worth trying? Meanwhile, I was still casting my pearls to swine, having affairs with completely inappropriate people, like rugby players and vegetable-delivery boys, for God's sake, and *not* cooking all the beautiful, refined dishes I had learned in France. One day my friend Steve Yeoman, who worked in publishing, said, 'I believe you have written a book about your life in France through your stomach?'

'Yes,' I replied brightly, 'but it's crap — you don't want to see it.'

'I'll be the judge of that. Where is it? Let me see it.'

'No. It's rubbish and I can't face more put-downs.'

'Give it.'

'No.'

'Give it.'

'O-kay, it's in my desk drawer.'

It was Steve who explained to me the correct way to submit a manuscript to a publisher.

'First of all, don't send it just anywhere, Peta. Go into a bookshop and see who publishes books like yours — certain publishers specialise in food literature. Then you put together your package. You can't make a publisher have to think; they have unsolicited manuscripts submitted to them every day. You make it simple: offer the publisher one chapter, a synopsis of the other chapters, recipes, photos, other info about yourself, who you think your market is and why what you have to say is different from what everyone else is saying. You choose maybe eight publishers and you send your proposal to them one by one. Wait for a reply, then send it to the next one. Don't nag them — wait for them to reply.'

Being impatient by nature and an early proponent of 'leaning in', I sent everything to all of the publishers on the same day and started calling them all exactly a week later with the word 'so?' They all sent me rejection letters, which I periodically take out and look at. I keep them in a shoe box. I feel like having them printed on toilet paper, then giving all the publishers a free packet with the message Kiss My Arse. I have now published 13 books, some bestsellers, some award-winning, all written the way anyone writes a book: you keep tapping until your fingers bleed.

One publisher said yes — Harriet Allan at Random House. She asked me to cut out half the recipes and double the story, because she felt it was the story that would sell it. They only printed 2,500 copies because few people thought it would sell, but before it was even published it was selected as one of the top 20 books published in New Zealand that year, 1995. I spent many happy hours in Harriet's office with photos spread all over the floor, treats I had brought her to eat, and trying to guess what gender of baby she had in her tummy. If you have a good publisher, you write the book for them.

I thought this was the only book I would write because I had told my story and that was that. I would go back to trying to push open the other doors in my magic circle. I didn't have to. *Fête Accomplie* opened the other doors all on its own. When this book was released, suddenly I had credibility, suddenly the travel agencies could place me, and mysteriously

TVNZ came calling. This book has been reprinted many times and is still my favourite book because I wrote in a very unguarded way.

Initially I found it very difficult to write about myself and my personal life as I felt it was no one's business, but Harriet said it wouldn't sell if I didn't fill in all the gaps. She wanted to know who my husband was, where he was, where I lived, how I learned to cook, the downside of my life in Paris, the failures as well as the successes. This is why the subtitle became *A New Zealander's Culinary Romance*. I wrote about the chefs I had learned to cook from, my restaurant in Paris, the fascinating people I knew, cooking in Burgundy and love affairs. Like *navarin printanier*, there's a lot thrown in there: husband, recipes, *foie gras* in bed, Russian princesses, disappointment, Champagne, gun fights and romance. To me it was a normal life, and lots of my friends in Paris lived like that — I knew ballerinas, artists, chefs, famous photographers, opera singers, actors. You didn't end up in Paris if you were ordinary.

In spite of the 'helpful' advice from agents and other readers of the original manuscript of *Fête Accomplie*, Harriet at Random published the story almost exactly the way I had written it. It was edited of course, but they chose to retain the open, frank way I wrote. For all the guilelessness, there was a lot I left out. When Harriet asked me to write more detail about my life, I first had to cross an invisible barrier: the barrier of my parents. The horror of them finding out what I had actually been up to in those 10 years in Paris — the poverty, the drugs, the men, the fabulous food, the disappointments, the illness, the fun — was the reason I had been so circumspect in the original version of the book. In later years, I was to write graphically about sex, which interviewers found shocking, but for me it is a story mixed with research, questions asked, education and attempts to make sense of life. One thing my life in France had taught me was that love and good eating go hand in hand — the two have roots locked deep in our collective consciousness. I think all writers write about love and life — it is the central theme and position of all books, whether they be fiction or non-fiction. Even if you are writing a recipe book, it is still about love and making people happy.

Fête Accomplie is also still my favourite book because it changed my life and took me from being a poor no-spring-chicken-chef to a poor no-spring-chicken-writer. I think I received a $1,500 advance, which

I spent on my first laptop. Once I had warned my mother about the content, I asked her whether she would create the cover painting and the illustrations. I sent her photographs of my tablecloths and cutlery from Paris, and she painted a scene of a woman sitting at a table eating.

I read this book on National Radio, and when it came to the part where my friend Willy died, I cried. So many people wrote to me and said they had to stop their car when that happened because they were crying, too. Unbelievably, that reading was still being played on National Radio in 2014. Lucky for them I didn't mention snorting cocaine off the top of toilet seats at La Coupole in Paris with my American boyfriend Ron; or the sexual assaults; or the time I almost died from eating a bad oyster; or the fashion *faux-pas* like when I shaved my head; or the attic apartment where I lived in the Marais that sprouted icicles on my bed in mid-winter; or the moment my lover Giles said he had just tested positive for AIDS. Somehow I survived all this and kept smiling.

Harriet was right about opening up, and I adjusted to exposing my private life by separating myself from the main character, Peta. She became someone else I was writing about, and I had no attachment to her story. This is still the way I write. I have no emotional attachment to the words in my books; otherwise I couldn't write them. Writing is a job like any other job: you sit down in a room on your own and write. It is a matter of discipline, sinking down into it like a form of hibernation and producing something by the end of the day. When I sink into it, I can write from nine in the morning until nine at night, only moving for food and not speaking to another human being all day. There are no set times to write. I write like most women write — when I have time and when everything else is done. I don't need to have peace and quiet necessarily. I wrote *Burnt Barley*, my book on Ireland, in my cousin Tricia's farmhouse kitchen in Tipperary surrounded by loud farmers, cats, sheep, birds, chooks, cooking and singing. If you've a good story to tell, it will pour out. I write on planes, on trains, in hotel rooms, while filming (filming television is very boring and long-winded). I get a lot of writing done in January, because the whole world is on holiday and no one wants to know me — it's heavenly.

Being sick is a good time to write. *Culinary Adventures in Marrakech* was written in one month from morning until night every day as I recovered from a bout of debilitating vertigo, which meant I could only function if I didn't move. Sitting rigid in front of a computer was perfect, and I was so stoned from the medication the hospital had given me that I was nothing short of loquacious. I try to write the way I speak, and it seems to work. Of *Fête Accomplie*, David Burton wrote in the *Evening Post*, 'a thoroughly compelling, stylish mixture of autobiography and recipes . . . Delicious, sensuous and free of pretension, the recipes beg to be tried'. It is still selling as an eBook, over 20 years after first publication. It was published in French by NiL, and I believe ruined by their changes. New Zealand is unusual in that publishers give you a say in the title and cover; overseas publishers do what they want.

My favourite recipe in this book is *navarin printanier*, because it's like a glamorous Irish stew and has everything in it to make you happy — lamb, sugar, turnips and peas. It is one of the most classic and loved dishes in French provincial cooking, best made in the springtime with early lamb and tender new potatoes. See overleaf for the recipe.

I had no intention of writing another book, but when Harriet heard I was making a food show on television she asked me to write about it. The great thing about your first book being mildly successful is that you no longer have to beg publishers; they commission you. The title of this book, published in 1996, was given to me by my brother Paul: *Don't Get Saucy With Me, Béarnaise*. The phrase comes from the 1981 Mel Brooks film *The History of the World: Part 1*. Our researcher on the show *Town and Country*, Laurence, took the photos for the book and snapped me lying on a bed of garlic with my head thrown back licentiously. This photo became the cover, and when I took it to France people asked me if it was a porn book — they were very disappointed to find only purple potatoes and staggering scenery inside. The book was shortlisted for a few awards, but unfortunately TVNZ was not impressed when they noticed I mentioned Maori cannibalism in the early days of New Zealand and the oft-repeated sight of dogs chasing the remains of human heads and bones down the street.

By this time, I had invested in the laptop — the iconic first-ever laptop by Apple, the PowerBook 100. Although it seems impossibly boring and clunky now, at the time this grey machine was considered light, well-

NAVARIN PRINTANIER

Serves 6

1 tablespoon oil
1 tablespoon butter
1½ kg boned-out shoulder of spring lamb, in chunks
2 tablespoons sugar
2 tablespoons flour
sea salt and freshly ground black pepper
2 large cloves garlic, finely chopped
1 teaspoon each of rosemary and thyme
1 bay leaf
2 tablespoons chopped flat leaf parsley
3 medium tomatoes, peeled and chopped
½ cup dry white wine
2 cups chicken or lamb broth or stock
12 each of small new potatoes, little carrots, little turnips and baby onions, peeled
300g peas, fresh green beans or asparagus in 4cm pieces

1. Preheat the oven to 180°C.

2. In a heavy-based pan, heat the oil and butter, and brown the lamb in it.

3. When done, remove to a heavy-lidded oven dish, sprinkle with sugar and flour, place over a medium flame and cook, stirring until the sugar and flour disappear.

4. Add the seasonings, garlic, herbs, tomatoes and liquids, stirring to mix in the flour and dislodge any bits stuck to the bottom.

5. Bring to a simmer, cover and cook in the oven for half an hour.

6. Wash the vegetables, and add all of them, except the greens, to the stew. Cover and continue cooking until the vegies are tender — maybe 15 minutes.

7. Cook the greens in salted water until *al dente* and add to the stew just before serving.

designed and the last word in fabulousness. It had a 16MHz processor, 2MB RAM and a 20MB hard drive. It cost me $1,000 and I had to buy an external floppy drive for $250. At the same time I bought my first cellphone: big, grey, looked like a military walkie-talkie, and you had to constantly recharge it, which took overnight to do. I became addicted to the portability of the laptop and have never owned a desk-top. I like the fact that I can follow the sun around the house when I am writing.

In the meantime, I had saved enough money for a long-overdue trip to France. Harriet said, 'You know what you have to do', and so I did. I had decided when I returned to New Zealand in 1990 that I would not go back to France as an ordinary civilian. When I went back I had to have something to say to my old friends and colleagues that would be more impressive than, 'I've done nothing and I'm still a well-dressed drifter.' Fortunately, writing and television had saved me from a life of quiet desperation, and, as the ball had been fortuitously kicked into my court, I bloody well wasn't going to let go of it. So, in 1997 I flew to France with my new favourite appendages, the laptop and the cellphone, to wander around, visit friends and write a culinary travelogue called *Salut!*

The French live in a country so beautiful that they have the most tourists in the world in spite of their efforts to humiliate them, and they still had, at that point, the best cuisine and wine in the world. My first book on France was mostly centred on Paris, where I had lived for 10 years, but this new book was to be much broader yet still free-range, in the sense that I wandered to where I wanted to wander and left out anything that didn't interest me. I visited Paris, Burgundy, the Upper Loire, the Dordogne, Provençe and the southwest, and was blown by the winds of work, festivals, love, circumstance and hunger.

I have never liked writing recipes, and always try to avoid doing so in every book I write. I am not a recipe writer and have nothing original to contribute to this genre; I have always wanted to write about other people who were genuinely talented and creative, and shine a light on them. In fact, I never intended to be a *food* writer. By the time *Fête Accomplie* was published and I was offered the job of presenting *Taste New Zealand* on TV in 1995, I had already decided to move away from food and become a full-time writer. What I was going to write about I didn't know (I think I intended to write fiction), but I was dragged back into food by the unexpected success of *Fête Accomplie* and *Taste New Zealand*, and I have, in a sense, been trapped in it ever since. Once you have a name for food, fashion, art or whatever, it is very difficult to change tack because the public simply won't let you. You have a job only if people want to buy what you are offering. To me, *Salut!* was to be a travel book, and I talked Harriet at Random House into not displaying the recipes (they are still there, hidden within the chapters).

It was heavenly being back in France after six years, and when I alighted from the plane in Paris I knelt down and kissed the tarmac. I went straight to the office of my French publisher NiL, who had translated *Fête Accomplie* and turned it into something uninteresting and unsellable. The clever original title became *Fêtes Gourmandes*, which was boring and gave you no clue of the eccentricity of the book, my mother's hand-painted cover had been exchanged for a dull brown scene, and they had cut all the photos out. I had a good time being wined and dined by the publicist, though, and she plied me with lots of gossip about their other writers. Those were the days; I bet they don't have the budget for that now.

For a sociable loner, I didn't fare too badly while writing *Salut!* — only a few tears, lots of laughter, many days of hibernation, a small handful of temper tantrums and unlimited nosiness. This is the character of the travel writer. I am always amazed at the ones who are nasty and lacking in grace: how do they inveigle people into talking to them? How do they get into people's homes? Who would feed the hand-biter, and how come they sell millions of books? And then, of course, there's the periodic loneliness or disappointment in a place that one isn't expecting. There's no such thing as a wonderful, beautiful or moving place; there is only your reaction and relationship to it that makes it worthwhile or not. In the introduction to *Salut!* I said that if I wasn't a writer I would have a potato stall in the south of France. Sixteen years later, I have a house in the south of France and eat lots of potatoes. In 2006 I rewrote and updated *Salut!*, added recipes and changed the name to *French Toast*. In 2011 it won Best Book on France in the Gourmand World Cookbook Awards.

In 1999 I decided to go to Ireland to meet my Irish mother's relatives and write about the food, the music and the *craic*. I didn't know what I would call this book, but as soon as I found out how Guinness is made I had it: *Burnt Barley*. I had now upgraded to the transparent coloured-plastic Clamshell Apple laptop: mine was orange with a little handle for carrying — so camp. By this time, cellphones were getting smaller and more colourful, too, so like everyone else I had to have one. It was all desperately chic and fun and I thought I was Audrey Hepburn; all I needed was a poodle and a French roll hair-do. I didn't go to Ireland with any romantic visions of accessing my family history, I wanted to eat and drink and sing; it was a job to me. I have never worked with tourism bodies in any country I have written about, and have rarely had any sponsorship or funding. Most of the travelling and research is self-funded because I wish to be free to tell the truth. The Irish wouldn't let it be just a job, however: they grabbed me by the heart the minute I arrived and didn't let go until I left. I went for a month, stayed for three, and left through a wall of tears. Total strangers would say to me, 'How long are you home for?', as if it was a mistake I had been born in New Zealand.

The Irish are so warm, so kind, so funny and so totally unattached to the concept of world time that there is no point in fighting them, and indeed you would be doing yourself a huge favour by joining them. So began the trip into my past and my family history, which took an hour on the train from Dublin to Tipperary but 49 years by the map of the heart. I think I laughed my entire way through those three months of singing in 'sessions' in the mountains until dawn, driving home drunk from the pub with every other single person on the dark country roads completely trashed, eating sponges at country fairs, falling for musicians, getting to know my family.

The Irish were a good influence on my writing. They are a people with a deeply rooted spirituality, which is linked to their extraordinary imagination and poetic but fatalistic way of looking at things — this has of course been of great benefit to Irish literature, giving it its density and complexity. Another important thing I learned in Ireland was how to drink whiskey properly. I used to scorn ice or water with whiskey, on the grounds that it takes them 16 years to extract the water, so far be it from me to put the water back in again. But my friend Eily taught me that 40 per cent proof is bloody strong and you can't go on for very long at that power level. Also, if you add a little water you can see the fumes lifting off, which opens the whiskey up, releasing the aromas.

Random House were always kind enough to give me big book

launches, and this one took place at the Irish Society on Karangahape Road in Auckland. I had sung on the stage at the Irish Society all my childhood, but sadly it doesn't exist anymore. The launch was like a country wedding with Irish food — soda bread, Guinness, smoked salmon, sponge cakes, ham sandwiches; Irish set dancing; an Irish band; anyone could stand up and sing a song; and there was even a fight. My parents and brothers and sisters came over all Irish and turned up from Sydney and Melbourne for the party.

The book received mostly good reviews, but there is always a (female) journalist who hates the fact that someone is travelling the world and writing books while she is sitting in a fetid office reviewing that book. I seem to have a black or white effect on people: either they can't stand me or they are very supportive and put up with my faults. I do care what people think, but only if they are cleverer than I am. Anyway, this reviewer was so furious with me for having a good time that she accused me of being on a paid junket and wouldn't be surprised at all if I suddenly decided I was Welsh and sailed off to claim my welcome in the hillsides, pretending I was a Taffy. Unfortunately for her, my father is half-Welsh, and I felt like turning up to her office with a leek and an offer to shove it where the sun don't shine. As mentioned, I pay all my expenses myself, which could never be reimbursed by the proceeds from a book sold only in New Zealand. My accountant actually told me that I was making zero income from my books and that writing them was a perverse waste of time. Then someone gives you a prize and you think it's worth it. *Burnt Barley* won Best Literary Food Writing in English from the World Cookbook Fair in Perigueux in 2000.

Now that I had written four books, I couldn't stop, and it seemed I had turned into a writer. I am often asked how you learn to write. You learn to write by reading and reading and reading. Read authors you admire, then sit down and write. If it won't come, keep sitting until something comes. Write anything, no matter how bad it is, because it gets you going. You can always go back later and throw in a few brilliant metaphors. Drinking helps. The first glass of wine makes you brilliant. The second one makes you diabolical. Any writer will tell you it is incredibly hard work and requires almost inhuman discipline. You write because you are driven to it and the sight of a finely tuned sentence is a beautiful thing.

In 2000 Harriet asked me to write a straight recipe book with no stories. I wasn't interested, but got talked into it because it was a collection of all my recipes; I didn't have to be inventive. To write a recipe for a book you have to test it many, many times. I have a colleague in New York, Rose Levy, who tests every recipe 21 times for a book. Nothing can be guessed, everything has to be measured, you have to assume that the reader is an idiot, and the ingredients have to be in the same order as the stages in the method. I like recipes that say, 'Here are the ingredients, do what you want, use your creativity.' I was right not to want to write a recipe book: the recipes themselves were okay, but there was no cohesion to the book. The only things I liked about it were the title and the hat I fashioned to wear on the cover, which was decorated in meringues. I didn't know what to call the book, until one night I woke up in the middle of the night, sat up and said, 'Insatiable', and that became the name of the book. To my utter astonishment, this book won Recipe Book of the Year from the New Zealand Guild of Foodwriters. I asked the imported American judge why, and this woman, who was a specialist consultant in recipe writing, said because the recipes are so well written.

Sometimes you start out with an idea for a book and it turns into something else. Not all of your ideas are going to work, and if a publisher doesn't think a concept will sell, they do their best to talk you out of it. I loved all the sad songs in Ireland and became fascinated by the culture and history of sad songs all over the world. I figured if singing sad songs made *me* happy, then other people would respond the same way, and that gave me the idea for my next book. I was going to call it '*Ne Me Quitte Pas*' (Don't Leave Me), but the sadness of it all threatened to close Random House down. I narrowed my thesis from the whole world to Portugal, Andalusia in Spain, and Morocco, and set off on my adventure of musical discovery, which turned out to be a huge, romantic, sad, violent story. But because I am so greedy, I found I couldn't write about anything, let alone singing, without bringing food into it, so the book turned into the story of the musical and culinary connections between these countries. In Portugal I listened to sad, wistful *fado* songs and ate salt cod, in Andalusia I listened to pain-infused flamenco and ate tapas, and in Morocco I listened to mesmerising classical al-Andalusian and

Arabic singing and ate *tagines*. I called the book *Sirocco* after the wind. The sirocco is a hot, oppressive and often dusty wind, usually occurring in the spring and sometimes in autumn, beginning in North Africa and Syria and eventually reaching southern Europe.

If you are a writer who manages to sell more than six copies of your books, other publishers approach you from time to time. When the independent publisher Exisle came knocking, promising the world, I thought it was perhaps time to ring in some changes and bring a bit of fresh air into my career. They convinced me that Random House were taking me for granted, they had connections in Sydney, which I wanted, and they wined and dined me until I agreed. Our first production meeting was in a café in Ponsonby, where they laid out a map of the world and said, 'Where do you want to go?' There and then we decided on Vietnam, which I knew nothing about but chose because of the French connection. I absolutely adored Vietnam, and took my friend Tanah along for company. The book became a quest for the perfect *pho*, that simple but complex soup which is Vietnam in a bowl, heaven in a spoon, culture in a sip. Vietnamese food is fantastic — very fresh, zingy and clean — and people still approach me in airports with that book under their arm. It was called *Noodle Pillows*, was published in 2003 and won Best Foreign Cookery Book in English at the Gourmand World Cookbook Awards in Perigueux. The book sold well in spite of what I regarded as poor production. Exisle seemed to have a slightly cavalier attitude, and I found they were not great to deal with on a business level. I regretted that they had lured me away from Harriet and felt guilty about it, although I still felt I needed a change.

Exisle asked me to write a book about New Zealand food and produce, with recipes, but despairing at the difficulties I had in working with them, on the eve of signing the contract, I bolted. Bernice Beachman from Penguin had spoken to me a few times, so I called her and asked whether she wanted this book. She did, agreeing with me that I needed to be relaunched as a writer, and suggested a beautiful design and typeface for the book, to which end she employed the clever Athena Sommerfeld. It had a hardback blue-chequer cover, striped tablecloth dust-jacket with blood-red tamarillos and gorgeous colourful titles inside. This is still the most beautiful of all my books, and it was one of those situations where people bought the book for the cover. Laurence Belcher took the stunning photos once again (as he had for *Don't Get Saucy With Me, Béarnaise*). *A Cook's Tour of New Zealand*, which published in 2005, sold a huge number of copies, Air New Zealand alone buying 10,000. It was a warm and affectionate romp through all that is good and pure in terms of produce in New Zealand, from olive oils to chicory-fed lamb; from boutique ice cream to creamy cheeses; from perfect oysters to exotic fruit and vegetables. New Zealanders have one of the most adventurous national palates I know of — we will try anything, and because we have such good growing conditions we understand and respect the meaning of the word *flavour*. We love the land, take pride in craftsmanship, and have a strong sense of integrity.

I like writing, but was tired of writing about food, and felt I didn't have any more to say about eating at this point in my life. I cast about for an idea for my next book and, with suggestions from other people, came up with a topic that had absolutely nothing to do with food and everything to do with naughtiness, women and life. It was 2008, I was 59, had been around the block a few times, and made enough dumb mistakes to figure I had something to say. I had never put all my eggs in one bastard, and my life certainly wasn't the one I had planned. I told Penguin it was going to be a bestseller, and they said, 'Yes, Peta, sure, we love your confidence.' I had never said I was going to write a bestseller before, but I had a feeling about this topic — addressing women. Like *Fête Accomplie*, I knew it was the right book at the right time.

I tried to call it *Beat Till Stiff*, but the publisher lay down on the floor and screamed, so I dropped it. Sadly, Bernice had decided to retire, and her place was taken by the wonderful Dorothy Vinicombe, and it was she who suggested the title *Can We Help It If We're Fabulous? And other thoughts on being a woman*. The cover was lipstick pink and had a cartoon woman sitting on the edge of a cocktail glass looking at herself in the mirror. I had a lot of fun writing this book, and it was so invigorating not to be writing about food. There were 10 chapters on topics I was interested in, from fashion to sex to happiness, and they had subtitles like 'Work — is it a personality disorder?', 'Men — so many men, so few bullets' and 'Beauty — nature is your enemy'. I had to call my parents in Sydney and warn them again that I was not a virgin and had written a chapter on sex. This book sold out in the first weekend it released, was on the bestseller list for three months, was sold to German and British publishers, and has been reprinted many times since.

At the same time, I was approached by the publisher PQ Blackwell, and started work on a very interesting and unusual project with Geoff Blackwell and Ruth Hobday. They were producing a coffee-table book of photographs by Italian photographer Fulvio Bonavia. The stunningly original and beautiful images were of women's accessories made of food — a handbag made of Parmesan cheese, a bracelet made of sage leaves, slippers made of aubergines, etc. They asked me to write accompanying captions, poems and text. For the photo of a ham ring, I wrote, 'The tender sweet delicate flavour and enticing perfume of silver-lined rose-pink prosciutto makes the platinum band blush with pleasure.' For the salami necklace: 'She had such a passion for salami that people said she was barmy. Smiling at them in response to the suggestion she wasn't too clever, she said, "You're only young once but you can be immature forever".' For the leek hat: 'A French gastronome named Savarin questioned the leek-as-hat plan. This stylish aberration had but one explanation: I leek, Monsieur, therefore I am.'

Flushed with the success of *Fabulous*, which sold many more copies than any food book I had written, I decided I was writing the wrong books. Penguin agreed, and in 2009 Dorothy asked me to write a book on men. In spite of years of selfless research, I didn't feel I understood one thing about men. I tell people I am a feminist and men are no longer the enemy, but this is a lie to make me look better adjusted and more socially evolved than I actually am. The truth is that, although I like men, have many male relatives and friends, have lived with them, married them, loved them, I don't *really* get them. As far as I am concerned, they are charming foreigners who speak an obscure Mongolian dialect; I nod my head in *faux* comprehension and hope they don't notice I don't speak Mongolian. I suspected it would be hazardous to my health to look into the heart of the male species, but there I was writing a whole book on them. I wanted to call this book 'Often Licked But Never Beaten', but ended up calling it *Just In Time To Be Too Late — why men are like buses*. It had a blue cover showing a cartoon woman waiting at a bus stop. Men are like buses, because you wait and wait, then three turn up at once and you have to choose.

When interviewing men for this book, I learned lots of good things about them, but also that they have three brains and don't seem to know how to use any of them, especially when it comes to Christmas and women. Dorothy and I gave the 10 chapters subtitles from Country and Western songs: 'Relationships — superficial manipulative bitch seeks nice guy to exploit'; 'Sex and Love — if you walk away from me I'll love you from behind'; 'Why Men Lie — feel free to kiss my ass on the way out, honey'. It was men's reactions to this book that were the most interesting. Men with a high level of security laughed their heads off, while insecure men said, 'This is actually not very funny, Peta.' Once again I had to warn my parents about the sex chapter. It didn't sell as many copies as *Fabulous*, I can tell you.

When I made the television series of my culinary tours in Marrakech, I decided at the last minute to write a companion book called *Culinary Adventures in Marrakech*. I took the Morocco section from *Sirocco*, updated it, added a lot more information on Marrakech, recipes and photos, and completed it in a month. How you write a book in a month is that you do absolutely nothing else: you get up in the morning and write, then go to bed at night, then repeat until done. This book, published in 2010, was actually rather gorgeous, designed and typeset by Sara Bellamy. It had burnished gold pages, lush vibrant illustrations, and Moroccan tile prints on the chapter pages. It had lots of photos, lots of stories and lots of recipes, but sadly no recipe photos, so it didn't sell as well as it might have.

In December 2010, I began writing an Agony Aunt column for *The Dominion Post*, which ended four years later, and can honestly say I had more fun saving the nation from themselves than I could ever have imagined. It started off in *The Dom Post*, then was syndicated to the Christchurch *Press*. I survived letters of complaint about my vulgarity and stupidity from (mostly elderly male) readers, formal complaints to the broadcasting standards committee, love letters and marriage proposals. People thought I made the letters up, but mostly I didn't: the most outrageous questions were from real people. The tone of the column was meant to be tongue-in-cheek, but you'd be surprised how many readers didn't appreciate that. My answers were funny and bossy when I could get away with it, but if I received a serious problem then I answered it seriously. The concept of an Agony Aunt column works because we are all flawed, we all have ridiculous problems with the neighbours, our sex lives, cooking, fashion, our pyjamas and the price of fish.

Finally, in 2011, I found the opportunity to use 'Beat Till Stiff' as a title, and talked Penguin into it by explaining that it was to be a book of transformation stories. As I explained to them, beating egg whites until they're stiff is a metaphor for life: just when you thought your existence would never be more than flaccid transparent snot, something happens to turn it into tight white light. The cover was orange and had a cartoon woman in a swimsuit riding on a kitchen whisk on the back. I agree with Joseph Campbell that we must be willing to abandon the life we have planned so as to have the life that is waiting for us. In this book, I explained to readers how I stopped strangling my mother, why redheads have more fun, whether having an orgasm really makes a difference to sex or world peace, and how to control the universe with egg whites. Once again, I had to warn my poor parents in Sydney about the sex chapter. My mother is 96 and almost blind from macular degeneration, so she asked the neighbour to read the book to her. Needless to say, the neighbour wished he had never been born, and Mum called me to say that she didn't understand a word of it and couldn't imagine how she and Dad had made six children without my advice.

In May 2012, I was in the Atlas mountains in Morocco when I received a text from the Cabinet Office of the New Zealand Government, asking if I could please answer the email they had sent me. Email and phone access was very difficult in the mountains, but I managed to access a hotel's email to find a form with the Queen's insignia, requesting me to accept or decline an invitation to be on the Queen's Birthday Royal Honour's List. I also had to assure them that there was nothing in my background that might, if I were to accept an Order of Merit, bring the New Zealand Royal Honours System into disrepute. I could only think of about 37 disreputable incidents in my background, but didn't believe they merited mentioning. My reaction to this news was surprise, as I didn't think I was the sort of person who would be honoured by the state — being far too unconventional. I am still astounded that the personality I was marginalised for as a child has somehow managed to channel itself into something constructive. Once over the surprise, I had to find a printer and a scanner in the mountains to fill in the acceptance form, which was quite a challenge. At one stage, I considered scanning it with my iPhone or simply standing on a mountaintop and yelling. There was this sense of urgency that if I didn't accept *right then* I would be plain Peta for the rest of my life.

It's all terribly secretive: you are not allowed to know who nominated you, and if you talk about it before the date you are taken out the back and shot.

Most people don't choose their work or contribute to good causes because they think they might receive a gong; it is something that has never entered our heads. But it is very humbling and surprisingly delightful to be acknowledged for a profession you love and work hard at. I was bestowed the Order of Merit for my services to television and writing, and upon reflection I realised how powerful the written word is and how you can convey messages, not only of teaching and informing, but also of hope, humour and beauty. Television is also very powerful because it reflects a culture back to itself. I was lucky to be there when New Zealand cuisine started taking off in the 1990s, so I feel part of the record of that time. I also realised I could drop my name and become Your Royal Fabulousness. I was in India at the time of the investiture in Wellington, so Government House kindly arranged a private one for me on 30 January 2013 in Auckland. It was a lovely ceremony, all my brothers and sisters and parents and friends were there, I received a pretty medal and the Governor-General Jerry Mateparae said he was happy to be giving the medal to someone who wasn't a sportsperson for a change.

At this point, I went on strike. After 13 books I couldn't face writing another one. Penguin asked me to write a memoir. My first reaction was that I was far too young and was nowhere near the end of my career, and my second was that I had already told so much in all my books, who could possibly want to know more? It would surely goad people into gnawing their own arms off. At that very moment, Nicky Pellegrino wrote a review of *Beat Till Stiff* in which she said she was frustrated, wanted to know more, and when was I going to write a proper memoir?

'See?' said Penguin.

'No,' said I.

A year went by and Penguin asked again. I said I would think about it and continued to enjoy life without the pressure of a book deadline. Eventually, I entered into discussions with them, but without enthusiasm. I needed help, expert advice and some sort of key to unlock the secret to this memoir — there had to be a point, a link, a hook, aside from 'this is my mad life blah blah blah'. The young editors at Penguin weren't terribly helpful and suggested 'read some memoirs'. In desperation, I called the one person whom I knew would have the key, the person who had the brains, experience and creativity to push me over the hurdle. I called my retired editor Bernice Beachman and invited her to lunch. Bernice gave me the key about 15 minutes into the lunch, and that was that: I had my link. She asked, 'What is happening in your life at the moment?' I said, 'Well, I'm still hosting my culinary tours . . .'

'No. What is *new* in your life?'

'I bought a house in Uzès in the South of France and am doing it up.'

'There it is. That's it. You hang the memoir around the do-up. It's a simultaneous story of the renovation of the house and how you came to this point in your life.'

'You're absolutely right — why couldn't I have thought of that?'

Then she added another piece of invaluable advice: 'Go back to Harriet at Random — she was always the best.'

'More Champagne, darling?'

At this point, Random merged with Penguin, and so it wasn't an issue. Harriet forgave me for deserting her years ago and said she would be interested in the book. When I said I wanted to call it *Never Put All Your Eggs In One Bastard*, she raised her eyes heavenward. I like saying that. As I said earlier, it comes from Dorothy Parker who, on the occasion of her abortion said, 'serves me right for putting all my eggs in one bastard'. If there was one person in the world who had never put all her eggs in one bastard, it had to be me. At the very same moment, I mentioned that I wanted to write a book based on my India tours. I had wanted to write it for ages and had asked my then business partner in my tours to take all the photographs. Years went by, he did nothing to help it materialise, and it was such a big project — I wanted to write about fashion, interior décor, food, friends and everything I loved about India — that I gave up on it. One day I was talking to my friend, food writer and photographer,

Julie Le Clerc, and told her about the India project. She immediately said, 'I'll do it with you. I would *love* to do it.' So the memoir was put on hold and we launched head-first into India.

The India book became *Hot Pink Spice Saga — an Indian culinary travelogue with recipes.* Julie's photos were fabulous, and in 2015 it won Best Culinary Travel Book from New Zealand from the Gourmand World Cookbook Awards and was shortlisted for Best in the World. The book is about all the people I encounter in my culinary tours of India, their stories and their recipes. We also visited other places like Delhi, Maheshwar and Fort Cochin. I first visited India in 2005 when I filmed a documentary on tea and another one on spices for TVNZ. Subsequently I was lured back to put together a culinary tour in 2008, and I have been hosting them every year since. India is a land of colour, noise, laughter, poverty, fabulous food and beautiful clothes.

Spice Saga is a very personal book about what Julie and I love about India — the huge differences in cuisine, culture and geography from state to state. It is a sublime country, ancient, challenging, almost overwhelmingly colourful, emotional, passionate and dangerously addictive. It has always been an intellectual and artistic powerhouse, but it is changing and now emerging as a financial and commercial force, too. Indians *love* Indian food, and 1.252 billion people can't be wrong — there wasn't one humble shack or one grand five-star restaurant kitchen we entered where we weren't received with open hearts and generosity.

CHAPTER 13

IN WHICH THE PROPERTY SITUATION
IN UZÈS PROCEEDS APACE.

Back in France, things were progressing at their usual lightning pace, as can be seen in the list below.

House renovation tasks completed:

_____
_____
_____
_____

CHAPTER 14

IN WHICH I FALL INTO TELEVISION.

In 1990, unbelievably, there were no cooking shows on television in New Zealand. I had arrived from France where there was a whole channel devoted to food shows, as there was in England and the United States. I made what I thought was a good pilot of a television cooking series with a friend, David Green, who directed and filmed it in a friend's kitchen. It was very funny: I was teaching the nation how to make an apple tart. David was off-set talking from the camera and asking me ridiculous questions as I cooked and explained my dish. He would say things like, 'Have you washed your hands?', 'What kind of weird apple is that? I've never seen a deformed apple like that', 'What colour is your lipstick and how does that contribute to the success of this tart?' Almost a decade later, that is exactly what Jamie Oliver did with his first cooking show: he talked to an off-set unseen person who asked him questions. David was there first — just saying. We sent this pilot to TV3 and TV ONE; it was ignored. When I called producers, they said, 'There's no market for cooking shows; maybe at 10 in the morning, but they don't rate.' I thought they were wrong and way behind the eight-ball.

At the time *Fête Accomplie* was published in 1995, I was corporate catering manager at Coopers & Lybrand, dressed in a navy skirt and white blouse, and was wondering how my life had come to this, when the phone rang. My assistant, Sharlene, picked it up, gave it to me and watched me like a hawk as I talked. The voice had said 'TVNZ', and she was star-struck already. When I put the phone down, Sharlene said I was white and she thought my parents had died in a five-car crash.

'What is it? What did they say?'

I sat down. 'My life is about to change,' I replied, and boy was I right.

I was 45. The caller was Irene Gardiner, executive producer of the lifestyle division at TVNZ. She had seen a review of *Fête Accomplie* in the paper and asked would I audition for a new show they were putting together? It was to be an hour-long weekly series called *Town and Country*, and the 12-minute food segment was to be called *Taste New Zealand*. I went in to meet Irene, and brought with me the pilot I had made with David. The director and researcher saw it and thought 'mmmmm'. Irene sounded like she was 18 on the phone, and I was terribly impressed that someone so young could produce the entire leisure programming for TVNZ. When I met her that fine sunny afternoon, I wondered why she wasn't on the other side of the screen. She was a bit older than 18, and her blonde good looks appeared to be exceeded only by her brains. *Town and Country* had evolved from *Open Home* and was an innovation of programmer Mike Lattin.

The audition was on the North Shore in the middle of nowhere, and cats and dogs fell out of the sky along with walls of water. I made a mental note to punish the person who had organised such a ridiculous location as I had to drive so slowly through this storm that I almost arrived a day late. As I knew my life was about to change, I took this audition very seriously and told myself that I would win it, even though the other eight auditionees were much more experienced and well-known than I was. I can't remember them all now, but I recall that Annabel Langbein and Vic Williams were on the list. I had left absolutely nothing to chance. They had given me a one-minute piece to camera to memorise, I had to cook a recipe all the way through without stopping, and I had to interview somebody about their food product. I went to a television speech teacher to learn how to do a piece to camera without blinking or stuttering, I practised my recipe over and over, and hoped my natural nosiness would help me in the interview. Later, I was told that none of the other auditionees had gone to so much trouble.

Waiting for me in the deluge were the producer Chris Wright and the researcher Laurence Belcher. I had to perform my cooking segment outside in the deafening rain, sheltered by the patio roof, then interview Laurence about the imaginary pork pies he was importing into New Zealand. By the end of the interview, I told him he could bugger off with his revolting pork pies and go back to where he came from. I said my piece to camera slowly and meaningfully, the way I had been taught, and they stopped me. 'Why are you saying it so slowly?'

'I thought that was how you do it.'

'Just talk normally at your usual speed.'

I drove home again in the deluge and had a lie-down. Christ, the stress of it.

A few weeks later, I received a call saying I had been shortlisted, it was now down to three people and could I come in for a second audition? *Shortlisted!* Surely I wasn't going to have to go through the process again?

I was later told that as far as they were concerned I had the job before they even had the first audition, but they had to go ahead with the full process for political reasons. So, why was I doing it again? More political reasons, I was told: the boss wanted someone else, everyone else wanted me. So, off I trudged to an address in Parnell, this time armed with a few centimetres of war paint applied by Renée in the TVNZ make-up room. I was asked to interview Judith Taberon, who had Ramses restaurant in those days. She turned up looking like a million dollars and made the interview easy for me. I went home and lay down again — talk about strain. The phone call came: I had the job. I was so convinced that my life would change that I immediately gave up my job at Coopers & Lybrand to concentrate fully on my little 12-minute food segments; you would think I had won the love-interest role in *War and Peace*. I knew I was going to miss that nasty navy-blue skirt and white blouse, but what could I do?

Town and Country: Jim Hickey covered the cars; Ngaire Fuata the passions; Tiffany de Castro demonstrated crafts; Dave Cull and Jude Dobson discussed homes; and Andy Dye was the spunky handyman. In the first series, Jude Dobson did the links, and in the second series, Susan Wood took over. Irene Gardiner was not remotely interested in food or lifestyle, but she was a brilliant producer who knew what would and what wouldn't work, what talent would fly and what wouldn't, what New Zealanders wanted and didn't want to watch. She spearheaded a lot of new successful programmes during her stewardship. In 2000, Irene left the internal production unit, went upstairs to commissioning, and stayed for three years. Initially, she was TV ONE's commissioning editor, then became the head of commissioning across the two channels. She said she never really enjoyed commissioning as much as running the production unit, so when a couple of the bosses that she had liked working with left, she decided to go, too. Mel Rakena took over from Irene downstairs for a year, and then the job passed into the capable hands of Simone McNaught.

We filmed 11 destinations of our food segment around New Zealand, from Dunedin to the Hokianga, telling the stories of the people, their produce, their recipes, their hopes and dreams. It screened on prime-time on TV ONE, and *Don't Get Saucy With Me, Béarnaise* is the book

I wrote about it. The big revelation for me was the wealth of regional products available in this country, and that a lot of them never left their province. We found pockets of people who still cooked the ethnic food of their ancestors. There were the Asians who were raising the standard and choice of seafood to unimaginable heights in New Zealand. There were tiny boutique cheesemakers making the most mouth-watering cheese. Queen scallops were being harvested, though no one knew of them except Dunedinites. There was Irish soda bread made in Christchurch, and trout you could only eat if you caught it yourself. We tasted wine in Queenstown that was matured in a huge cave tunnelled out of a mountain, and wine that grew out of black rocks. We ate flounder straight from the Hokianga Harbour, and cheesecakes made from quark, not to mention homemade prosciutto and mozzarella. And what about your mountain oysters? You haven't tasted New Zealand until you've tasted sheep testicles.

In spite of the series being very successful, the following year TVNZ decided to change the name and the channel, which just about did it in because it absolutely wasn't a TV2 show. It became *New Zealand Living*, and ran for 22 episodes. Nevertheless, I won an international silver award for Best Food Presenter of a Food Segment from the World Food Media Awards in Australia. Okay, so it wasn't an Oscar, but it made up for all the prizes I didn't receive at school. I don't recall any thank-yous or acknowledgement from the powers-that-be at TVNZ, and the highest compliment Chris ever paid me for all my one-take pieces to camera was, 'It'll have to do.' But he did teach me how to present, as prior to this I had never seen a television camera. Irene was the only person who ever asked me how I was doing. She alone gave me positive and helpful feedback.

At some point, another presenter asked me if I knew what my personal presenter ratings were. I said I didn't know what he was talking about. Some time later a person in the know at TVNZ told me about what are called 'qualitative ratings', done by a company called Magid, which analyses presenters, shows, commercials, whatever, to determine their popularity and relevance levels. This person had got hold of my rating, which was very high. I was told that a television station will never reveal what your Magid rating is because it would give you too much negotiating power for your contracts. They don't want you to get a big head. So, I understood that the way you keep talent happy and producing good work at TVNZ was to ignore them and make them think they were lucky to be alive.

My agent at that time was Robert Bruce, who knew how to be careful when negotiating contracts. It is very hard to find out from other presenters what they are being paid because their contracts forbid them to tell, thus keeping them powerless in negotiations. The advantage of a good agent is that they know what everyone else is being paid, they have developed good relationships with the producers, and they know your worth, rather than what *you* think it is.

The director Chris Wright was BBC-trained and he knew how to tell a good story and make a good coherent show — it was thanks to his skills that this series had such high-production values in spite of our small budget. At least in those days there was *some* money; now, there is none. Our researcher Laurence travelled all over New Zealand with us, buying the food, prepping the cooking shoots, taking the photographs and picking up everything I left behind, be it sunglasses, boxes of food, cardigans, scripts. He was also hilarious to work with, so we had such a good time on those shoots. Sadly, the money became tighter so Laurence's job was axed, and we really missed him.

I was very much just employee front-person in these shows: the research was done by Laurence and the scripts and story written by Chris. I had only to turn up in my Zambesi clothes and cook and talk. At the beginning it was very formal and I had no input in the way information was given. I had to learn one-minute pieces to camera perfectly, word for word, and memorise questions for the interviews; there was no room for me to express things in my own way. Because 22 episodes was a lot to get through, Chris now had to farm out some of the work to other directors. It was when I started working with different directors and camera people that things loosened up and they encouraged me not to learn things by rote but to be more myself and more spontaneous. Along with Chris, I worked with some wonderful directors like Michelle Bracey, Katherine Downs, Michelle Arden, Karen Mackenzie and Carolyn Sylvester. Great camera persons included Richard Williams and Dave Caldwell, who said when I complained about being filmed in the unflattering midday sun:

'What can I do, Peta? You didn't get the job for your looks.'

'But, Dave, Susan Wood just told me in the make-up room that any presenter over 40 should always be filmed with a pro-mist on the camera lens.'

'Well,' said he, 'when you turn 40, I'll buy you one.'

The way I dressed had always been Irene's idea. Believe it or not, in my daily life I do not wear three kilos of jewellery, centimetres of make-up and over-the-top clothes. Irene loved the incongruous side of a food presenter wearing fabulously inappropriate clothes and Swarovski chandelier earrings while interviewing a farmer in a potato field. It was she who insisted on the rings, designer clothes and hair-dos. This was fine with me, because I thought it was funny and I was still suffering post-traumatic stress disorder from the navy skirt and white blouse. I was dressed by Zambesi, Scotties and Trelise Cooper. TVNZ had an arrangement with these designers that I would buy some clothes and borrow some, dry-clean them and return them. This was common practice with all TV presenters. This seemed to work fine until one day, after I had been doing the show for many years, I went into Trelise Cooper as usual, picked out my clothes for the season and went up to the counter for the paperwork. Everything was wrapped up, I picked up the huge package and was given a bill for the full amount (by shop assistants I had been dealing with for years).

I said, 'No, I don't get a bill, you have an arrangement with TVNZ.'

They replied that everything had changed and they didn't do deals anymore — I had to pay for the clothes now.

This was from a company I had given free marketing to by wearing their clothes on screen. I had written about them, and our association was well known as viewers were always asking me where I got my clothes. I had to put all of the clothes down in front of a full shop of people staring at this scene with fascination, and walk out. It would have been very easy to have taken me aside, but instead I was told at the counter once the package was in my hands. I felt humiliated in front of the whole shop. And that is how I stopped wearing Trelise Cooper clothes. Forever.

Every so often, a viewer would write in to the production company and complain about the sordidness of me cooking with my rings on, or the fact that I had tasted something with my finger then tasted it again with said finger. This unhealthy behaviour was surely giving the nation bad hygiene messages at best and botulism at worst. I was not allowed to answer these letters due to it being unacceptable to tell viewers to question their parentage and to sit on something pointy, so the line-producers answered them, saying Peta was deeply concerned by their letter and would change her ways immediately. So, Irene would tell me to take my rings off while cooking, but we would film a few shows and the powers-that-be would view them and the cry would go up: 'Put the rings back on — it's not the same without the diamonds!' When we were filming in India, Chris actually received a phone call ordering me to put my rings back on.

The following year, 1998, it became obvious that the *Taste New Zealand* segment was rating the highest in the series, so *New Zealand Living* was dropped and *Taste New Zealand* became its own half-hour show, back on TV ONE where it belonged. We filmed 13 episodes for prime-time, the ratings were ridiculously high, and it was nominated for Best Television Food Show in the World Food Media Awards and was a finalist in the Qantas Media Awards. We did it again the following year, and in 2000 the show reached number two in the country and number one in the 25–55 age demographic.

Every year, I thought it would be the last time, and every year I dragged out the navy skirt and white blouse and looked at them, and every year we were still there. It certainly wasn't a given, though. Several times, TVNZ almost dumped *Taste New Zealand*, but Chris always dreamed up a new, fresh way of doing it, and we were saved. They even brought in an expert television critic from England to critique the show, the content, me, etc. She gave me such a bad report that we all burst into laughter: we realised that her criticism of my voice, my delivery and my appearance was exactly what the viewers loved. After they had read the bad report, Irene said, 'Carry on as normal.' Meanwhile the series was being sold all over the world, and in 2001 it won Best Electronic Media Award from the New Zealand Guild of Food Writers.

In 2002, my taste buds went awry and I accepted a request to audition for a position as panellist on a new 5.30pm advice show to be called *How's Life?*, produced by Greenstone. I turned up and the audition room was full of all sorts of over-qualified hopefuls willing to make fools of themselves. Kerre Woodham threw herself into the room still putting her foundation on and said, 'Oh God, a room full of A-type personalities — this'll be fun!' She was a genuine and funny woman then, and she still is.

Coming from presenting a high-rating show, it was strange being in this room, and I felt out of place, but I gave the audition and won one of the panellist jobs. It was explained to us that the panellists would rotate evenly, but as the show progressed through its dire lifetime, it was apparent that there was a handful of preferred panellists and I wasn't one of them, so thankfully I wasn't called often. The pay was derisory. The host, glamorous Charlotte Dawson, was a good presenter whom I ended up liking, but inexplicably she was given a hard time by the public. She was mouthy and funny, but very sensitive and took criticism to heart. She left New Zealand and continued her career in Australia, but sadly, in spite of all her success, the black dog got her and she committed suicide in 2014. Back in 2002, our troupe of wildly diverse panellists sat around solving the nation's sordid problems, some of which were so horrendous that the producer had to call the police. Some were so stupid you had to thank God you had two legs and two arms, and some were genuinely interesting and thought-provoking.

The actress Robyn Malcolm was lovely, earnest and caring, Merepeka Raukawa-Tait from Women's Refuge was a great person, gave good advice and hated being fussed with in the make-up room. I love having stylists do my hair and make-up, as it is a form of relaxation for me and I can look like Julianne Moore instead of the ordinary person I am. Merepeka, though, usually said:

'Okay, that's enough — *stop!*'

Colin Hogg, whom I have always liked, said to me, 'I read an interview you gave where you were putting men down and I thought "what a ball-breaker", but you're actually rather nice.'

Cindy Gibbons, who owned a plus-size women's clothing store, was adorable and beautiful. Paul Henry was unrepentantly right-wing but lots of fun and very hard-hitting in his advice. (He was obviously practising for his future role on *Breakfast*.) Jude Dobson was as sensible as you would expect. Christine Rankin insisted on wearing huge unfashionable earrings, but I liked her — she was a spunky lady. Suzanne Paul talked a lot about sparing the rod. Colin and I used to look at each other and go cross-eyed. Marcus Lush was, I think, the most popular panellist with his intelligent and witty answers, but the most sexy one was Julia Hartley-Moore, the famous private investigator whose mission it is to root out and expose dastardly philandering husbands. In the green room, she told us great stories of her antics, and we laughed until the tears rolled down our cheeks. We loved Julia.

How's Life? was a strange experience because of the contrast with *Taste New Zealand*, but it rated well. Due to the nature of the show, abusive emails were periodically sent in to the presenters, which, amazingly in my case, were passed on to me. I was very shocked by this, and wondered what possible advantage there could be in the producer doing that. My *Taste New Zealand* viewers berated me in the street, 'Peta Mathias, how could you lower yourself to participating in this rubbish show? You have sullied yourself.' Fortunately, *How's Life?* lasted only another year, not leaving me enough time to 'ruin my fabulous reputation' any further, nor learn any more tricks from Julia. She said it was so easy to catch unfaithful men that she almost felt bad taking money for it. Women are much better at hiding their philandering and hardly ever get caught; in fact, it rarely even enters men's heads that their wives would be doing the same thing as they are.

That same year we made another series of *Taste New Zealand* and also a new one on wine, with me and Timothy Giles, called *Toast New Zealand*. In 2003, I was a guest presenter on Jam TV's *Intrepid Journeys*, produced by Mel Rakena and Jane Andrews. Jane had directed some episodes of *Taste New Zealand*, so I was lulled into a false sense of security due to my friendship with them. To this day, it is the most remembered TV appearance I have ever done, and most people still think it was an episode of the international series *Taste Takes Off*. Irene said to Mel, 'Don't take Peta — she'll die. There's no lipstick in Bolivia, there are mountains and no good food.' Needless to say, this made me determined to do it. As it turned out, we all almost died, and lipstick was the least of my problems.

The weather was much colder than we were prepared for, Mel became ill and I arrived with bronchitis, then got severe altitude sickness. We all had to suffer through the conditions: we half-slept, rigid, fully dressed and wondering why we were doing it. I never managed to grasp why people think hardship is enjoyable. Neither my mother nor the Virgin

Mary turned up to save me, so I realised in Bolivia, in 25-below and having not washed for five days, that there is, as I had long suspected, no God. The upside was we had wine, Bolivian hooch, coco leaves and chocolates for our production meetings. With adventure travel, you're right in there with the locals — there's no observing through Prada sunglasses from a comfortable distance. It was intense and confronting. If you complained, the Bolivians smiled and said, 'This is how we live all our lives and we're happy and our ancestors are in those mountains and this is our place.'

In 2003, I also presented the television version of the World of Wearable Art show on TV ONE. This was lots of fun because I got to wear the most outrageous outfits imaginable. One of them, which I still have in my wardrobe, was a winged apparition of orange and purple with a hooped skirt and shawl. I even bought orange lipstick to go with it. At this stage, I still had the blonde streak in my red hair, so you could see me coming for miles, but my niece said, 'That blonde streak is SO five minutes ago, Aunty,' so it went and was never seen again. Meanwhile *Taste New Zealand* was still going great guns, and again won Best Electronic Media Award from the New Zealand Guild of Food Writers, plus the Supreme Award for the most outstanding entry overall. We even made a special Christmas show that year, in which I made the mistake of involving my family, who were so hopeless and terrified of the camera that some of them actually became sick with the stress of it. Everyone said, 'Wow, what a sweet family — how did *you* happen?'

In 2004, Chris finally talked TVNZ into an international series, but we stayed close to home. Travelling outside New Zealand to film was right up my alley, and allowed me to indulge the gastronomad within. Chris and I couldn't wait to jump on planes and go somewhere. *Taste Takes Off* was filmed around the Pacific Rim, but it was a start. Who knew where it would lead, so off we flew to such exotic climes as Hawaii, Australia, Vietnam, Thailand, California, Vancouver, Chile, Fiji, Malaysia and Mexico. My favourites were Vietnam, because I had written a book on Vietnam and loved the food culture, and Oaxaca, because I knew absolutely nothing about it and had never been to Mexico.

In Malaysia, I teamed up with my friend the celebrity TV chef, Chef Wan, which is like saying I teamed up with the Queen. He is so famous in Malaysia that he gives the word new meaning. He was very camp, told lots of gossip about the Malaysian royal family, introduced me to Chow Kit Market in Kuala Lumpur, and taught me to make prawn *sambal* and the exotic rice dish *nasi ulam*. In Hawaii, I ate fabulous rare tuna hamburgers and palm-heart salads. In Victoria, I steamed Murray River cod in beer. In Thailand, we nearly expired in 42-degree heat and my entire dialogue while I was there was reduced to two words: 'air' and 'conditioning'. What happens to make-up in that heat is that it runs down your face as you are doing your piece to camera or putting together your green papaya salad. In every destination we filmed, I wore the clothes of that country, so there were some startling outfits best left to the annals of history. I vaguely remember wearing a shocking pink *áo dài* with platforms and chopsticks in my hair in Vietnam.

Santiago in Chile was interesting because they are very conservative dressers, and everywhere I went women would come up to me in the street and tell me I wasn't Chilean. They would say, 'You're wearing Eee-say Mee-shak.' I had no idea what they were saying until Chris translated, 'I think they're saying Issey Miyake.' For a country that has such fabulous produce all year round, it was surprising that they are not terribly good cooks. The seafood selection was fantastic and so was the wine. Fiji was quite stressful, as we were still filming pieces to camera in the sunset as we were driving to the airport to go home, but they did teach me a really good fresh chutney: see opposite.

Cooking in Oaxaca was smashing and surprisingly good. It is a big centre for chocolate, where they drink it rather than eat it. Our local chef, Susana Trilling, taught me a very sexy chocolate pudding involving Mescal, grainy Oaxacan chocolate and *tuna* (a red cactus fruit). That Mexican show was wonderful and won the Electronic Media Culinary Quill from the New Zealand Guild of Food Writers.

In 2005, we filmed another *Taste Takes Off* series in Australia, England, India, China, New Orleans and Sri Lanka, simultaneously shooting a documentary on tea and one on Ireland. The Ireland one won Best Television Magazine Programme at the Qantas Media Awards. We filmed *yet another* series of *Taste New Zealand*, and then another one in 2006. In 2007, we made a series called *A Taste of Home*, about immigrant

GRILLED TUNA WITH SPICED EGGPLANT AND COCONUT CHUTNEY

Serves 4

FOR THE CHUTNEY

- 2 cups freshly grated coconut
- 1 cup chopped fresh coriander
- 3 tablespoons lemon juice
- 2 teaspoons grated fresh ginger
- ½ teaspoon sea salt
- ½ teaspoon freshly ground pepper

1. In a bowl, mix all of the chutney ingredients together. Set aside to mingle flavours.

FOR THE EGGPLANT

- 1 large onion, chopped
- 6 cloves garlic, chopped
- 1 small red chilli, chopped (or more if you like)
- ½ cup vegetable oil
- 1 vanilla bean, grains removed
- 1 teaspoon ground ginger
- 1 teaspoon ground cardamom
- 1 teaspoon freshly grated nutmeg
- ½ teaspoon salt
- 4 medium eggplants

1. In a mortar and pestle, grind the onion, garlic and chilli with some of the oil until well combined into a pulp.

PTO

2. Add the vanilla bean and other spices along with the remaining oil and mash again, to a lumpy but fairly smooth consistency.

3. Lengthwise, cut the eggplants into 4 slices. Put the eggplant in a bowl with the crushed spices and smother both sides of the eggplant.

4. Grill on both sides until golden.

FOR THE TUNA

4 x 200g tuna steaks
vegetable oil
sea salt and freshly ground pepper

1. Generously coat the tuna in oil and sprinkle with salt and pepper.

2. Grill on high heat for 1½ minutes on each side. It should be medium–rare.

TO SERVE

Serve the tuna and eggplant on a plate together, with the coconut relish in a side-bowl. Eat with your fingers like they do in Fiji.

families in New Zealand and their cuisine: the French, Iranians, Iraqis, Koreans, Indians, Russians, etc.

It was during the pre-production for *A Taste of Home* that I first had any inkling that TVNZ might be cooling towards me. I knew these shows couldn't last forever, so why not say that? In mid-year I had written confirmation from the commissioning editor and the executive producer of the lifestyle unit that the new series had been confirmed, and asking me to start thinking about salary, hair, clothes and stories. Then I suddenly heard that the funding had been withdrawn and given to another show, so we wouldn't be making *A Taste of Home*. The executive producer said she had no agreement with me; so I went straight to my lawyer with my written agreements, and months of sizzling letters were exchanged between said lawyer and TVNZ. I told this story to Susan Wood, who said, 'Why are you buggering around with the commissioners? Go straight to the top — call Rick Ellis and tell him what's going on.' So I did. Within a few days, my series had mysteriously got its funding back and we were all go.

Lovely Dana Youngman took over from Chris Wright as producer. At the end of the shoot for the series, it was understood that there would be another series in 2008. But the day I walked out of the production office was the last thing I ever saw of TVNZ or the lifestyle unit. I never filmed another series for them. They never told me we wouldn't be filming, no one ever said thank you for 12 years of service to TVNZ, no one ever acknowledged me in any way. One day I existed and the next day I didn't. I still don't know why. Maybe it was the fact I had defended my job and the series with the help of my lawyer? Maybe after 12 years of highly rating shows I wasn't flavour of the month anymore? The poor corporate culture at TVNZ ensured that presenters were, and still are, treated like this all the time. And I was nobody; remember what happened to Judy Bailey, John Hawkesby, Richard Long . . .?

In March 2008, I was filming an advertisement for a wine company and started chatting to the cameraman, Jeff Avery.

'Why haven't I seen your series on TV recently? When are you making another one?' he asked.

'I don't think my shows are being made anymore.'

'Why?'

'I don't know. Nobody at TVNZ will talk to me.'

'You can't be serious.'

'Dead serious.'

'Well, you're not going to sit on your bum and feel sorry for yourself, are you? It's well past time you set up your own production company and started making television the way you want to make it.'

'Oh no, I don't want the burden of a production company. I don't know how to produce — I'm an entertainer.'

'I'll do it with you: come and have lunch with me.' So I did, and by the end of lunch we had a production company. This is a man I had never met before. The next day Jeff's wife called me and said, 'Hi, Peta, I'm Jane Avery. I'm in on it with you two artists and I'll be producing and directing.'

'*Choice.*'

That's how we met and that's how we became the Red Head Media Group. The first DVD we made for public sale was strictly cooking only. We shot 10 recipes in my friends Colleen and Steve Murphy's kitchen in Grey Lynn, and enthusiastically called it *Peta Unplugged: 10 Fabulous Recipes for Summer Entertaining*. I think we sold it for thruppence to the Food Channel. Of all the complicated stuff I demonstrated in those recipes, the most popular was the simplest: broad bean, pea and Parmesan mash (see opposite). Jeff and his family are now addicted to it, and, every time I make it, people act as though they have never eaten a pea before. The secret is that it is full of salty Parmesan cheese and lots of fresh mint. I was inspired by Jamie Oliver making something similar in one of his shows, but I have never figured out how he got the mozzarella to fall out of heaven onto his broad beans in the garden.

After that, we decided to make food/travel shows of my international culinary tours. The first one was on Marrakech, suggestively titled *Peta Unplugged in Marrakech*. We made it with our own money and filmed the entire six episodes in three weeks, just the three of us. There was no director, but Jane was the one who knew what was going on in terms of the story. We all knew how to make television, so we turned the switch on and went for it. Jane sorted the post-production, Jeff edited it in his under-the-house editing suite, and we sold it for peanuts to Prime and

BROAD BEAN, PEA AND PARMESAN MASH

Serves 8 as a snack / Makes 5 cups

800g fresh broad beans in the pod (or 400g frozen)
500g fresh peas in the pod (or 250g frozen)
handful of fresh mint leaves
2 cloves garlic, peeled and chopped
1 teaspoon sea salt and freshly ground black pepper to taste
½ cup extra virgin olive oil
100g freshly grated Italian Parmesan cheese
1 baguette, sliced
300g buffalo mozzarella cheese

1. Pod the fresh broad beans and peas or defrost the frozen broad beans and peas.

2. Blanche in boiling water for 1 minute. Drain. Skin the broad beans.

3. Place the broad beans, peas, mint, garlic, salt, olive oil and Parmesan cheese in a large mortar and pestle and mash until the paste is thick and rough. Add the pepper and more salt, if you like, to taste. (You could pulse everything in a food processor, but if you don't have a mortar and pestle it would probably be better to crush it all together in a bowl with a potato masher or on your chopping board with a fork so you don't make the mixture too smooth.)

4. Toast or grill the bread on both sides and top generously with the mash. Plop torn mozzarella on top.

the Food Channel. We couldn't sell it to TVNZ because they would likely have 'ghetto-ised' it — screened it at a dead hour when no one was watching. As badly as Prime paid, at least they put it on at prime-time in the evening, even it if *was* up against impossible competition like Rick Stein and Masterchef on the other channels.

The following year, 2009, we made a series on Uzès and the south of France and sold it to Prime and SBS 2 in Australia. This series we also paid for ourselves, along with lots of help from Lysianne Boissy d'Anglas of Gard tourism and Patricia de Pouzilhac of Languedoc-Roussillon tourism, which was fantastic. The Uzès tourism department did absolutely nothing to help — they didn't even turn up to the launch in Uzès. We gave our shows to TVF, a distribution company in London, who sold us to lots of countries we had never heard of. The next series we wanted to make was on India, which was bound to be easy considering the heat, the bureaucracy and the hordes.

It's great making television with Jeff and Jane because we are all unplugged and have similar ideas. We don't like long pieces to camera, we like to be able to take advantage of good shots and situations quickly, we like an intimate, emotional presenting style, and don't worry too much about whether my earrings are banging against the microphone or not. The anal-compulsiveness of conservative television filming is unbelievable, and I had no idea that most of it was unnecessary until I stopped doing it. At the beginning, I was always saying to Jeff, 'Is it okay if I say this? Can you see my mike? Is this dress too low?' and he would say, 'Hey, baby! It's your show, you're the boss — now you do what you like. If you think it's okay to mix coffee into your lamb stew, go ahead, be my guest, I trust you.' I would look at Jane, and she would say, 'Peta, you're free.'

Taste New Zealand is the longest-running food show ever screened on New Zealand television — 12 years — but it's only now that I feel I have found what it takes to hold an audience.

CHAPTER 15

IN WHICH I INDULGE MY INNER
GASTRONOMAD AND GET PAID FOR IT.

In the interests of continuing my scheme for world domination, which started when I moved back to New Zealand in 1990, I finally did dip my toe into the tour business. It was the ideal way to make a living from my wanderlust and desire for food, and as I had long been living an unplanned life and accepted that I suffered from incurable marital dyslexia, why not? I began by jointly hosting a big culinary tour of northern Italy and southern France. It was organised by a travel agency: Julie Biuso hosted the Italian side, and I took over on the border and hosted the French side. I don't know about Julie's side, but the guide/manager we had on the French side was absolutely horrendous — she seemed to hate food and hate the fact that we were interested in gastronomy. To this end, she repeatedly reiterated how disgusting we were every time we tried to eat.

A few years later, I hosted another big culinary tour through northern Italy with an agency. We had some very wild guests on this tour, some of whom were either psychopaths, drunks or criminally boring. But two of the normal clients, Verna (also known as Mini) and Luis (also known as Luigi), are still my friends. The one person who saved this tour was the fabulous Italian manager/guide Antonella Laurenza, also known as Bubu the Original. Antonella, whom we called Citronella, gave up her room so two fighting friends on the tour could be separated, went out at night to find the lost drunks, sang to keep us happy, counselled the nutty, made me laugh until I cried, and generally made life worth living. We still write to each other, and she never forgets my birthday.

The problem with these slightly out-of-control tours, I figured, was that a travel agency was running them, not me. It was the agency that found the hotels and restaurants, but often they were not up to standard at all, and of course I got the blame. I also felt that client misbehaviour would not happen if the tour groups were smaller and I could pay 100 per cent attention. So, I reduced the numbers who could come to 10, and maybe a few extras if they begged. I decided that if I was to host any more tours, ever, I personally had to visit the hotels and sleep in the beds beforehand, I personally had to eat in the restaurants and cooking schools, and I personally had to know every single person I dealt with on the tour — every hotel manager, every chef, every tour guide. This all had to happen long before any more clients paid money to go anywhere with me. Even *my* free-range standards were way above anything an agency could aspire to. By this time, I had written quite a few books and had been on television for years, so I was familiar and trusted as someone who knew what they were talking about and who undertook rigorous research — so I wanted to deliver on that. I was originally going to set up a culinary week in Burgundy where I lived briefly, but my head was turned by my first visit to Uzès, and the rest is history.

On that first visit to Uzès in 2005, I went to a party and met New Zealander David Horsman. Drinking *rosé*, we sat outside on a low wall while I told him my cooking-school idea and he told me about his newly renovated *mas* in the countryside nearby. We made a date for me to look at it as a possible venue and to meet his English wife, Celia. Their traditional *mas* turned out to be a large, low, rectangular farmhouse with a sprawling roof covering everything, including all extensions. As was normal practice, it was built from stone taken from the surrounding fields and plains, and in places the stone created beautiful patterns. The ground floor, covered by solid vaulting, contained the stables for the smaller animals and a storeroom for winemaking tools. Harvested goods, hams and sausages were kept in the cold-room nearby. A stone staircase went up to the covered *couradou* terrace, which led to the terracotta-tiled kitchen. Also off the *couradou* was the *magnanerie* cocoonery, used for growing silkworms. The bedrooms were entered from the kitchen, which also opened to a small wooden staircase that led to the attic. In some *mas*, the house is divided into two parts by a corridor, one for the master and one for the farmer.

The site of Mas Bonnafoux dates back to Roman times. To the south, it overlooks a peaceful valley of vineyards, fruit trees and native woodland, and beyond that is a ninth-century Knights Templar fort: the Arque. To the north, across woods, the land stretches to the last ramparts of the Cévennes Mountains. When David and Celia bought the *mas*, it was a ruin, as Celia described: 'thick with spirits and heavy with the past'. We toured the *mas*, walking through the cocoonery, which was now the living room, tastefully decorated with sculptures, art, antiques and contemporary furniture.

David and Celia's kitchen was airy and spacious, with a central work area, which seemed to me to be fine for a cooking class. I imagined my grateful students sitting around it on bar chairs, hanging on my every word as I elucidated the secrets of a *grand aïoli*. We sat on the elegant colonnaded stone terrace overlooking the vineyards, landscaped gardens and swimming pool, and talked. I mapped out how I wanted my cooking school to be, then raced home to Gina's house in Uzès and spent the next two months testing recipes, eating, trying them out on the household, writing them up and drawing up schedules. This was exciting. This was a new project. I decided the cooking-school experience would be a week long, and include accommodation, cooking lessons, vineyard visits, guest chefs, picnics, restaurants, market shopping and general immersion in the sunny, intoxicating Languedoc lifestyle. There was no cooking school in Uzès, so everyone I knew thought the idea was a good one. The set-up went pretty smoothly. All the activities would happen *chez* David and Celia, and the clients would sleep in nearby village hotels.

My initial concept was a cooking school, and it was only ever going to be in Uzès and four weeks a year. The first year, 2006, I nearly died of exhaustion because I did all the teaching every day, most of the shopping, and all of the worrying. I fretted all night instead of sleeping, and would sit up at 4am and say into the darkness, 'OMG, I forgot the anchovies.' Everything had to be perfect all the time, though David and Celia didn't understand why my attention to detail in the cooking lessons was so important. Nor did I in the end, as I realised I was not Ruth Pretty and didn't have a staff of 20, and so could loosen up a bit.

Initially, David and Celia were employed by me, but they quickly became partners. They were very good at looking after the clients, organising and making everything seem luxurious. David put a lot of work into designing and producing brochures, and Celia made gorgeous tablecloths and aprons. We were very professional and classy all day, then it would all go bonkers in the evening when we got drunk. On top of all of this, I also had to be chauffeur part of the time, which was tiring and scary for me as I wasn't used to driving on the right side of the road, wasn't used to driving late at night after a hard day's work, and certainly wasn't used to having precious clients in the car. Things had to change, so I decided to relieve the pressure in the future by reducing the cooking classes and including more visits and activities so that the 'school' was more of an 'experience', like a week-long house party.

The following year, we ran it again. However, in 2007, David and

Celia split up and put the *mas* up for sale, so sadly I was to lose the lovely Celia as a partner and I would have to find a new place to host the culinary week. However, I already knew Sylvie and Jean-Marc, who owned Mas des Oules outside Uzès, which was fully equipped with a professional kitchen, huge swimming pool and lots of accommodation. The *mas* was not as upmarket as David and Celia's place, but it was much more practical. And so Mas des Oules became my new venue over the subsequent years.

David and I remained as business partners and, not long after all these changes, were sipping *kirs* at L'Oustal café in Uzès and came up with the idea of expanding the culinary weeks to another destination. We figured we had worked so hard to put the concept together, how complicated could it be to turn it into a moveable feast? I had written a book on Morocco, which David had visited, so we jumped on a plane to Marrakech and undertook the first recce. I subsequently went back a few times, and we hosted the first Marrakech trip in 2008. I had eaten North African food in Paris when I lived there, and I like it because it is aromatic, served in an unusual way, and you can eat it with your fingers.

Marrakech is a great destination for a tour, because it is lush, affluent, Euro-influenced chic, has outrageously exotic nightclubs, designer kaftans, *tagines*, sushi, sexy North-African cool and drop-dead stylish accommodation. Forget hashish, backpacks, dodgy carpets and 3,000 ways to make couscous — Marrakech has hit the big time. When I was not out researching, I was sitting on my bed at the *medina* hotel I still use for the tours, Hotel du Trésor, sipping mint tea and eating pomegranates and chocolates. It is quite hard organising schedules in the south of France as everyone is very *mañana mañana*, but Morocco is much worse — they have absolutely no concept of time. In Marrakech, everyone thinks I have a compulsive-obsessive disorder. They can't understand why my clients and I need all of these outrageous commitments. If you ask musicians three months in advance to turn up at your party, you can forget it: they can't even *think* that far in advance, let alone remember to turn up.

Each year, I turn up in Marrakech a week in advance to beat everyone into submission — I couldn't possibly rely on emails and rock up the day before. I talk to every single person I will be working with, sleep in the beds, ride the camels, check out anything that's new, and eat the food again and, if it's not good enough, change it. That is why I am still finalising the dreaded schedule right up until the night before the group arrives. What does stand me in good stead in all my destinations is the professional friendships formed, distinguished by the respect we all have for each other, and their longevity. I have been working with the same people since the first tour, which is why they are so personal and convivial. The star person in Marrakech is the Italian owner of our hotel, Adriano Pirani — the fixer from heaven. He knows everyone, throws the best parties, is very naughty and fun, and endlessly generous.

As I mentioned earlier, I eventually filmed a six-part television series with Jeff and Jane not just on my Uzès tour and the south of France but also another on the Marrakech tour. And a further book also poured forth: *Culinary Adventures in Marrakech*. During filming, Jeff and Jane went local immediately, and it was thanks to their ability to go with the flow that the series was so immediate and alive.

I first visited India in 2005 when I filmed a documentary on tea and another one on spices for TVNZ. Subsequently, I was lured back by Robyn Bickford and Manav Garewal, who used to manage Opou Lodge in Gisborne and had become managers of the five-star resort Amanbagh in deepest darkest Rajasthan. Robyn suggested I host one of my culinary tours in Rajasthan, basing it at Amanbagh. So, in 2008, back I went to India to set up my first India tour, and I have visited every year since. Robyn and I plotted what we would include in the 10-day experience. At calm, enchanting Amanbagh, I sipped pomegranate juice while listening to the *bansuri* flute, with monkeys and peacocks crossing before me. Dressed in beautiful Indian clothes, I dived into the kitchen to make buffalo-milk feta, yoghurt and haloumi. I learned Rajasthani dishes, went into the villages to learn how to make butter and grind wheat, and went shopping for Kashmiri shawls and hand-blocked cotton in Jaipur.

In 2009, David and I turned up at Amanbagh with our clients for our welcome feast, which was truly, deeply, madly fabulous. Upon arrival we were greeted by the entire staff of the hotel lined up at the entrance. I almost burst into tears. On the floor of the main area was a huge design — made with lentils — of a kiwi and a kangaroo, and the pathways were decorated with colourful patterns created by flower petals. During the rooftop candle-lit dinner of Rajasthani specialties, the *bansuri* played. Amanbagh was a haven of peace, beauty and sophisticated food. We went for walks through the villages, meditated, did yoga, visited the temple, got massaged, had dinner in a fifteenth-century *chhatri* folly in the middle of a dry lake, which was all lit up with fairy lights and had sparkly orange lengths of fabric floating from the roof. We had cooking lessons, made shopping trips, visited the tiger reserve at Sariska, and took picnics by the lake. Our last-night feast was another low-key affair: a five-course Rajasthani dinner by the pool, with fireworks, dancing girls, musicians . . .

The following year, we decided to open the tour up, as Robyn and Manav were transferred to the luxurious Lodhi in Delhi and it wouldn't be the same at Amanbagh without them. We settled on four destinations: Delhi, Jaipur, Goa and Kolkata. This changed the following year when we discovered the tea plantations, so added Darjeeling and dropped Delhi. India is like Morocco in that it is devilish to organise anything but *so* worth it in the end. The four destinations we visit were chosen for the clear contrast in cuisine: in Rajasthan it is austere desert food mixed with rich Mogul food; in Goa it is a mix of Indian and Portuguese, and, unlike many Indians, they eat pork and beef; in Kolkata it is harmonious and extravagant Bengali food with an English influence; and in Darjeeling it is Nepalese-influenced with lots of meat and fermented foods.

I had always wanted to lead tours to Italy, but then my epicurean colleagues began asking me if I knew about the Basque Country.

'You know,' they said, 'that's where Juan Mari and Elena Arzak have their restaurant — molecular cuisine and all that stuff.'

This, along with elBulli down the coast in Catalonia, were only the most famous three-star restaurants in the world at that time. A few years previously, I had been to a molecular cuisine demonstration in Adelaide, which had starred Ferran Adrià and Juan Mari Arzak. The class was at some ungodly hour like 9am, and they both seemed hungover from the night before, appeared barely conscious and were reeking of cigarettes. They didn't speak one word of English and stood on the stage turning water into spaghetti and olives into liquid balls. I was enchanted and thought, 'These are my kinda guys.'

I began looking into the Basque Country, speaking to people in the know and dreaming about discovering this odd part of the world that is half-Spanish and half-French. I found an outfit online called San Sebastián Food, told them I was approaching from the east and drove myself from Uzès to San Sebastián with the help of the miraculous TomTom GPS system. TomTom has changed my life and taken all the stress out of driving. I find it truly magical that I can drive for six-and-a-half hours, listen to great music, have absolutely no sense of direction and calmly park outside my hotel in another country whose street signs I don't understand.

In Spanish Basque country, they speak Spanish and Basque, and on the French side they speak French and Basque. In San Sebastián, I met up with friends, who dragged me from *pintxos* bar to *pintxos* bar. This Basque version of *tapas* (pronounced 'pinchos') are more refined than the better-known Spanish dishes, being delicate but tasty, sophisticated and varied. They are ideal for grazing. The likelihood of growing fat on them or indeed on water spaghetti is pretty slim. I had the most fantastic time eating in San Sebastián, Bilbao, Laguardia and Getaria, driving all around the coast and through the mountains and meeting the friendly Basque people, who love singing and eating fish and meat in equal measure. San Sebastián is the perfect city, a magical city no less, and easy to fall in love with. Nestled by the sea, it is very beautiful, with both traditional and avant-garde architecture; it is clean, rich, relaxed, safe, and has a huge cultural life. Jon from San Sebastián Food helped me a lot, sent me to a fantastic fish-cooking lesson, and introduced me to Basque cider and *txakoli* (a slightly fizzy, dry white wine). I have an outrageous guide/manager from San Sebastián Food who now works with me — the gorgeous, loud, funny, sexy Eli Susperregui.

At the end of my research trip to San Sebastián, Jon asked me whether I had made reservations for a meal at Arzak. I sheepishly said regrettably no, but it was too late as you have to reserve there months in advance. As I was driving to Rioja, my mobile rang — it was Jon.

'Turn around immediately. I have got you into Arzak for lunch.'

Cripes. I turned around and arrived at my hero's gastronomic temple in very casual travelling clothes and said, 'Hello, I'm Peta.' From that moment on, my life went up a notch. They seated me all on my own at the best table. Everyone talked to me — the waiters, *maître d'*, *sommelier*, the chefs. For a three-star restaurant, it is small and amazingly fun, which is typical of the Basques. People (rich people, admittedly) were there with their kids and grandparents, talking loudly and all completely obsessed with the food. The owners, Juan Mari and Elena, are unpretentious, and the atmosphere in the restaurant is chatty and lively, like a bistro. This is typical of Basque hospitality. The father-and-daughter duo spend most of the service in the restaurant talking to the customers, whom they treat like old friends. They came over to my table many times to talk about the food and how much they love Australia. (She speaks in English and he speaks in French.)

'New Zealand.'

'Oh, yes, well, same thing.'

'Not the same thing.'

In between gasps, I wrote everything down and took photos. Elena allowed me into the kitchen to look around: 35 chefs all on top of each other — about one chef per customer. Customers can also eat at the chef's table in the kitchen. The food was heavenly and unusual — employing smoke and mirrors everywhere: *foie gras* spiced with tea and coffee; lobster with tapioca; 'monkfish at low tide', with blue *curaçao* stars, pink seaweed tempura and oyster-flavoured edible shells; lamb with sheep-milk curd tempura rolls and chard; basil sorbet with warm-chocolate emulsified marbles. When it was time to leave and I asked for the bill, they said:

'Peta, you have come so far to see us and we are so happy to meet you, we couldn't possibly ask you to pay.' At which point I stood in the foyer in my old shoes and burst into tears.

I have gone back every year to eat at Arzak, taking with me bouquets of flowers for Elena. I am usually with someone, and I still can't induce them to accept my money. Over the years, I have been on tours of the whole building, the kitchens, the laboratory, the fabulous wine cellar, the spice room . . . and every year they treat me like royalty. The former *maître d'*, Jacopo Focacci and I still talk to each other on Facebook.

I have also tried other three-star restaurants in San Sebastián: Martín Berasategui and Mugaritz, which are very different though equally fabulous. But I always go back to Arzak because they are so much fun and don't take themselves seriously at all. Last time I was there, we had: an *amuse-gueule* served on a squashed tonic tin; an *entrée* served on small stones; a fish dish served on a transparent plate set over an iPad screening the surf and sea, with the sound of crashing waves; steak set on a plate also on an iPad screening flames, with a soundtrack of a burning fire; tapioca floating in a bowl full of smoke; a funky glass plate where it's hard to tell which are the flowers printed on the glass and which are the 'ladybirds' you are supposed to be eating. It's not your average bistro.

On my first trip, well stuffed, I lurched over to the other side of the Basque Country and found myself in the beautiful fishing town of St-Jean-de-Luz. Here I holed up at Hôtel La Devinière, right in the middle of town. It is so lovely, this hotel, that I still stay there with the gastronomads every year. The owner, Bernard Carrère, is slightly eccentric and calls me 'La Princesse' and bows when I walk in. (I do feel there's not enough bowing and scraping in my life.) I had already done a lot of research, but Bernard, who just happens to belong to Slow Food and just happens to write about food and wine, was very helpful in his slightly unfocused way. He's very artistic and funny and a great ideas man; meanwhile it is up to me to make sure things actually happen and people sign on the dotted line.

Bernard sent me to the best chilli people in Espelette, the best vineyard Brana, the best restaurant in St-Jean-de-Luz 'Zoko Moko', the gâteau Basque museum, the fabulous market, and had me walking along the unendurably pretty sea front, protected by three walls and lined with Belle Époque houses. They love piggies in this area, and are famous for the cured hams and charcuterie. I put the Basque trip up on my website, sent out a newsletter and, far from no one knowing anything about the Basque Country, everyone seemed desperate to come, so the first 2011 tour filled up in nanoseconds. This tour still fills in nanoseconds every year.

One happy day, I received an email from an Australian company specialising in online bookings for culinary tours all over the world. They wanted me to go to the heel of Italy to write about a Puglian cycling tour company called Southern Visions who were branching out into food tours. They wished to break into the Australian and New Zealand markets. I suggested my producer Jane come along and make a video of the experience, and we struck a deal with the New Zealand edition of the *Australian Women's Weekly* for the story. Puglia is a place no one knows about, a secret part of Italy far from the glamour of Rome, Venice and Tuscany, but I had always wanted to go there because of an Italian chef I knew who cooked this cuisine. She is the best pasta maker I have ever met. Australian TV chef Lyndey Milan and a journalist from the *Australian Financial Review* came, too, and we all flew from New Zealand and Australia to Puglia, spent four days there and flew home again.

I returned exhausted, ecstatic and deeply in love. Not in love with a Puglian man (although they are very lovable and are specialists in the all-over hug), but in love with a beautiful, generous and traditional land. We were dragged out to very late-night dinners, put our arms around 3,000-year-old olive trees, learned how to make *orecchiette* pasta by hand and how to eat *cialledda* — a watery mix of tomato, cucumber, green pepper, onion, garlic, olive oil and water, which you throw your *crostini* into, scrunch up and eat with a spoon. We also got drunk and sang all night, and anyone who knows the wonderful Lyndey will know who sang the loudest. I wrote four genuinely untested Puglian recipes in the Hong Kong airport lounge, someone else cooked them in Auckland, and the day after I arrived home I did a semi-conscious photo shoot on Puglia with the *Australian Women's Weekly*. To my surprise, there were very few faults in the recipes and it all looked quite good.

Of course, I had to add Puglia to my gastronomic tours, so I took another recce later in the year with David and set up an inaugural tour for 2014. We put a schedule together with help from Ali and Antonello of Southern Visions, tasting lots of Negroamaro, Primitivo and Susumaniello wines and eating heroic amounts of pasta, fish and vegetables. The Puglians are a proud people, perhaps more prone to reflection than their excitable northern cousins.

Puglia was very poor, but they could grow wheat, olives and grapes really well, so their cuisine is driven by fresh ingredients cooked very simply; there is no pretentiousness or fake artiness. They also have a long coastline, so are inundated with fish and seafood, the favourite being little sea urchins in early summer. Because there is a lot of wheat, there is not only a lot of pasta but a lot of bread, the best being the heritage-protected *pane di Altamura*, made with semolina and only available in the beautiful city of Altamura. Puglia is also famous for *burrata* (mozarella filled with cream) and *vincotto* (reduced grape must). The fabulously preserved architecture is heart-stopping, from the Baroque magnificence of Lecce and other smaller but no less superb towns, to the delightfully eccentric cone-shaped *trulli* in Alberobello. You don't know how much you miss Puglia until you leave it, then you long to return to their gentle ways and honest food.

I can't tell terrible stories about my clients, partly because there aren't many and partly because I wish to continue my tours. I was right about reducing the size of the tours to 10 people and being much more hands-on: this diminished bad behaviour drastically. Also, we made the tours more expensive, figuring that if you had to pay a decent price for it, you might have resolved your problems before you arrive. New Zealanders are very easy to get along with, and people with alcohol issues are usually the only ones to cause ripples in our happy house party. Australians are outgoing and often very witty. However, a bad apple will turn the whole case bad if you don't jump onto them very quickly. The worst-ever clients were on an India trip, and if I could have thrown this ghastly couple into a hole in the jungle I would have. They went troppo in Goa, but in the end the other clients turned on them and sorted them out.

Overwhelmingly, people are there to learn about the culture, have a good time and relax, and overwhelmingly they are adorable. I have many returnees and one Australian lady came to three tours in one year! Sometimes a group of 10 friends will take over a whole tour, which is great as they already know each other and are ready to party. I still take everything far too seriously, worry constantly that the week might not be exemplary, the sheets not perfectly ironed and that I am not being fabulous enough. Every destination I choose, I choose because I have an intimate connection to it and it has to have a strong food culture.

At the end of 2013, David and I parted ways, and I now run the tours with my fabulous PA Rosie and local professional managers in each destination. In 2015, I added New Zealand to the tours — half the week in Hawke's Bay and half in Auckland. I also visited Vietnam again after a 10-year absence and started hosting tours there in April 2016. And now I've gone and added a Tamil Nadu tour in South India. *Et vogue le navire* — and the ship sails on . . .

CHAPTER 16

UZÈS AND LA MAISON DE LA DILIGENCE.

The deconstruction and reconstruction of the house continued through the French winter, and in June 2015 I turned up to spend the summer in Uzès, teaching cooking classes, writing, organising the expanding culinary tours long-distance with Rosie, and sweating. There was a heat-wave in Uzès, and living in a rented house without air-conditioning reminded me how glad I was I had insisted on it in the new place. As soon as I arrived, I ran up the road to see my house, dreading it, fearing what I would find, almost with my hands over my eyes. Although I knew what the plans looked like, I couldn't picture what it would be like in reality with the space added from the ruin behind the original house. I so hated that little original hovel where I had to live in such small rooms that I feared the new house would be similar, even though I had been inspired by Gina's open-plan home and had said: no rooms, no walls, no claustrophobic divisions.

I was with my niece Estée and her boyfriend when I saw it, and we all gasped. In front of us was what seemed like a *huge* three-storey loft, straight up and down. It didn't remotely resemble the original hovel, in fact it was a completely new building — the hovel had gone. The addition of the land behind had made a *big* difference, the ceilings had been raised and there was a third floor.

The entire front of the building was open, waiting for the steel frames and big windows to go in. The ground floor, which would be one big kitchen, had the beginnings of a bathroom made by Gina's wonderful Swiss carpenter, Hans, and the steel girders on the ceiling were visible as intended. Wide stairs lead up to the first floor. The completely open living level was laid with pine floors and housed the huge Louis XIV chimney, though it had been dismantled and was in pieces. A ladder led through a hole to the second floor, housing the bedroom and a big airy terrace already sporting its steel railing made by Gina's blue-eyed iron man, Yanick.

Many layers went into the making of the ground floor — 11 centimetres in all by the time all of the tubes and wires had been laid, a few layers of concrete, insulation and eventually fancy tiles. Gina was at the house every day supervising things, as was I, except that in my case I didn't know what I was talking about. I barely knew what a hammer looked like. I would wander in, fanning myself in a summer dress, and say 'nice wall', and wander out again.

I was so enchanted with the new house after everything I had been through that I decided to have a roof party, even though the roof had gone on ages ago. My friends and I (Amy the winemaker, Gina and Pierre, amongst others) sat in the dust on the second floor, admired the completely open wall where the windows would go, enjoyed the view of the neighbour's garden and trees, sipped Amy's wine and ate cheese. Despite the house costing twice as much as I wanted it to, I was now prepared to swallow the bills because I could see how dramatic and sleek it was going to be. I had never envisaged embarking on such a big, complicated project, but now that it was half done, and, with such extreme care being taken by Gina and the builders, I could see a future living in it as the fittest pensioner in town, running up and down those two flights of stairs, developing thighs of steel.

Gina was brought up in a late-nineteenth-century ex-hotel, Hôtel Jura, in Langenthal, Switzerland. She believes her passion for old buildings originates from her childhood of living in this extravagant building. It was thought at the time of construction that Langenthal was going to be a tourist destination and was called 'little Venice' due to the regular floods that swamped it. When the river broke its banks, it flowed right by the hotel, and a flood day meant a no-school day, so was quite exciting. The town's footpaths were a foot higher than the street, and all of the houses had bridges.

Gina's father, a dentist, bought the hotel and installed his practice on the ground floor, where the hotel's restaurant, kitchen and dining room had been. This ground floor had 5-metre high ceilings, and the best part was the old ballroom, which was now used as a church and was just under her bedroom window. She listened to hymns being sung as she drifted off to sleep. The family home took up the whole of the beautiful, spacious first floor. The three floors above this had been transformed into apartments, two on each floor, one of which housed her grandmother. On the very top floor were the maids' rooms or *chambres de bonne* where, later on, Gina would hide her first lovers. At the very, very top were vast attics, and Gina told me she can still smell the wood they were constructed from. The basement was of rammed earth and housed the wine cellars. Another very grand part of the house was the monumental staircase, with its cast-iron railings and ornamental tiles on each landing. She was so fascinated by this staircase that, when she was seven, she intentionally leaned over from the first floor to see what she could see, and toppled down to the ground floor, breaking her arm and teeth.

Gina bought her first-ever house at the age of 22 with the help of her parents. It was a derelict farm built in 1740, with an outdoor toilet, big stables and 10 hectares of land with 100 fruit trees. After a huge amount of reconstruction done by her and the workers, she turned it into a gorgeous jewel, which was, 17 years later, bought by one of the singers in ABBA and her husband.

'He was a German prince, who bought the house because his grandmother's house in Sweden looked similar. During the Second World War, his family had to leave Germany and go there. He was born after the end of the war, was an architect and very charming. He did some more work on the house, and his work was very good. Unfortunately he died a few years after he bought my farmhouse, and his wife couldn't stay there anymore because she was so upset and sold it.'

The next house Gina bought was a bourgeois mansion in Burgundy, 'Le Monestier' — again, a ruin, which she and her husband, Michael, renovated and turned into a luxury guest house. After this came the Château de Saint Victor des Oules outside Uzès, a deserted *château*-cum-hotel, which had been decorated and restored in bad taste. Gina fell on it, and with much hard work and her (by now) theatrical taste, turned it into a gorgeous and chic B&B. The *château* was surrounded by a park that had housed a few ruined houses, which she also restored. After that she bought a huge derelict barn in Saint-Laurent-la-Vernède, again outside Uzès. This was a unique building and a challenging project, but Gina threw herself into it, conjuring her old/new magic, and sold the whole do-up project to a buyer before the work had even begun.

It is now that the story joins up to when I first met Gina and Michael not long after they had bought the hotel l'Albiousse in Uzès, where I lived during my first summer in 2004. They had horses and dogs and realised after a few years in town that they missed the countryside and needed a house where there was lots of room for the animals. They sold l'Albiousse and bought le Domaine de Castelnau, a four-storeyed mansion outside Uzès, where I also lived in one of the houses on the property one year. When Gina and Michael split up, they sold Castelnau, and Gina again bought a do-up, a big old garage with a little flat, situated in the centre of Uzès. This was another property where I lived one summer. I had hated it, but Gina was to turn the garage into a split-level Baroque loft with an outdoor part for summer rentals, and she lives in the small flat herself. The whole place looks like a dramatic theatre set.

When I bought my house in Uzès, I could see — because it was so ugly and unlovable — that I needed something quite different for the transformation, and Gina was the only person who could do it and interpret my professional and lifestyle needs. She has known me for so long that she understood I would be up for anything. She doesn't plan the same thing for every house, but rather adapts her design to what she has been given to work with and the desires of the owner. She asks the client what the point and end use of the house will be, so when I told her cooking school, she immediately moved the kitchen and dining room from the first floor to the ground floor and put in a bathroom so there would be a natural separation between the cooking school and the private levels above. She would never use colour in her own home, preferring a dusky palette, but in mine she understood immediately that she would have to create light with lots of colour. Because she knows how hot it is in Uzès in the summer and how desperate you are to be outside, in the absence of a garden she created a big terrace at the top.

The most difficult challenge for Gina was the fact that the house was very hemmed-in and hard to access. She also had to talk her regular workers into doing it; a proposition they weren't too enchanted by. The build was a real drag for all concerned, not to mention my immediate neighbours, whom Gina plied with cakes and wine. The easy part was the big bash where most of the original house disappeared; the hard part was building a new modern house within the old walls that ended up being about 120 square metres, plus the big terrace.

The house is made of brick, with very thick insulation, and Gina hopes that the sun will flow in through the large windows in the winter, thus helping to heat the house. The terrace floor had to be made of concrete, not wood like the rest of the house, and old-style tiles were found and installed in the traditional way on the roof, some of them being made of glass to let more light in. One old beam had been saved from the original house and another one found by the builder. When I asked Gina if she was cured of fixing up old houses and taking on almost impossible projects, she said:

'Absolutely not — I am already looking for another project, and if I don't find one I will just have to sell my place and find another do-up.'

One fine day I walked up the road to the house and found the steel window frames had been installed. Because in France you are not allowed to look down on your neighbours, I was forbidden to have windows on all sides of the house but one. I was allowed a window on one other side, but it had to be clouded. Thank God we had decided to have nothing but windows on the one permitted front wall or I would be crawling around in the dark writing angst-ridden novels about life in a primeval swamp. Having made the build so difficult for us, to Gina's pleasure, the Bâtiments de France are now showing photos of my house façade in meetings as an example of a good modern solution in a heritage context.

Next the industrial spiral staircase went in, giving easy access to the top floor. Then it struck me. The kitchen's on the ground floor, the bedroom's on the third floor — what about my cup of tea in the morning? We decided that each floor would have a little kitchen set-up with mini fridge and kettle. In fact, it looked like the whole house was turning into one big, three-level kitchen — which was absolutely fine with me. This house is about having lots of areas to entertain, rest, talk, work and read.

I went to the Basque Country to host my culinary tour and returned in July to find the double-glazed windows had gone in, so I had to have a window party. Can I say how very easy it is to have a party in a construction site, because there is no kitchen so no expectation of food. You rock up with some good Languedoc wine, some plastic glasses, open the new windows, close them again and call it a party.

Gina's fearlessness and cleverness in the design was becoming evident to my worried friends. The Louis XIV chimney had been reconstituted, repaired, installed on the second floor and made to work by a very expensive specialist, who charged €3,000. There it stood: majestic, masculine and graceful all at the same time, a simple but stylish monument to the past and the only thing in the house that was actually very old, except for the two ancient buttress stands on the ground floor. Yanick, the iron, tile and wall man, had explained to me that the stands were a *monument classé*, and I pointed out that I was also a *monument classé* and they'd better hurry up with the work.

Needless to say, everyone periodically disappeared and reappeared in August, and I knew the house wouldn't be finished as agreed, but as I could see that the major work was done, I chose to be at one with the universe regarding the rest.

In rural France they have a clever post-box system where you buy a certain large post-box with a lock and key and the postman has a master key for all of them. This allows him to deliver parcels when you are absent, instead of you having to walk around the town looking for them for the next week. As the French adore bureaucracy, you practically have to produce your parents' marriage certificate at the post office to retrieve the parcel. Gina had a label made for my post box that covered absolutely every aspect of my life so there would be no mistaking who lived there: my name, the name of the house (Maison de la Diligence), and the name of my business (Fête Accomplie).

Amy told me about made.com, so I went online and ordered some funky stackable chairs for the kitchen table, only I made a mistake and ordered six raspberry chairs instead of two, so ended up with 12 chairs in total, the other six in a range of different colours. Gina, who owned a castle so has quite a lot of furniture lying around the place between Uzès and Switzerland, asked me whether I wanted her lounge set of couch, three armchairs and coffee table. This furniture is ornate fake Rococo and had belonged to her aunt but looked exactly like my mother's dining-room curtains. Gina spray-painted the fabric black, and we bought some fuchsia paint to cover all the wooden parts.

In keeping with my desire to use old and new, on-cycle anything that could be on-cycled and control costs, we combed flea markets and garage sales. We took ourselves off to the Saturday antiques market at

OLIVE OIL ICE CREAM

Makes 1.2 litres

> 875ml full fat milk
> 250ml cream
> 220g caster sugar
> 10 egg yolks
> 75 ml extra virgin olive oil (a fruity one)
> vanilla seeds from 1 pod
> pinch of sea salt flakes and more to serve

1. Heat the milk, cream and sugar in a large pot, stirring to help the sugar dissolve. Remove from the heat when it starts to boil.

2. Beat the egg yolks in a large bowl with a wooden spoon. Slowly pour the hot milk mixture into the yolks, stirring constantly.

3. Pour all of this back into the pot and cook over a low heat, stirring all the time. It takes about 10 minutes and should end up being thick enough to coat the back of the wooden spoon.

4. Pour the mixture back into the bowl, and gradually stir in the olive oil, vanilla seeds and sea salt. Cool and then chill until cold.

5. Process in an ice-cream machine.

TO SERVE

Drizzle with olive oil and sprinkle with sea salt.

Villeneuve-lès-Avignon and found stashes of fabulous old Sarreguemines plates, covered in flowers, birds and leaves. Another time I found some little Italian yellow-and-green splash bowls in which to serve my olive oil ice cream (see opposite).

To distract me from the long wait for the house to be completed, some friends and I drove down to Saintes-Maries-de-la-Mer in the wild Camargue to watch a *Corrida Flamenca*, a Spanish bullfight with a live gypsy flamenco band. I wrote about the *corrida* in my book on men, *Just In Time To Be Too Late*. In the south of France they have Spanish and Portuguese *corridas*: the Portuguese fight is longer, structurally different, the bull's horns are taped and it is not fought to the death; the Spanish one is faster, cleaner, more dangerous and the bull dies.

I was horrified by the first bullfight I went to years ago, but then I learned something about it and began to understand the moves or *passes* and the brilliance of the toreadors and horse — not to mention the brave bull. The moment of truth is called the *descabello*: the sword goes through the neck, straight into the heart, and the bull drops almost immediately. The bull is much bigger, faster and more vicious than the toreador, and the only reason the fighter normally wins is because he has a bigger brain. This *corrida* had two toreadors: the brilliant Sebastián Castella and the flamboyant female fighter Léa Vicens. It's unusual to have female fighters, but they do exist. Léa was very fast and close to the action with her skilled horse, and played to the audience. Sebastián was breathtakingly tall, dark and handsome. I can't explain it but I love the *corrida*. It has everything: passionate music, cleverness, drama, tragedy, ritual, superstition and exceedingly uncomfortable seats. It even has food, the tender *Brouffado*.

I started looking for someone who could paint a large Arabesque design on one of the living-room walls, and threatened to paint the iron railings on the terrace purple. Gina and Pat managed to side-track me by suggesting I plant purple bougainvillea instead, and train it to grow down the right side of the house. I also wanted a gin corner on the terrace with all the herbs and spices that go into making gin, and an exotic herb corner with Vietnamese mint, curry leaves and Thai basil. If I could have fitted a

BROUFFADO: BULL OR BEEF STEW WITH ANCHOVIES AND CAPERS

Djouti, my butcher in Uzès, sells bull meat. It is not from fighting bulls, it is from bulls bred for eating, so the meat is tender and not strong-tasting.

Serves 6

FOR THE STEW

- 1.5kg *paleron* (shoulder or topside bull or beef) cut in 6 thick slices
- 1 large onion, sliced
- 6 cloves garlic, chopped
- 3 tablespoons capers
- strip of fresh or dried orange zest
- 2 bay leaves
- 6 cloves
- freshly ground black pepper
- ¼ teaspoon nutmeg
- ½ cup olive oil
- ½ cup red wine vinegar

FOR THE PASTE

- 6 anchovies soaked in milk
- 1 clove garlic
- 1 tablespoon olive oil

FOR THE GARNISH

- 6 anchovies
- gherkins
- chopped flat-leaf parsley

1. Preheat the oven to 150°C.

2. In an ovenproof dish layer the slices of bull or beef, onion, garlic, capers, orange zest, bay leaves, cloves, pepper, nutmeg, olive oil and vinegar on top of each other.

3. Cover and cook in the oven for 3½ hours.

4. Pound the anchovies, garlic and olive oil to a paste. Add a little hot water and combine well.

5. Transfer the meat from the oven to a warm platter and stir the anchovy paste into its remaining juices. Heat through and pour over the meat.

6. Put the garnish of anchovies and gherkins on top, and sprinkle with a little parsley.

TO SERVE

Serve with Camargue red rice or pasta.

golden swimming pool up there, I would have. We decided to put a fridge on the terrace so that my friends, family and I would never be short of chilled *rosé*.

Not requiring anything fancy, I went out to buy a basic cooker, and returned with one of the most expensive French stoves on the market: a Lacanche with two ovens, gas hobs and a shiny turquoise front. This I matched up with a retro pastel-blue Smeg fridge and dishwasher. The man in the appliance shop said, '*Ça alors!*' I assured him he hadn't seen anything yet — I was looking for some colourful floor tiles. Gina and I trawled through the online offerings of Carocim, the French tile company. I tried to buy something bright, but Gina once again steered me in the direction of a more subtle look. Eventually, we chose one called Poétique Clair, which involved muted blue, pink, yellow and green.

I went for a walk in Uzès and found a stunning German-made linear crystal chandelier to hang over the teaching table in the kitchen. It cost a fortune, but I was in love with it and kept going back and staring at it. Gina knew the Swiss woman who owned the shop, and she agreed to sell it to me at a big discount. I was in heaven. Who else in the world has a linear chandelier hanging over their kitchen sink? For good measure, I went back and bought her other round chandelier for the dining-room table. The chandeliers weren't going to be the only source of extravagant lighting. Gina bought some hanging lamps made of white feathers, and I had brought a kit-set kina Trubridge lamp from New Zealand, which she put together. She found it so hard to assemble that she requested I never put another in front of her again. On the website it said 'assembly time 45 minutes' — you wish. It is turquoise on the inside and plain bamboo plywood on the outside and very beautiful. These lamps are wildly popular in France and you even see them in restaurants in Uzès.

Then I had to think about the teaching table for the kitchen, which Hans the carpenter was going to make. Hans was at this stage making all the built-in cupboards, drawers and wardrobes in the kitchen and bedroom. He is the master of the complicated space and of the practical solution. As I had insisted on a completely open house with no rooms or walls, there was little room to hide things, so he suggested clever storage ideas under the stairs, on top of wardrobes, using every corner. All this house-design stuff is completely foreign to me, so it was interesting watching how Gina and Hans came up with design ideas. I asked him to make a long teaching table on wheels, with a shelf underneath for pots and pans, and a zinc top. And while he was at it, I decided he could also cover all my other benches in zinc. I have always loved zinc for its old-fashioned charm and its ability to make me think I am in a bar in Paris. I could see little violet artichokes, golden tomatoes and white asparagus all over the table.

In the middle of all this, while I was also running my cooking lessons in the rented house in August, the *New Zealand Woman's Weekly* turned up to do a story on my life in Uzès. Normally a magazine shoot lasts about four hours and involves many people; a wardrobe person, who brings a huge selection of clothes; a make-up artist; a hairdresser; a stylist to oversee the whole look, the photographer; the photographer's assistant; maybe the journalist and the magazine editor. The editor usually wanders in, says, 'I don't want that theatrical eye make-up, thanks,' answers a few *very important* calls on her mobile and walks out again. This shoot went on for three days with one photographer, a journalist and *moi*. I had to fix my own make-up and hair, use my own clothes and smile for three days in 35-degree heat. It was the hottest summer anyone could remember, and here was my glamorous pensioner life reduced to blotting sweat off thick inexpertly applied make-up and 'pulling through' as the photographer diplomatically called 'stop slouching'. The photographer was my friend Sally Tagg, the fabulous artist, so if anyone could make a girl look good, Sally could.

We visited all of my favourite shops, markets and restaurants, and wandered out in the evenings to see what was going on. This proved to be an absolute delight: in one single evening, we fell upon a choral concert in a church; a horse and cart; a night market selling amongst other things Virgin pendants; people dancing the tango in the courtyard of the *mairie*; and a beautiful swan fountain. *And* my make-up didn't slide off. It's always depressing to see what a dramatic improvement make-up brings to one's appearance, because one is too lazy to do it normally. Lipstick doesn't count — there is absolutely no excuse for anyone over 30 not to wear lipstick.

In August, the electricity folk turned up to dig huge holes in the ground to lay their cables outside the house. As the house is so hard to access and so hemmed-in, they had to leave their big truck outside in the narrow street, meaning the street residents couldn't drive down the road for a few hours. This was the last straw for them and drove them into a righteous fury. The French had a revolution, don't forget. They leaped on the blower to the Comité de Quartier des Bourgades, who got on the blower to Gina. The Comité explained to her that the locals were complaining that my house was taking far too long to build and that there was never anyone there working and that they were going to legally put a stop to the build. In spite of the fact that no one was ever there, the neighbours were sick of the noise and sick of not being able to drive down the street. (The street had been blocked maybe twice for an hour in nine months.)

Fortunately, it wasn't me the Comité called or he would have learnt a few new words in a foreign language. Gina, Miss Diplomacy, explained that, *au contraire*, the build had started in December, it was now August, the project was extremely complicated and it was a miracle it had progressed so quickly. She also reminded him that there was another restoration going on in another house a few doors down, which was very simple but had taken more than a year so far. Sanity was restored. This, I might say, from a Comité who when I, a woman living alone, was having problems with the young people next door two years previously had refused to help me. When I told Yanick, who was at that very moment singing his head off while gib-stopping, he roared, '*Ils n'ont qu'à se faire foutre!*' I couldn't help but agree.

At the end of August, I had to leave Uzès, so I needed to pack up everything in the rented house — straw hats, antique plates, chandeliers, writing desk, bed, art, Olivades tablecloths, Moroccan wedding blanket, cook books, gigantic wardrobe full of Indian shawls, Marni frocks, Souleiado outfits and every variety of shoe imaginable — and move it into the new house ready or not. Mind you, is a house ever finished? There'll always be maintenance to do, a new piece of furniture to squeeze in, pictures to rearrange, a new colour to try on the wall or on drapes or cushions. The point is, I now have a house to keep tweaking, where once I had a bombsite, a few plans and a bank balance.

When I flew back to New Zealand for work to pay for the spending spree, I left behind a dream house, not quite finished but almost. I am not quite broke but almost. In the end, I regret nothing. Almost.

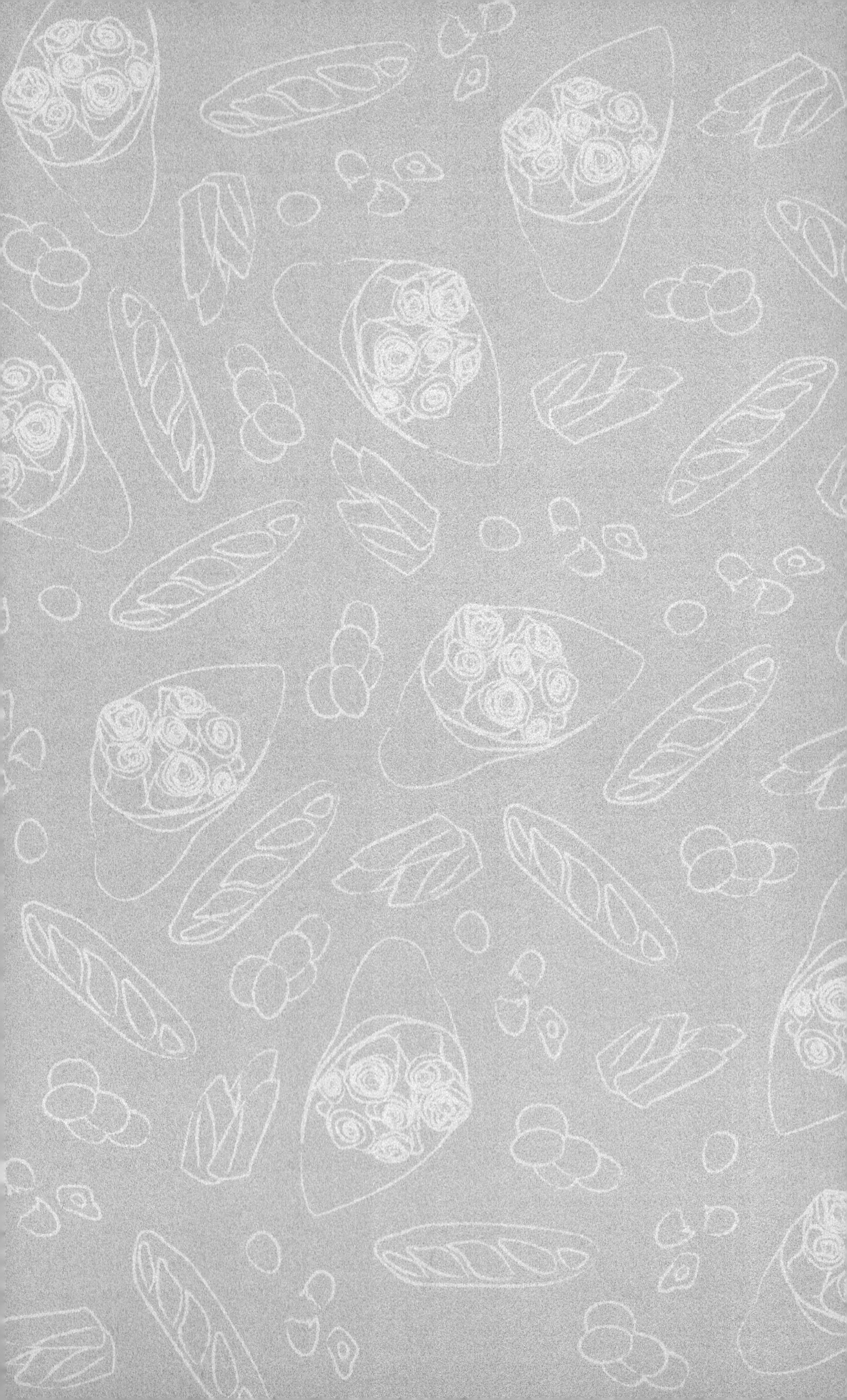

POSTSCRIPT

Being a nurse had been perhaps not a dream but a goal, and I have long since ticked that off the 'to do' list and marked it 'never to do again'. I hated it and was terrible at it because I was in the wrong job, but it was worth graduating because it taught me the value and discipline of hard work, and the ability to dress while walking there. Likewise, counselling and running restaurants have been ticked off my list and left behind. My subsequent goals of making television programmes, writing books, running tours — even singing — have all been fulfilled, and I keep them turning like plates on a stick. I was stupid to stop singing for 20 years — if I hadn't I could have been a professional singer by now and had a life of hardship, lung disease and cheap hotels — but I went on to have a life of adventure, romance and French food. *And* cheap hotels.

And I haven't completely missed out on life as a performer. Years ago, one of my brothers suggested I perform stage shows, and I thought what a good idea, but never found the time. In March 2012, I finally got around to it, with my partners in the production company, Jane and Jeff Avery, producing and directing it. We tour New Zealand every year with our rollercoaster of a show, work hard, have fun, and I get to explain to the audience how beating things until stiff can change your life. There's a cooking segment on the ironing-board cook-top, singing, an agony section to straighten out life's problems, readings from my books, and a big fat excuse to wear completely outrageous dresses. Not long after starting this new extension to my career, I became a pensioner, so now finally I am rich — $565.66 every fortnight — I try not to spend it all at once in the same shop.

Looking back at the younger me, I wonder if I was liberated or commitment-phobic. I think I was liberated. Regrets are for the birds, although I have a few, and I was extremely lucky to become a woman in the era of sexual and social revolution, when sex was clean and the air dirty. Now it's the opposite, so it's as well I made the most of it when I could. However, I am lucky to be alive, having taken too many risks with hitch-hiking and wandering around the world on my own. And liberation didn't always come quickly in all things; it took me a while to release myself from worldly possessions. Of course, building and furnishing my new house proves I'm not exactly free, but I'm still a nomad, happy to lock my new front door to head off somewhere else. I no longer lug around far too many suitcases with far too much in them. Nowadays, I pack one bag, take half the stuff out, then lock it. I've learnt that regardless of where you are going or for how long — you need only one suitcase.

As I have already written elsewhere, when we were young, my friends and I had no idea of the power we had over men — though it transpired we were the point of their lives. Sometimes we found how to use that power, sometimes we even abused it. Now, I realise, I am a girl's girl, not a man's girl, and I can't thank my girlfriends over the years enough for looking after me when the chips were down. Generally men didn't look out for me, women did. When everyone said I would end up old, tragic and alone because I more or less didn't want children, I was right to trust my instincts that I would have made a frustrated, neurotic mother. I'm glad I didn't put all my eggs in one bastard. Sure, if you are happy and loved at 25, the chances are you will be happy and loved at 65, right on to 95. But I wasn't happy, and when the man of my dreams ripped my still-beating heart out of my chest, I freely confess I became a bit bitter and twisted. But, eventually, I discovered that although you can't miraculously remove pain, singing and music come close to doing so because they turn pain into beauty. It was in Paris that I opened my heart and started singing again.

When I was a young nurse and counsellor, I couldn't possibly have guessed that, even though I was very greedy, food would become my job and greatest joy. It turns out that cooking is a short-cut to love. I discovered that cooking and eating are the cheapest and easiest way to make yourself and others happy. Thank God that happiness is fleeting, because it necessitates frequent repetition.

Building my own house meant reducing my dreams and intentions to what was available, to the demands of French bureaucracy, what the neighbours would sell me, building regulations, a limited budget, and many more restrictions besides. But the result has also been enriched by unexpected finds, such as a Louis XIV chimney, by talented and inspired builders, by perseverance, by the genius of Gina, the generosity of friends and by the meals that have been and will be shared there. We think our lives are a result of the choices we have made and we beat ourselves up if things didn't work out the way we planned, but those choices weren't entirely made by us — they were a result of the social times we were born and live in.

The belief that your life can only be meaningful if you follow the path of wifehood and motherhood is an ideological conceit, designed to keep women in their place. The meaningful life is the life where you have followed your own path and not necessarily the one expected of you. Life hasn't turned out at all as I thought it would — it has turned out to be better — so my advice is stay open and embrace Plan B. You can't do everything, even though your parents will have told you that you are beautiful and can succeed at anything. That's not true; they only say that to cut down on psychiatry bills later. I was averagely good-looking but not gorgeous, would never have been a brain surgeon, didn't start writing or making television until I was 45, and did quite well in fields I hadn't even thought of in my twenties. For a sociable loner and extremely late developer, I'm not doing too badly so far.

This goes to prove that you can bugger around for 35 years, figure out some goals and, bar a few wanderings off the path, achieve those goals over 30 years and still be only 65. Going by my parents' extreme longevity, this leaves me with another 35 years to knock off the rest of my goals. Fingers crossed.

LIST OF ILLUSTRATIONS

PAGE 7   Peta and her father, 1967
PAGE 13   The dismantled Louis XIV chimney

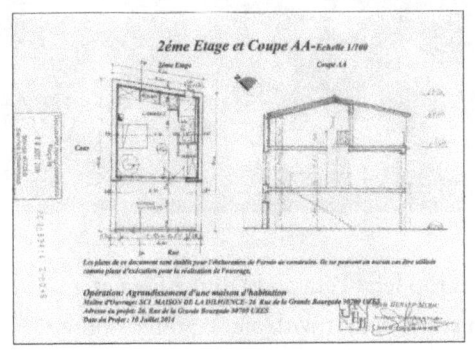

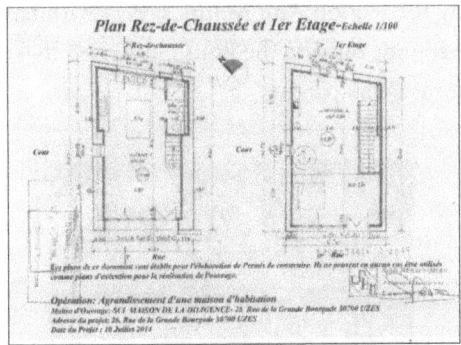

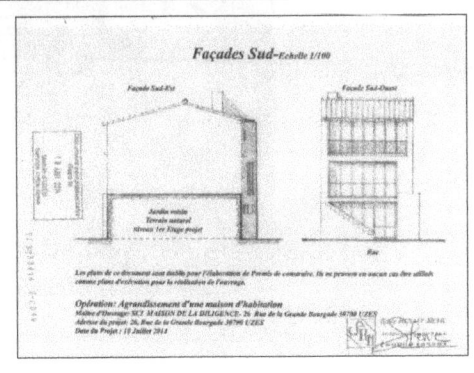

PAGE 17   The Uzès house plans

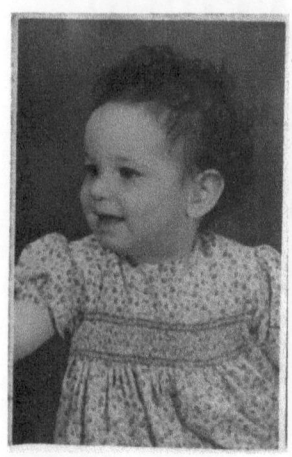

PAGE 39   (Clockwise from top left) Peta and family; Peta as a toddler; Peta in straw boater with some of her siblings, ready for school; Ann Mathias; Peta with family and friends outside the house in King Edward Avenue, Epsom; Peta's parents

PAGE 59   (From top) Peta strolling in Place aux Herbes; the Duché, the Duke's castle in Uzès | *Photos used with kind permission of Sally Tagg*

PAGE 79   (Clockwise from top) Peta with her parents at Top of the Town restaurant, Auckland, around 1970; the new house in Epsom; school days; Peta becoming Joan Baez, 1965

PAGE 91   The original state of the house in Uzès and (bottom left) the unattainable garden

PAGE 107   (Clockwise from top left) Peta as a fully fledged Joan Baez; Peta starched to within an inch of her life; Peta and friends; Nurse Peta, 1970s

PAGE 125 The Uzès house begins to take shape; (top right) Gina stands behind Yanick and another of the builders

PAGE 133 Peta in floppy hat with Paula, Richard and Ratty, some of the numerous flatmates she lived with, 1971

PAGE 151 Peta in Canada with assorted friends in assorted guises, 1970s

PAGE 167   Peta on her wedding day, 1984

PAGE 177   (From top) Peta with siblings Keriann, David, Jonathan, Desirée and Paul, 1987; another photo from Peta and Alexy's wedding, 1984

PAGE 187   (From top) Peta with her parents receiving her gong, 2012; Peta in meringue-infested hat

PAGE 209 Peta with the official notice of her building work
PAGE 211 Peta and Ruth Pretty filming for *Taste New Zealand, 1990s* | *Photos used with kind permission of Ruth Pretty*

PAGE 229 (From top) Peta on tour in India, singing with twin sisters in a village in Rajasthan; Peta in the 1990s
PAGE 241 The house almost complete; (bottom right) Peta pointing to Yanick, the builder responsible for getting it there

PAGE 257 Princess Peta going to the Strauss ball, 1971

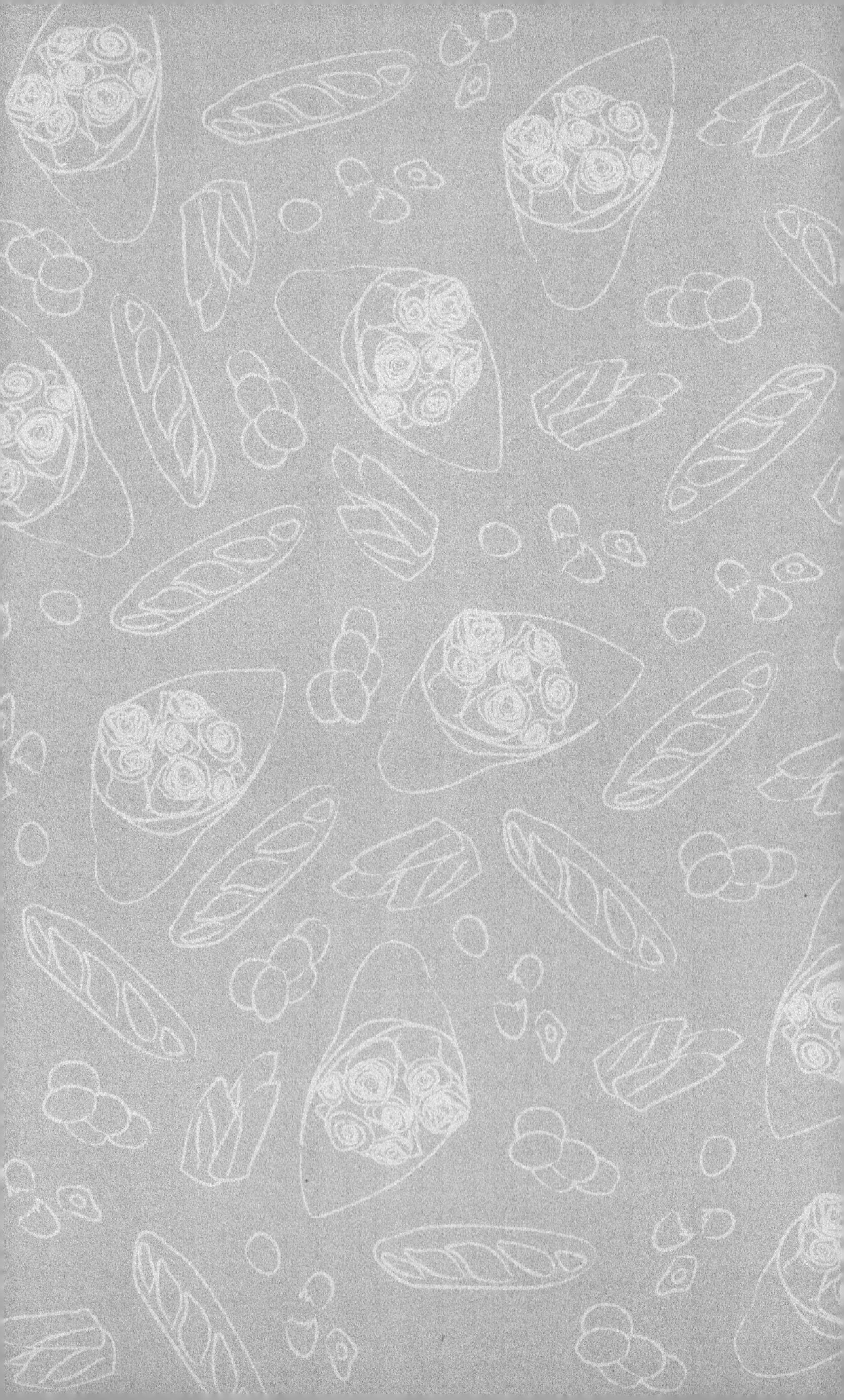

INDEX OF RECIPES

A

Anchovies and Sage Leaves in Tempura Batter 128

B

Baking & Desserts
    Chocolate Baklava 161
    Chocolate and Olive Oil Mousse with Sea Salt 76
    Ginger Madeleines 20
    Honey and Spice Cookies 89
    Olive Oil Ice Cream 248
    Oreillettes 78
    Sarah's Bran Muffins 139
Baklava, Chocolate 161
Beef
    Brouffado: Bull or Beef Stew with Anchovies and Capers 250
    Steak and Chips 155
Boiled Chicken with *Béchamel* Sauce 185
Bran Muffins, Sarah's 139
Bread
    Tastou 105
Broad Bean, Pea and Parmesan Mash 227
Brouffado: Bull or Beef Stew with Anchovies and Capers 250

C

Chicken
    Chicken with *Béchamel* Sauce, Boiled 185
    Roast Chicken 50
Chips 155
Chocolate Baklava 161
Chocolate and Olive Oil Mousse with Sea Salt 76
Chocolate, Philippe Deschamps's Hot 69
Chutney, Coconut 223
Cookies, Honey and Spice 89

D

Desserts *see* Baking & Desserts
Drinks
    Philippe Deschamps's Hot Chocolate 69

E

Eggplant and Coconut Chutney, Grilled Tuna with Spiced 223

F

Fennel and Pastis Soup with Quenelles 23
Fish
    Anchovies and Sage Leaves in Tempura Batter 128
    Fish Pies, Smoked 55
    Grilled Tuna with Spiced Eggplant and Coconut Chutney 223

G

Ginger Madeleines 20
Grilled Tuna with Spiced Eggplant and Coconut Chutney 223

H

Honey and Spice Cookies 89
Hot Chocolate, Philippe Deschamps's 69

I

Ice Cream, Olive Oil 248

L

Lamb
    Lamb with Pélardon Goat Cheese and Lavender 99
    Navarin Printanier 194

M

Madeleines, Ginger 20
Mash, Broad Bean, Pea and Parmesan 227
Mousse, Chocolate and Olive Oil with Sea Salt 76
Muffins, Sarah's Bran 139

N

Navarin Printanier 194
Nut Loaf with Roasted Tomato Sauce 148

O

Olive Oil Ice Cream 248
Oreillettes 78

P

Philippe Deschamps's Hot Chocolate 69
Pies, Smoked Fish 55
Potatoes
    Chips 155
    Smoked Fish Pies 55
    Potatoes in Duck Fat 132

Q

Quenelles 24

R

Roast Chicken 50
Roasted Tomato Sauce 149

S

Sarah's Bran Muffins 139
Sauces & Relishes
    Béchamel Sauce 185
    Coconut Chutney 223
    Roasted Tomato Sauce 149
Smoked Fish Pies 55
Snacks & Starters
    Anchovies and Sage Leaves in Tempura Batter 128
    Broad Bean, Pea and Parmesan Mash 227
    Tastou 105
Soup, Fennel and Pastis with Quenelles 23
Steak and Chips 155

Stew
   Brouffado: Bull or Beef Stew with Anchovies and Capers 250
   Navarin Printanier 194

T

Tastou 105
Tempura Batter, Anchovies and Sage Leaves in 128
Tomato Sauce, Roasted 149
Tuna with Spiced Eggplant and Coconut Chutney, Grilled 223

French Toast

peta mathias

EATING AND LAUGHING YOUR WAY AROUND FRANCE

French Toast is a totally pleasurable insight into the sensual delights of France through the eyes and taste buds of Peta Mathias, television personality and food writer. The former owner of a restaurant in Paris, Peta knows how to get the most out of every minute she spends there. Savour crusty breads and fruity wines, endless varieties of olives and mushrooms, and experience the open-armed hospitality of Peta's friends and hosts. Staying in apartments, châteaux, old churches and even the odd garden shed, Peta explains how to choose the best produce available — and how to banter with local stallholders. Share her evenings spent in village squares, feasting and laughing the night away.

Essential reading for anyone planning a trip to France, *French Toast* is crammed full of information about travel, regional food specialties and culture. Written with Peta's trademark verve and love of life, this is as close to being in France as you can get.

Also available as an eBook

Hot Pink Spice Saga

AN INDIAN CULINARY TRAVELOGUE WITH RECIPES

Peta Mathias

Julie Le Clerc

Peta Mathias and Julie Le Clerc are in love with food, in love with travel and in love with India. In her exuberant, evocative and hilarious style, Peta relates how they got to know this fascinating country through its cuisine: be it street food, feasts, or an everyday meal cooked on the floor of a tiny shack. They have travelled to tea plantations in the mountains, stayed in palaces and slept on a train: that 'wonderland of unmitigated, primeval swamp muck'. While Peta has led various culinary tours, Julie has established a patisserie in an upmarket New Delhi hotel. This is no superficial flirtation with the country, but a full-blown love affair.

The over 60 recipes showcase distinct regional traditions, passed on from the generous people they have met. Carefully chosen and adapted to be easy for the home cook, they are all mouth-wateringly delicious. Julie's fabulous photographs convey the colour of the country, and are almost good enough to eat.

Can we help it if we're Fabulous?

And other thoughts on being a woman

peta mathias

Available as an eBook

The irrepressible Peta Mathias is a woman who has never been afraid to embrace life with all its glorious inconsistencies, joys and heartbreaks. While we know her as an engaging television presenter, an inspiring food writer and a delightful raconteur, in *Can We Help It If We're Fabulous?* Peta instantly becomes every woman's confidante, as she shares with us the wisdom she has learnt over her years of living outrageously. She is a woman who appreciates the importance of a gorgeous pair of shoes and the perfect shade of lipstick. She knows the value of good friends, great music, lively conversation, beautiful surroundings and a one-way ticket to an exotic destination. And having loved and lost — more than once — Peta also has her own theories on why relationships begin and end. And then there's the sex chapter!

Inspirational, razor-witted and irresistibly funny, *Can We Help It If We're Fabulous?* is Peta Mathias at her wisest — and naughtiest. This book is for each and every fabulous woman out there.

Just in Time to be Too Late

WHY MEN ARE LIKE BUSES

peta mathias

Available as an eBook

In her bestselling guide to womanhood *Can We Help It If We're Fabulous?*, the irrepressible Peta Mathias shared with us her thoughts on being a woman. In *Just In Time To Be Too Late*, she turns her attention to what it means to be a man in the twenty-first century.

What makes men cry? Why are Bad Boys so irresistible? What exactly is the point of sport? To what extent is a man's self-worth connected to his job? What do men look for in a relationship? Why do men lie? What do they need to be happy? And, of course, why are men like buses?

Though she has been married and has had her fair share of meaningful relationships and flirtatious dalliances, Peta is the first to admit that she knew very little about the opposite sex when she began work on this book: 'A virgin would know more about men than I do because she's probably listened more.'

Just In Time To Be Too Late is an account of Peta's discoveries on delving deeper into the mysterious world of men. It is a highly personal and frequently hilarious pilgrimage that will resonate with women everywhere.

By the author of Can We Help it if We're Fabulous?

Beat Till Stiff

A Woman's Recipe for Living

peta mathias

Available as an eBook

'Beating egg whites till they're stiff is a metaphor for life — just when you thought your existence would never be more than flaccid transparent snot, something happens to turn it into tight white light.'

Once a counsellor, nurse and cook and now a writer, television presenter and all-round fabulous woman, Peta Mathias is the queen of transformation. In *Beat Till Stiff*, Peta shares lessons learnt in her pilgrimage through life, such as how she stopped strangling her mother, why redheads have more fun, and whether having an orgasm really makes a difference to sex, procreation or world peace.

In her bestselling guide to womanhood, *Can We Help It If We're Fabulous?*, Peta shared with us her thoughts on being a woman. In *Just In Time To Be Too Late*, she turned her attention to what it means to be a man in the twenty-first century. This time around, Peta covers topics she considers important, naughty or personal — all with a bent towards life's many transformations.

Some of the essays in *Beat Till Stiff* are scurrilous, many are funny and others autobiographical, but all are thoroughly entertaining.

Peta Mathias

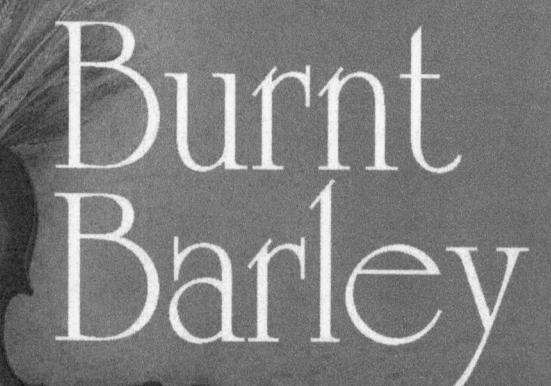

Burnt Barley

How to eat, dance & sing your way around Ireland

Available as an eBook

If Peta hadn't known of her Irish ancestry, her love of potatoes would have betrayed it. Peta always connects with a place through its food, and in visiting the country of her forebears she set herself a difficult task. But it didn't take long for Peta to find the world-class restaurants hidden up windy cobbled streets, to savour the delights of grand country cooking, high-quality primary produce and seafood from sleepy fishing villages. She dances her way from such traditional fare as Guinness, barmbrack and black and white puddings to refined fusion dishes of roasted tomato and goat cheese charlotte with lentils and basil oil and cured wild salmon, topped off with slugs of fine Irish whiskey.

In this wonderful account of travelling through Ireland, Peta searches for its gastronomic heartland, introduces us to her intriguing relatives, discovers that her other love — music — is intricately intertwined with Irish social life and eating habits, and spins tales both traditional and true.

Fête Accomplie

A New Zealander's Culinary Romance

PETA MATHIAS

Available as an eBook

A New Zealand nurse opening a restaurant in Paris? Sheer cheek and blind determination led Peta Mathias to fulfil her long-held ambition . . . rising from dishwasher to French chef and forging a life filled with sensuous gastronomic experiences. The wonderful recipes Peta cooked during her extraordinary time in France are intermingled here with her lively account of the exotic French lifestyle and colourful characters she encountered.

For more information about our titles visit
www.penguin.co.nz